Programming Grails

Burt Beckwith

Beijing · Cambridge · Farnham · Köln · Sebastopol · Tokyo

Programming Grails

by Burt Beckwith

Copyright © 2013 Burt Beckwith. All rights reserved.

Printed in the United States of America.

Published by O'Reilly Media, Inc., 1005 Gravenstein Highway North, Sebastopol, CA 95472.

O'Reilly books may be purchased for educational, business, or sales promotional use. Online editions are also available for most titles (*http://my.safaribooksonline.com*). For more information, contact our corporate/institutional sales department: 800-998-9938 or *corporate@oreilly.com*.

Editors: Mike Loukides and Meghan Blanchette	**Indexer:** Judy McConville
Production Editor: Kristen Borg	**Cover Designer:** Karen Montgomery
Copyeditor: Absolute Services, Inc	**Interior Designer:** David Futato
Proofreader: Linley Dolby	**Illustrator:** Robert Romano

May 2013:   First Edition

Revision History for the First Edition:

2013-04-22:   First release

See *http://oreilly.com/catalog/errata.csp?isbn=9781449323936* for release details.

ISBN: 978-1-449-32393-6

[LSI]

Table of Contents

Preface

I started using Grails in early 2008, about a month before the 1.0 release. Much has changed since then, but many aspects are still very much the same. Grails continues to be the fastest way to develop an application on the JVM and, as an added bonus, is a lot of fun. Grails saves you a tremendous amount of time by handling the plumbing work that you would ordinarily have to do yourself if you were using another framework, and you can save even more time by using some of the hundreds of plugins that are available. Plus, because you are targeting the JVM, the whole JVM ecosystem is available, and you can use any library that isn't already included by Grails or a plugin.

I have always had a need to know how things work. Open source software makes that possible, because you can read the code, and it is particularly helpful when debugging since you can step into library and framework code from your IDE. But Grails adds a layer of opacity by providing so much dynamic behavior. All that magic is great when everything works, but when you have problems, it can be hard to know where to even start looking. When I started using Grails, I spent many hours exploring the internals, not only to understand how what I was seeing was possible, but also to determine whether the problems I was seeing were Grails issues or problems in my code. That experience was a large part of the motivation behind writing this book; I hope that by shining a light on some of the inner workings and motivations behind Grails features, your path will be easier.

Who This Book Is For

This book is intended for experienced developers. This primarily includes Grails developers who want to dig deeper into the architecture and understand more about how Grails works its magic and how it integrates with Groovy, Spring, Hibernate, and other technologies. Developers with experience in similar frameworks such as Spring MVC, JEE, or Ruby on Rails should find this book useful in understanding how Grails implements features to which they are accustomed.

This should not be your first Grails book, since it presumes a good deal of previous experience and understanding, so be sure to read a more comprehensive Grails book first.

Other Resources

There are many resources available if you would like to find out more about Grails and Groovy.

There is a significant amount of information at the Grails site (*http://grails.org*), in particular the reference documentation (*http://grails.org/doc/latest/*). Likewise, the Groovy site (*http://groovy.codehaus.org/*) has years of collective information available. For a more general overview of Grails, there are two books available that cover Grails 2: *The Definitive Guide to Grails 2* by Jeff Brown and Graeme Rocher (Apress), and *Grails in Action, Second Edition* by Glen Smith and Peter Ledbrook (Manning). *Programming Groovy, Second Edition* by Venkat Subramaniam (Pragmatic Programmers) is an excellent resource for Groovy, and the second edition covers Groovy 2, and *Groovy in Action, Second Edition* by Dierk König et al. (Manning), when finished, will be a comprehensive reference for all things Groovy.

There are several conferences around the world that feature Grails and other Groovy-based technologies:

Spring One 2GX (http://springone2gx.com/)
> This is the largest and is held in the fall; it includes five tracks on Spring Framework technologies and four Groovy and Grails tracks

Groovy and Grails Exchange (http://skillsmatter.com/event/groovy-grails/groovy-grails-exchange-2013)
> Held in London each year in December

GR8Conf US (http://gr8conf.us/)
> Held in Minneapolis each spring

GR8Conf Europe (http://gr8conf.eu/)
> Held in Copenhagen each spring

Greach (http://greach.es/)
> Held in Madrid each winter

All of these conferences have a significant amount of content on a wide range of technologies in the Groovy ecosystem, and they attract the top experts in the field as speakers.

Grails also has a strong user community. The User (*http://grails.org/Mailing+Lists*) mailing list is quite active and is great place to ask questions. There are dozens of user groups across the globe, and hopefully one near you. See the group list page (*http://grails.org/User+Groups*) at *grails.org* for the active groups, and if there isn't one nearby, create one! Groovy Blogs (*http://www.groovyblogs.org/*) is a blog aggregator that includes posts about Groovy and Grails technologies. It's a convenient way to stay aware of what's going on, and I recommend adding its Atom or RSS feed to your news reader. I write a regular "This Week in Grails" (*http://burtbeckwith.com/blog/?cat=32*) blog series that lists Grails- and Groovy-related blog posts, tweets, job postings, and upcoming conferences and user group meetings each week.

Conventions Used in This Book

The following typographical conventions are used in this book:

Italic
>   Indicates new terms, URLs, email addresses, filenames, and file extensions.

`Constant width`
>   Used for program listings, as well as within paragraphs to refer to program elements such as variable or function names, databases, data types, environment variables, statements, and keywords.

`Constant width bold`
>   Shows commands or other text that should be typed literally by the user.

`Constant width italic`
>   Shows text that should be replaced with user-supplied values or by values determined by context.

 This icon signifies a tip, suggestion, or general note.

 This icon indicates a warning or caution.

Using Code Examples

This book is here to help you get your job done. In general, if this book includes code examples, you may use the code in this book in your programs and documentation. You do not need to contact us for permission unless you're reproducing a significant portion of the code. For example, writing a program that uses several chunks of code from this book does not require permission. Selling or distributing a CD-ROM of examples from O'Reilly books does require permission. Answering a question by citing this book and quoting example code does not require permission. Incorporating a significant amount of example code from this book into your product's documentation does require permission.

We appreciate, but do not require, attribution. An attribution usually includes the title, author, publisher, and ISBN. For example: "*Programming Grails* by Burt Beckwith (O'Reilly). Copyright 2013 Burt Beckwith, 978-1-44932-393-6."

If you feel your use of code examples falls outside fair use or the permission given above, feel free to contact us at *permissions@oreilly.com*.

Safari® Books Online

Safari Books Online is an on-demand digital library that delivers expert content in both book and video form from the world's leading authors in technology and business.

Technology professionals, software developers, web designers, and business and creative professionals use Safari Books Online as their primary resource for research, problem solving, learning, and certification training.

Safari Books Online offers a range of product mixes and pricing programs for organizations, government agencies, and individuals. Subscribers have access to thousands of books, training videos, and prepublication manuscripts in one fully searchable database from publishers like O'Reilly Media, Prentice Hall Professional, Addison-Wesley Professional, Microsoft Press, Sams, Que, Peachpit Press, Focal Press, Cisco Press, John Wiley & Sons, Syngress, Morgan Kaufmann, IBM Redbooks, Packt, Adobe Press, FT Press, Apress, Manning, New Riders, McGraw-Hill, Jones & Bartlett, Course Technology, and dozens more. For more information about Safari Books Online, please visit us online.

How to Contact Us

Please address comments and questions concerning this book to the publisher:

O'Reilly Media, Inc.
1005 Gravenstein Highway North
Sebastopol, CA 95472
800-998-9938 (in the United States or Canada)
707-829-0515 (international or local)
707-829-0104 (fax)

We have a web page for this book, where we list errata, examples, and any additional information. You can access this page at *http://oreil.ly/programming-grails*.

To comment or ask technical questions about this book, send email to *bookques tions@oreilly.com*.

For more information about our books, courses, conferences, and news, see our website at *http://www.oreilly.com*.

Find us on Facebook: *http://facebook.com/oreilly*

Follow us on Twitter: *http://twitter.com/oreillymedia*

Watch us on YouTube: *http://www.youtube.com/oreillymedia*

Acknowledgments

Several people helped to make this book what it is today. Thank you to Peter Ledbrook for suggesting the idea at SpringOne 2GX 2011. My initial response was no, that there was no way that I would have the time to devote to a book. That was true, but I did it anyway, and it seems to have worked out okay. I would also like to thank Mike Loukides for supporting Grails at O'Reilly; I am hopeful this will be the first of many O'Reilly Grails and Groovy books.

I was fortunate having Meghan Blanchette as the book's editor. Thank you for your patience, advice, and for keeping everything on schedule.

Graeme Rocher and Tomas Lin were the technical reviewers. They carefully read the book and found numerous mistakes and omissions, and made extensive suggestions. Andrew Eisenberg also provided valuable feedback on the AOP chapter. Thank you all for making this a better book than I could have alone.

Many thanks to the Grails, Groovy, and tools teams at SpringSource for creating these amazing technologies.

And, finally, thank you to my wife, Maria. I know it can be hard being married to someone who spends as much time staring at a computer screen as I do. Thank you for your patience and support.

CHAPTER 1

Introduction to Groovy

We can't talk much about Grails without a solid understanding of Groovy, because it's so integral to how Grails works.

Groovy is a JVM language with a primary goal of extending Java. By adding a Meta Object Protocol (MOP) to enable metaprogramming, Groovy adds powerful capabilities that enable dynamic programming (changing and adding behavior at runtime), domain-specific languages (DSLs), and a huge number of convenience methods and approaches that simplify your code and make it more powerful.

Groovy compiles to bytecode just like Java does (although it creates different bytecode). As Java developers, we tend to think that only `javac` can compile source code to create *.class* files, but there are many JVM languages that do as well (including Groovy, JRuby, Jython, and hundreds more). There are also libraries such as BCEL (*https://commons.apache.org/bcel/*) that you can use to programmatically create bytecode. As a result, Groovy and Java interoperate well; you can call Java methods from Groovy and vice versa, a Java class can extend a Groovy class or implement a Groovy interface, and in general, you don't need to even think about interoperability because it "just works."

The Groovy equivalent of `javac` is `groovyc`, and because it compiles both Groovy and Java code, it's simple to use for your project code. Of course in Grails applications, we rarely even think about this process (except when it fails) because Grails scripts handle that, but if you're manually compiling code (e.g., in a Gradle (*http://gradle.org/*) build or with Gant (*http://gant.codehaus.org/*)), it's about as simple as working with Java code.

Installing Groovy

Ordinarily, Grails developers don't install a Groovy distribution, because each version of Grails ships with the `groovy-all` JAR with which it was developed. Groovy is a fundamental part of Grails, so using it in a Grails application is trivial. But it's easy to install if you want to use Groovy outside of Grails, for example, for scripting or to run standalone utility applications. Just download the version you want (*http://groovy.code haus.org/Download*), unpack the ZIP file to your desired location, set the `GROO VY_HOME` environment variable point at the location you chose, and add the `$GROO VY_HOME/bin` (or `%GROOVY_HOME%\bin` in Windows) directory to the `PATH` environment variable. That's all you need to do; run `groovy -v` from a command prompt to verify that everything is working.

If you're using Windows, the download page has installers that will install the distribution and configure the environment.

There is also a new tool, GVM (Groovy enVironment Manager). It was inspired by the Ruby RVM and rbenv tools, and it will install one or more versions of Groovy, as well as Grails, Griffon, Gradle, and vert.x. It uses the bash shell, so it works in Linux, OS X, and Windows, if you have Cygwin installed. It's very simple to use, and if you have projects that require different versions of Groovy, it's easy to switch between them. See the GVM site (*http://gvmtool.net/*) for usage information.

Groovy Console

The Groovy console is a great way to prototype code. It doesn't have many text editor or IDE features, but you can run arbitrary Groovy code and inspect the results. You can run it in debug mode and attach to it from a debugger (e.g., your IDE) to dig deeper and look at the call stack. It's convenient to test an algorithm or a fix, or to do what-if experiments. And you don't need to create a class or a `main()` method—you can execute any valid code snippet. If Groovy is installed and in your `PATH`, run the console by executing `groovyConsole` from the command line. I encourage you to test out the code examples as they're shown to make sure you understand how everything works.

The Groovy console is also a part of Grails—you can run `grails console` from the command line and start the Grails version of the console. It's the same application, but it also has Grails-specific hooks like easy access to the Spring `ApplicationContext` and automatic application of the `PersistenceContextInterceptors`. You can use it to call Grails object relational mapping (GORM) methods, services, and pretty much anything in your application that isn't related to an HTTP request. As a plugin author, I often troubleshoot bean definition issues by running the following (as shown in Figure 1-1):

```
ctx.beanDefinitionNames.sort().each { println it }
true
```

This grabs all of the Spring bean names (a `String[]` array) from the `ApplicationCon text` (the `ctx` binding variable), sorts them (into a new `List`), and prints each name. The `true` statement at the end is a trick to avoid printing the entire list again in its `toString()` form, because the console treats the last statement as the return value of the script and renders it in the output window.

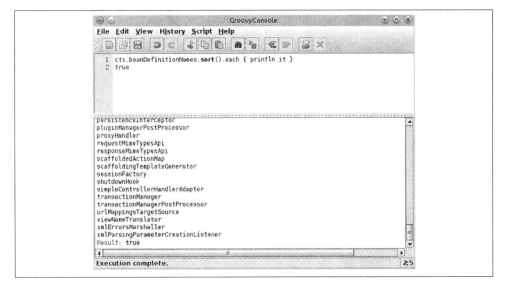

Figure 1-1. Grails console

Optional Typing

One of Groovy's strengths comes from its support of optional typing. You can define the types of variables, method parameters, method return values, and so on, like you do in Java, but you often don't need to. Groovy determines the actual type at runtime and invokes the methods on the objects if they exist (or if you've added support to the metaclass; more on this later). The approach used is often called *duck typing* (*https:// en.wikipedia.org/wiki/Duck_typing*); i.e., if it walks and talks like a duck, consider it a duck.

This isn't the same as weak typing. The objects themselves have a concrete type (unlike JavaScript, C, Perl, and so on), but you're not restricted by the compiler to only invoke methods defined in the specified type of the object. If the object supports the call, it will work.

In fact, you're not even restricted to hardcoding the method or property names. You can dynamically invoke a method or access a property value by name:

```
def person = ...

String methodName = ...
def value = person."$methodName"(1, 2)

String propertyName = ...
def otherValue = person."$propertyName"
```

Collections and Maps

Creating and populating Java collections might not seem that bad if you haven't seen how it's done in Groovy, but once you have, you won't want to go back. Here's some code to add a few elements to an `ArrayList` in Java:

```
List<String> things = new ArrayList<String>();
things.add("Hello");
things.add("Groovy");
things.add("World");
```

And here's the equivalent code in Groovy:

```
List<String> things = ["Hello", "Groovy", "World"]
```

The difference is rather stark, and using more idiomatic Groovy (there's not much need for generics in Groovy), it's even cleaner:

```
def things = ['Hello', 'Groovy', 'World']
```

Note that here I'm taking advantage of Groovy's support for declaring strings using single or double quotes; this is described in more detail later in the chapter.

There isn't a separate syntax for a `Set`, but you can use type coercion for that. Either:

```
Set things = ['Hello', 'Groovy', 'World']
```

or:

```
def things = ['Hello', 'Groovy', 'World'] as Set
```

The syntax for a `Map` is similar, although a bit larger, because we need to be able to specify keys and values delimited with colons:

```
def colors = ['red': 1, 'green': 2, 'blue': 3]
```

We can make that even more compact because, when using strings as keys that have no spaces, we can omit the quotes:

```
def colors = [red: 1, green: 2, blue: 3]
```

You might be wondering what the type of these collections is—some funky Groovy-specific interface implementations that handle all the details of the Groovy magic happening under the hood? Nope, `Lists` and `Sets` are just regular `java.util.ArrayList` and `java.util.HashSet` instances. Maps are `java.util.LinkedHashMap` instances instead of the more common `java.util.HashMap`; this is a convenience feature that maintains the order in the map based on the declaration order. If you need the features of other implementations such as `LinkedList` or `TreeMap`, just create them explicitly like you do in Java.

Lists and Maps support array-like subscript notation:

```
def things = ['Hello', 'Groovy', 'World']
assert things[1] == 'Groovy'
assert things[-1] == 'World'

def colors = [red: 1, green: 2, blue: 3]
assert colors['red'] == 1
```

Maps go further and let you access a value using a key directly as long as there are no spaces:

```
def colors = [red: 1, green: 2, blue: 3]
assert colors.green == 2
```

Properties

You've heard of POJOs—Plain Old Java Objects—and JavaBeans. These are simple classes without a lot of extra functionality and, in the case of JavaBeans, they follow conventions such as having a zero-argument constructor and having getters and setters for their attributes. In Groovy, we create POGOs—Plain Old Groovy Objects—that are analogous and work the same way, although they're more compact.

Consider a POJO that represents a person in your application. People have names, so this Person class should have firstName, initial, and lastName attributes to store the person's full name. In Java, we represent those as private String fields with getter methods, and setter methods if we're allowing the attributes to be mutable. But often we don't do any work when setting or getting these values—we just store them and retrieve them. But dropping this encapsulation and replacing each private field, getter, and setter with a public field would be limiting in the future because, at some point, there might be a reason to manipulate the value before storing or retrieving it. So we end up with a lot of repetetive boilerplate in these POJOs. Sure, our IDEs and other tools can autogenerate the code and we can ignore it and pretend that it's not there, but it is, and it unnecessarily bulks up our codebase.

Groovy fixes this mess for us by automatically generating getters and setters for public properties during compilation. But that's only the case if they're not already there; so this gives you the flexibility of defining attributes as public fields while retaining the ability to override the behavior when setting or getting the values. Groovy converts the public field to a private field but pretends the public field is still there. When you read the value, it calls the getter; and when you set the value, it calls the setter.

Consider this POGO:

```
class Thing {
    String name
    int count
}
```

The default scope for classes, fields, and methods is public (more on this later), so this is a public class and the two fields are public. The compiler, however, will convert these to private fields and add getName(), setName(), getCount(), and setCount() methods. This is most clear if you access this class from Java; if you try to access the name or count fields, your code won't compile.

Although Groovy generates getters and setters for you, you can define your own:

```groovy
class Thing {
    String name
    int count

    void setName(String name) {
        // do some work before setting the value
        this.name = name
        // do some work after setting the value
    }
}
```

and in this case, only the setName(), getCount(), and setCount() methods will be added.

You can also have read-only and write-only properties. You can create an immutable read-only property by making the field final and setting it in a parameterized constructor:

```groovy
class Thing {
    final String name
    int count

    Thing(String name) {
        this.name = name
    }
}
```

Because it's final, the compiler doesn't even generate a setter method, so it cannot be updated. If you want to retain the ability to update it internally, make the field private and create a getter method. Because it's private, the compiler won't generate the setter:

```groovy
class Thing {
    private String name
    int count

    String getName() { name }
}
```

You'll need a parameterized constructor to set the value, or set it in another method. Creating a write-only property is similar; use a private field and create only the setter:

```groovy
class Thing {
    private String name
    int count
```

```
    void setName(String name) { this.name = name }
}
```

 In general, it is safe to replace getter and setter method calls with property access; for example, person.firstName is a lot more compact than person.getFirstName() and equivalent. One case where it's not safe is with the getClass() method and Maps. If you try to determine the class of a Map instance using the .class property form of the getClass() method, Groovy will look up the value stored under the "class" key and probably return null. I always use getClass() even when I know the object isn't a Map just to be on the safe side.

Using the AST Browser

During compilation, Groovy represents your code in memory as an Abstract Syntax Tree (AST). The Groovy console's AST browser is one way to see what is going on under the hood. There are several compilation phases (parsing, conversion, semantic analysis, and so on), and the AST browser will show you graphically what the structure looks like at each phase. This can help to diagnose issues, and is particularly helpful when you write your own AST transformations, where you can hook into the bytecode generation process and add your own programmatically. Figure 1-2 shows the state at the Class Generation phase.

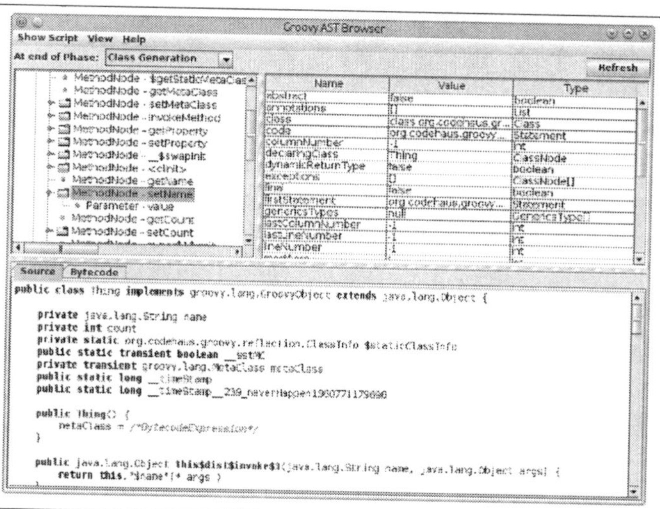

Figure 1-2. AST browser

Decompiling with JD-GUI

I highly recommend decompiling Groovy *.class* files to get a sense of what is added during the compilation process. It's one thing to believe that getters and setters are added for you, but it's another to actually see them. And there can be a lot of generated code in some of your classes; for example (jumping ahead a bit here), Grails uses several AST transformations to add compile-time metaprogramming methods to controllers, domain classes, and other artifacts. JD-GUI (*http://java.decompiler.free.fr/?q=jdgui*) is an excellent free decompiler that I've had a lot of success with. Figure 1-3 shows an example class.

Figure 1-3. JD-GUI

Decompiling with javap

Another option that doesn't require third-party software is `javap`, which is part of the JDK install. Running it with no switches will display the method signatures, e.g., `javap target/classes/com.foo.Bar`, and passing the `-c` switch will decompile the code into a readable form of the bytecode, not the Groovy or analogous Java source; e.g., `javap -c target/classes/com.foo.Bar`. The output isn't anywhere near as readable as what you get with a decompiler like JD-GUI, but it can be more convenient for a quick look.

Closures

Closures are an important aspect of Groovy. As a Grails developer you'll use them a lot; they define controller actions (although in 2.0, methods are supported and are preferred) and taglib tags and are used to implement the `constraints` and `mapping` blocks in domain classes, the `init` and `destroy` blocks in `BootStrap.groovy`, and in fact most of the blocks in the configuration classes in grails-app/conf. They also provide the functionality that makes builders and DSLs so powerful. But what are they?

A closure is a block of code enclosed in braces. Closures are similar to function pointers in C and C++ in that you can assign them to a variable and pass them as method parameters and invoke them inside the methods. They're also similar to anonymous inner classes, although they don't implement an interface or (at least explicitly) extend a base class (but they can be used to implement interfaces—more on that later).

A closure can be as simple as:

```
def hello = { println "hello" }
```

A closure can be invoked by calling its call method:

```
def hello = { println "hello" }
hello.call()
```

but Groovy lets you use a more natural method call syntax (it invokes the call method for you):

```
def hello = { println "hello" }
hello()
```

Like methods, closures can have parameters, and there are three variants. In the hello example, because there's nothing declared, there is one parameter with the default name it. So a modified closure that prints what it's sent would be:

```
def printTheParam = { println it }
```

and you could call it like this:

```
printTheParam('hello')
```

You can omit parentheses like you can with method calls:

```
printTheParam 'hello'
```

Named arguments use -> to delimit the parameters from the code:

```
def printTheParam = { whatToPrint -> println whatToPrint }
```

and, like method arguments, they can be typed:

```
def add = { int x, int y -> x + y }
```

If the closure has no arguments, use the -> delimiter and the it parameter will not be available:

```
def printCurrentDate = { -> println new Date() }
```

You can determine the number of parameters that a closure accepts with the getMaximumNumberOfParameters() method and get the parameter types (a Class[] array) with getParameterTypes().

A closure is a subclass of `groovy.lang.Closure` that is generated by the Groovy compiler; you can see this by running:

```
println hello.getClass().superclass.name
```

The class itself will have a name like `ConsoleScript14$_run_closure1`. Nested closures extend this naming convention; for example, if you look in the *classes* directory of a Grails application, you'll see names like *BuildConfig$_run_closure1_closure2.class*, which are the result of having `repositories`, `dependencies`, and `plugins` closures defined within the top-level `grails.project.dependency.resolution` closure.

The dollar sign in the class and filename will look familiar if you've used anonymous inner classes before. In fact, that's how they're implemented. They're different from anonymous inner classes in that they can access nonfinal variables outside of their scope. This is the "close" part of closure—they enclose their scope, making all of the variables in the scope the closure is in available inside the closure. This can be emulated by an inner class by using a final variable with mutable state, although it's cumbersome. For example, this Java code doesn't compile, because `i` isn't final, and making it final defeats the purpose, because it needs to be changed inside the `onClick` method:

```
interface Clickable {
    void onClick()
}

int i = 0;
Clickable c = new Clickable() {
    public void onClick() {
        System.out.println("i: " + i);
        i++;
    }
};
```

We can fix it with a final `1-element array` (because the array values are still mutable):

```
final int[] i = { 0 };
Clickable c = new Clickable() {
    public void onClick() {
        System.out.println("i: " + i[0]);
        i[0]++;
    }
};
```

but it's an unnatural coding approach. The Groovy equivalent with a closure is a lot cleaner:

```
int i = 0
def c = { ->
    println "i: $i"
    i++
} as Clickable
```

So how does Groovy break this JVM rule that anonymous inner classes can't access nonfinal variables? It doesn't—it uses a trick like the one above. Instead of using arrays like the above example, there's a holder class, `groovy.lang.Reference`. Enclosed variable values are stored in final `Reference` instances, and Groovy transparently makes the values available for you. The only time you'll see this occurring is when you're stepping through code in debug mode in an IDE.

Interface Coercion

The previous example demonstrates interface coercion; because the `Clickable` interface has only one method, the closure can implement that method if it has the same parameter type(s). The `as` keyword tells the Groovy compiler to create a JDK dynamic proxy implementing the interface. This is the simple version, but it also works for interfaces with multiple methods.

To implement an interface with more than one method, create a `Map` with method names as keys and closures with the corresponding parameter types as values:

```
import java.sql.Connection

def conn = [
    close: { -> println "closed" },
    setAutoCommit: { boolean autoCommit -> println "autocommit: $autoCommit" }
] as Connection
```

One useful aspect of this approach is that you aren't required to implement every method. Calling `close` or `setAutoCommit` will invoke the associated closures as if they were methods, but calling an unimplemented method (e.g., `createStatement()`) will throw an `UnsupportedOperationException`. This technique was more common before anonymous inner class support was added to Groovy in version 1.7, but it's still very useful for creating mock objects when testing. You can implement just the methods that will be called and configure them to work appropriately for the test environment (e.g., to avoid making a remote call or doing database access) and switch out the mock implementation in place of the real one.

Programmatic Closures

Although it's rare to do so, you can create a closure programmatically (most likely from Java). You might do this if you have some reason to implement some code in Java but need to pass a closure as a parameter to a Groovy method. The `Closure` class is abstract but doesn't have any abstract methods. Instead, you declare one or more `doCall` methods with the supported call signatures:

```
Closure<String> closure = new Closure<String>(this, this) {
    public String doCall(int x) {
        return String.valueOf(x);
```

```
    }
    public String doCall(int x, int y) {
        return String.valueOf(x * y);
    }
};
```

This can be invoked from Groovy just like one created the typical way:

```
closure(6) // prints "6"
closure(6, 2) // prints "12"
closure(1, 2, 3) // throws a groovy.lang.MissingMethodException
                 // since there's no 3-param doCall()
```

Owner, Delegate, and this

this inside a closure is probably not what you expect. Intuitively, it seems like it should be the closure itself, but it turns out that it's actually the class instance where the closure is defined. As such, it's probably not of much use—the owner and delegate are much more useful.

The *owner* of a closure is the surrounding object that contains the closure. It functions as the target of method invocations inside the closure, and if the method isn't defined, then a MissingMethodException will be thrown. In this example, if we create a new class instance and call the callClosure method (new SomeClass().callClosure()), it will print Woof!, because the dogAndCat closure calls the existing woof method, but it will then fail on the meow call because it doesn't exist:

```
class SomeClass {

    void callClosure() {

        def dogAndCat = {
            woof()
            meow()
        }

        dogAndCat()
    }

    void woof() {
        println "Woof!"
    }
}
```

You can assign a *delegate* for a closure to handle method calls. By default, the delegate is the owner, but you can change it with the setDelegate method. This is frequently used when parsing DSLs. The DSL can be implemented as a closure, and inner method calls and property access can be routed to a helper (i.e., the DSL builder), which implements the logic required when a method or property is called that's not locally defined but is valid in the DSL.

One example is the mapping block in Grails domain classes. This is a static closure that, if defined, will be used to customize how the class and fields map to the database:

```
class User {
    String username
    String password

    static mapping = {
        version false
        table 'users'
        password column: 'passwd'
    }
}
```

If you were to invoke the mapping closure (User.mapping()), you would get a MissingMethodException for each of the three lines in the closure, because the owner of the closure is the User class and there's no version, table, or password methods (and none added to the metaclass). It's more clear that these are method calls if we add in the optional parentheses that were omitted:

```
static mapping = {
    version(false)
    table('users')
    password(column: 'passwd')
}
```

Now we see that it's expected that there's a version method that takes a boolean parameter, a table method that takes a String, and a password method that takes a Map. Grails sets the delegate of the closure to an instance of org.codehaus.groovy.grails.orm.hibernate.cfg.HibernateMappingBuilder, if you're using Hibernate; otherwise, it'll be an analogous NoSQL implementation if you're using a different persistence provider, and that does have a version and a table method as expected. There's no password method though. But there's missing-method handling that looks for a field of the same name as the missing method, and when it finds a match and the parameter is a map, it uses the map data to configure the corresponding column.

So this lets us use an intuitive syntax composed of regular method calls that are handled by a delegate, usually doing a lot of work behind the scenes with a small amount of actual code.

Groovy's Contributions in the War Against Verbosity

One of Groovy's most popular features is its reduced verbosity compared to Java. It's been said that Groovy is a "low ceremony" language. If you're new to Groovy, you may not yet appreciate how much less code it takes to get things done compared to Java, especially if you use your IDE's code-generation functions. But, once you get used to

Groovy, you might find that you don't even need to use an IDE anymore, except perhaps when you want to attach a debugger to work on a particularly gnarly bug.

You've already seen how property access and the compact syntax for collections and maps can help condense your code, but there are a lot more ways.

Constructors

It's rare to see constructors in Groovy classes. This is because the Groovy compiler adds a constructor that takes a Map and sets field values to map values where the key corresponds to a field name. This gives you named parameters for this constructor syntax, so it's both more convenient and clearer which values are which. For example, a simple POGO like this:

```
class Person {
    String firstName
    String initial
    String lastName
    Integer age
}
```

can be constructed by setting some or all of the field values:

```
def author = new Person(firstName: 'Hunter', initial: 's', lastName: 'Thompson')
def illustrator = new Person(firstName: 'Ralph', lastName: 'Steadman', age: 76)
def someoneElse = new Person()
```

In the examples, I'm taking advantage of Groovy letting me omit the [and] map characters, because it makes the invocations cleaner.

This is especially useful for classes with many fields; in Java, you have to either define multiple constructors with various signatures or pass lots of nulls where you don't have a value.

However, note that the Map constructor relies on the default constructor that's added to all classes that don't define any explicit constructors. It calls that constructor, then sets properties from the provided Map (this is defined in MetaClassImpl.invokeConstructor(), if you're curious). But if you declare one or more parameterized constructors, the compiler doesn't generate an empty one for you, and the Map constructor will fail.

Also, because it's not a real constructor that's added to the bytecode, you can use this with Java classes that have a default constructor, too. So you could replace this code:

```
MutablePropertyValues propertyValues = ...
def beanDef = new GenericBeanDefinition()
beanDef.setBeanClassName('com.foo.bar.ClassName')
beanDef.setAutowireMode(AbstractBeanDefinition.AUTOWIRE_BY_TYPE)
beanDef.setPropertyValues(propertyValues)
```

with this:

```
MutablePropertyValues propertyValues = ...
def beanDef = new GenericBeanDefinition(
    beanClassName: 'com.foo.bar.ClassName',
    autowireMode: AbstractBeanDefinition.AUTOWIRE_BY_TYPE,
    propertyValues: propertyValues)
```

Checked Exceptions

Groovy also relaxes the requirement to catch and declare checked exceptions. Checked exceptions are widely regarded as a failure in the Java language, and a lot of the time, there isn't much you can do once you catch one. So in Groovy, you don't have to wrap calls to methods that throw checked exceptions in try/catch blocks, and you don't have to declare checked exceptions in method signatures.

For example, consider java.sql.SQLException. A lot of the time, a SQLException will be caused by one of two things: temporary connectivity issues with the database and errors in your SQL. If you can't connect to the database, you probably just have to punt and show an error page, and bad SQL is usually a development-time problem that you'll fix. But you're forced to wrap all JDBC code in try/catch blocks, thereby polluting your code.

You can still catch checked (and unchecked) exceptions in Groovy, and when you can handle an exception and retry or perform some action after catching it, you certainly should. It's a good idea to also declare thrown exceptions in your method signatures, both for use by Java and also as a self-documenting code technique.

Groovy Truth

In Java, only boolean variables and expressions (including unboxed Boolean variables) can evaluate to true or false, for example, with if checks or as the argument to assert. But Groovy extends this in convenient ways. null object references evaluate to false. Nonempty collections, arrays, and maps; iterators and enumerations with more elements; matching regex patterns; Strings and GStrings (and other implementations of CharSequence) with nonzero length; and nonzero numbers and Characters will all evaluate to true.

This is especially helpful with strings as well as with collections and maps. So, for example, you can replace:

```
def someCollection = someMethod(...)
if (someCollection != null && !someCollection.isEmpty()) { ... }
```

with:

```
def someCollection = someMethod(...)
if (someCollection) { ... }
```

and:

```
String s = someMethod(...)
if (s != null && s.length() > 0) { ... }
```

with:

```
String s = someMethod(...)
if (s) { ... }
```

Semicolons

Semicolons are for the most part unnecessary in Groovy, the exception being the traditional for loop (although you'll most likely prefer the semicolon-free Groovy for/in
version). Also, if you want to have multiple statements on one line, you still need to
delimit them with semicolons.

Optional Return

You can omit the return keyword in a method or closure, because Groovy treats the
last expression value as the return value if you don't use return.

Scope

Scope modifiers are often omitted in Groovy because the default scope is public. You
can still define private or protected fields and methods. Because package scope is the
default in Java and there's no keyword for that, Groovy added the groovy.trans
form.PackageScope annotation in version 1.8 for classes, methods, and fields.

Parentheses

You can often omit parentheses in method calls. This is only true if the method has
arguments, because otherwise the call would look like property access. So, for example,
all but the last of these are valid:

```
println("Using parentheses because I can")
println "Omitting parentheses because I can"
println()
println // not valid; looks like property access
        // for a nonexistent getPrintln() method
```

You can't omit parentheses from the right side of an assignment, however:

```
int sum = MathUtils.add(2, 2) // ok
int product = MathUtils.multiply 2, 2 // invalid, doesn't compile
```

Default Imports

Another space saver is the extended list of default imports. Java automatically imports
everything from the java.lang package, and Groovy extends this to include java.io.*,

java.net.*, java.util.*, groovy.lang.*, and groovy.util.*, as well as the java.math.BigDecimal and java.math.BigInteger classes.

Differences Between Java and Groovy

In general, you can rename a *.java* source file to *.groovy* and it will still be valid, although there are a few exceptions.

Array Initialization

Because Groovy uses braces to declare closures, you cannot initialize an array the standard Java way:

```
int[] oddUnderTen = { 1, 3, 5, 7, 9 };
```

Instead, we create the array using List syntax and cast it to the correct array type:

```
int[] oddUnderTen = [1, 3, 5, 7, 9]
```

or:

```
def oddUnderTen = [1, 3, 5, 7, 9] as int[]
```

in and def Keywords

One other gotcha is that in is a keyword, used by the Groovy for loop, (e.g., for (bar in bars) { ... }); def is also a keyword. So Java code that uses either of these as a variable name will need to be updated.

do/while Loops

There is also no do/while loop in Groovy, so any code like this will need to be reworked:

```
do {
    // stuff
}
while (<truth expression>);
```

for Loops

Another small difference is that you can't initialize more than one variable in the first part of a for loop, so this is invalid:

```
for (int count = someCalculation(), i = 0; i < count; i++) {
    ...
}
```

and you'll need to initialize the count variable outside the loop (a rare case where Groovy is more verbose than Java!):

```
int count = someCalculation()
for (int i = 0; i < count; i++) {
    ...
}
```

or you could just skip the whole `for` loop and use `times`:

```
someCalculation().times {
    ...
}
```

or a range with a loop, if you need access to the loop variable:

```
for (i in 0..someCalculation()-1) {
    ...
}
```

Annotations

Annotation values that have array types use a different syntax in Groovy than Java. In Java, you use { and } to define multivalued attributes:

```
@Secured({'ROLE_ADMIN', 'ROLE_FINANCE_ADMIN', 'ROLE_SUPERADMIN'})
```

but because these are used to define closures in Groovy, you must use [and] instead:

```
@Secured(['ROLE_ADMIN', 'ROLE_FINANCE_ADMIN', 'ROLE_SUPERADMIN'])
```

Groovy Equality

The previous examples will cause compilation errors if you rename a `.java` class to `.groovy` and try to compile it, or copy/paste Java code into an existing Groovy class. But checking for object equality actually works differently in Groovy.

In Java, == is mostly used for comparing numbers and other primitives, because comparing objects with == just compares object references but not the data in the instances. We use the `equals` method to test if two objects are equivalent and can be considered equal even though they're not the same instances. But it's rare to need the == object comparison, so Groovy overloads it to call `equals` (or `compareTo`, if the objects implement `Comparable`). And, if you do need to check that two references are the same object, use the `is` method—e.g., `foo.is(bar)`.

Groovy's == overload is convenient and avoids having to check for null values, but because it works differently than the Java operator, you might want to consider not using it. It's simple enough to replace `x == y` with `x?.equals(y)`, which isn't that many more characters and is still null-safe. Working with both Java and Groovy will keep you from introducing subtle bugs in your Java code. (I'm speaking from experience here....)

Multimethod Dispatch

Overloaded method selection is another runtime difference between Java and Groovy. Java's type checking is stricter, so it uses the compilation type of a variable to choose which method to call, whereas Groovy uses the runtime type, because it's dynamically checking all method invocations for metamethods, `invokeMethod` interception, etc.

So, for example, consider a few versions of a `close` utility method:

```
void close(Closeable c) {
   try { c.close() }
   catch (e) { println "Error closing Closeable" }
}

void close(Connection c) {
   try { c.close() }
   catch (e) { println "Error closing Connection" }
}

void close(Object o) {
   try { o.close() }
   catch (e) { println "Error closing Object" }
}
```

In Java, this code will invoke the `close(Object)` variant, because the compiler only knows the compile-time type of the `connection` variable:

```
Object connection = createConnection(); // a method that returns a Connection
// work with the connection
close(connection);
```

But, if this were Groovy, the `close(Connection)` method would be chosen, because it's resolved at runtime and is based not on the compile type but the actual runtime type of the `connection`. This is arguably a better approach, but because it's different from the Java behavior, it's something that you should be aware of.

Groovy Strings

There are multiple ways to express string literals in Groovy. The approach used in Java —double-quoted strings—is supported of course, but Groovy also lets you use single quotes if you prefer. Multiline strings (sometimes called *heredocs* in other languages) are also supported, using triple quotes (either single or double). `GStrings` make things a lot more interesting, though.

The biggest benefit of `GStrings` is avoiding the clumsy string concatenation that's required in Java:

```
String fullName = person.getFirstName() + " ";
if (person.getInitial() != null) {
   fullName += person.getInitial() + " ";
```

```
    }
    fullName += person.getLastName();
```

Using a `StringBuilder` (the preferred approach when concatenating in a loop) wouldn't be much better in this case. But using a `GString` (along with property syntax), we can join the data in a single line of code:

```
def fullName = "$person.firstName ${person.initial ? person.initial + ' '
: ''}$person.lastName"
```

`GStrings` also work with multiline strings as long as you use three double quotes; this is convenient for tasks such as filling in templates for emails:

```
def template = """\
Dear $name,

Thanks for signing up for the Ralph's Bait and Tackle online store!
We appreciate your business and look forward to blah blah blah …

Ralph
"""
```

Here, I'm using the backslash character at the beginning of the string to avoid having an initial blank line. You can use three single quotes to create multiline strings, but they behave like regular strings that use single quotes, in that they do not support expression replacement.

Using the subscript operator lets you conveniently access substrings:

```
String str = 'Groovy Strings are groovy'
assert str[4] == 'v' // a String of length 1, not a char
assert str[0..5] == 'Groovy' // the first 6 chars
assert str[19..-1] == 'groovy' // the last 6 chars
assert str[15..17] == 'are' // a substring in the middle
assert str[17..15] == 'era' // a substring in the middle, reversed
```

Static this

Unlike Java where the `this` keyword only makes sense in instance scope, `this` resolves to the class in static scope. One use of this feature is when defining static loggers. In Log4j and SLF4J, you can define a logger with a class or the class name (or any string you like), but in Java, there's no way (no convenient one anyway) to get the class name in static scope. This can lead to copy/paste problems. For example:

```
private static final Logger LOG = Logger.getLogger(Foo.class);
```

has the class hardcoded, so if you forget to change it and copy that to a different class, you'll be logging as the wrong category. Instead, in Groovy, you can use:

```
private static final Logger LOG = Logger.getLogger(this)
```

which is more portable (and similar to the analogous instance version `private final Logger log = Logger.getLogger(getClass())`).

The Groovy JDK (GDK)

The Groovy JDK (GDK) is a Javadoc-style set of pages (*http://groovy.codehaus.org/groovy-jdk*) that describe methods added to the metaclass of JDK classes to extend them with extra functionality and make them easier to work with. There are currently over 1,000 methods listed. I strongly encourage you to check out the information there and familiarize yourself with what's available. You may find that you've coded something that was already available and, in general, will probably realize that you're working harder than you need to by not taking advantage of these built-in methods and features.

DefaultGroovyMethods and InvokerHelper

Many of the methods added to JDK metaclasses are implemented in the `org.code haus.groovy.runtime.DefaultGroovyMethods` (*http://bit.ly/115J5MB*) class. At its largest, this was a gigantic class (over 18,000 lines) with around 1,000 methods. In recent versions of Groovy, this large class is being refactored into several more focused classes, including `ResourceGroovyMethods`, `IOGroovyMethods`, `StringGroovyMethods`, and others. Many of the convenience methods that you use on a regular basis are implemented here, for example, the `sort` method that's added to the `Collection` interface (it sorts lists and creates sorted lists from nonlist collections) is implemented by the `public static <T> List<T> sort(Collection<T> self)` method. It's interesting to browse this class to see how things work under the covers, and you can use these methods yourself (although this is an internal class, so there may be some risk using it directly, because it's not a public API class).

`org.codehaus.groovy.runtime.InvokerHelper` is another utility class with a lot of interesting functionality that you should check out.

Metaprogramming and the MOP

Groovy's Meta Object Protocol (MOP) is the key to Groovy's power and it's what enables most of its coolest features. Every class gets a metaclass, which intercepts all method calls and enables customization of how methods are invoked, and also enables adding or removing methods. This is what makes Groovy a dynamic language; unlike Java, which compiles methods into class bytecode and doesn't allow changes at runtime. Because Groovy's MOP is intercepting all method calls, it can simulate adding a method as if it had been compiled in at startup. This makes JVM classes *open classes* that can be modified at any time.

And that's just runtime metaprogramming; with compile-time metaprogramming using Abstract Syntax Tree (AST) transformations, you can also add actual methods to the class bytecode that are visible from Java.

Every Groovy class implements the `groovy.lang.GroovyObject` interface (it's added by the compiler) that includes these methods:

```
Object invokeMethod(String name, Object args)
Object getProperty(String property)
void setProperty(String property, Object newValue)
MetaClass getMetaClass()
void setMetaClass(MetaClass metaClass)
```

 Java classes can also implement `GroovyObject` to add Groovy-like behavior. The most convenient approach for this is to subclass the `groovy.lang.GroovyObjectSupport` adapter class, which implements the interface and provides sensible default implementations of the methods that can be overridden as needed.

When you invoke a method in Groovy (including accessing a property, because that calls the corresponding getter method), it's actually dispatched to the object's metaclass. This provides an AOP-like interception layer. The calls are implemented with reflection, which is slower than direct method invocation. But each new release of Java adds reflection speed improvements, and Groovy has several optimizations to reduce the cost of this overhead, the most significant being call site caching. Early versions of Groovy were quite slow, but modern Groovy has seen huge performance boosts and is often nearly as fast as Java. And because network latency and database access tend to contribute most to total web request time, the small increase in invocation time that Groovy can add tends to be insignificant, because it's such a small percentage of the total time.

Adding Methods

The syntax for adding a method at runtime is essentially just one that registers a closure in the metaclass that's associated with the specified method name and signature:

```
List.metaClass.removeRight = { int index ->
    delegate.remove(delegate.size() - 1 - index)
}
```

The `List` interface has a `remove` method, but this addition removes the item considering the position from the right instead of the left like `remove`:

```
assert 3 == [1, 2, 3].removeRight(0)
assert 2 == [1, 2, 3].removeRight(1)
assert 1 == [1, 2, 3].removeRight(2)
```

Recall that closures have a delegate that handles method calls invoked inside the closure. When adding methods to the metaclass, you can access the instance in which closure is invoked with the `delegate` property; in this example, it's the list instance that `remove Right` is called on.

Intercepting Method Calls

Because all Groovy objects implement `GroovyObject`, you can override the `invokeMe thod` method in your class to handle method invocations. There are a few variants of behavior though. By default, it's only called for methods that don't exist (analogous to `methodMissing`, which we'll see in a bit), so for example:

```
class MathUtils {

    int add(int i, int j) { i + j }

    def invokeMethod(String name, args) {
        println "You called $name with args $args"
    }
}

def mu = new MathUtils()
println mu.add(2, 3)
println mu.multiply(2, 3)
```

will generate this output:

```
5
You called multiply with args [2, 3]
```

because there is an `add` method but no `multiply`. If we change the class to implement the `GroovyInterceptable` marker interface (which extends `GroovyObject`):

```
class MathUtils implements GroovyInterceptable {
    ...
}
```

then the result is a `java.lang.StackOverflowError`. Hmmm. What's up there? We tend to think of `println` as just an alias for `System.out.println`, but it's actually a metamethod added to the `Object` class that calls `System.out.println`, so it will be intercepted along with the calls to `add` and `multiply`. So the fix is to use `Sys tem.out.println` directly:

```
class MathUtils implements GroovyInterceptable {

    int add(int i, int j) { i + j }

    def invokeMethod(String name, args) {
        System.out.println "You called $name with args $args"
    }
```

```
    }

    def mu = new MathUtils()
    println mu.add(2, 3)
    println mu.multiply(2, 3)
```

and then we'll see this output:

```
You called add with args [2, 3]
null
You called multiply with args [2, 3]
null
```

getProperty and setProperty

Overriding getProperty and/or setProperty always intercepts the property gets and sets, so the output of:

```
class Person {
    private String name

    def getProperty(String propName) {
        println "getProperty $propName"
        if ('name'.equals(propName)) {
            return this.name
        }
    }

    void setProperty(String propName, value) {
        println "setProperty $propName -> $value"
        if ('name'.equals(propName)) {
            this.name = value
        }
    }
}

def p = new Person(name: 'me')
println p.name
```

will be:

```
getProperty name
me
```

You might have expected to see output indicating that setProperty was called, since the map constructor is used and it sets property values from the map, in this case the name property to 'me'. But the implementation of this feature bypasses setProperty (this seems like a bug). But if you explicitly set the property:

```
p.name = 'you'
```

it works as expected:

```
setProperty name -> you
```

methodMissing and propertyMissing

GroovyObject doesn't have `methodMissing` or `propertyMissing` methods, but if you implement one or both of them, they'll be called for undefined method calls and property accesses. The signatures are similar to `invokeMethod` and `getProperty`:

```groovy
class Person {
    String name

    def propertyMissing(String propName) {
        if ('eman'.equals(propName)) {
            return name.reverse()
        }
        throw new MissingPropertyException(propName, getClass())
    }

    def methodMissing(String methodName, args) {
        if ('knight'.equals(methodName)) {
            name = 'Sir ' + name
            return
        }
        throw new MissingMethodException(methodName, getClass(), args)
    }
}

def p = new Person(name: 'Ralph')
println p.name
println p.eman

p.knight()
println p.name
```

which results in the output:

```
Ralph
hplaR
Sir Ralph
```

and, if you try to access a property or method that doesn't exist or have special handling (e.g., `println p.firstName` or `p.king()`), then you'll get the standard `MissingPropertytyException` or `MissingMethodException`.

There are also static versions of `methodMissing` and `propertyMissing`, `$static_methodMissing` and `$static_propertyMissing`.

```groovy
class Person {
    String name

    static $static_propertyMissing(String propName) {
        println "static_propertyMissing $propName"
    }

    static $static_methodMissing(String methodName, args) {
```

```
            println "static_methodMissing $methodName"
        }
    }

    println Person.foo()
    println Person.bar
```

The output from the above code is:

```
static_propertyMissing foo
static_methodMissing foo
null
static_propertyMissing bar
null
```

$static_methodMissing works slightly differently from methodMissing in that if there's no method with the specified name, it looks for a closure property with that name to invoke as if it were a method. This results in a message about a missing foo property and a missing foo method.

Operators

Groovy adds several operators to the standard set of Java operators.

Null-Safe Dereference

The most commonly used is the null-safe dereference operator, ?., which lets you avoid a NullPointerException when calling a method or accessing a property on a null object. It's especially useful in a chain of such accesses where a null value could occur at some point in the chain.

For example, you can safely call:

```
String name = person?.organization?.parent?.name
```

and if person, person.organization, or organization.parent are null, then null is returned as the expression value. The Java alternative is a lot more verbose:

```
String name = null;
if (person != null) {
    if (person.getOrganization() != null) {
        if (person.getOrganization().getParent() != null) {
            name = person.getOrganization().getParent().getName();
        }
    }
}
```

Elvis

The Elvis operator, ?:, lets you condense ternary expressions; these two are equivalent:

```
String name = person.name ?: defaultName
```

and:

```
String name = person.name ? person.name : defaultName
```

They both assign the value of person.name to the name variable if it is "Groovy true" (in this case, not null and has nonzero length, because it's a string), but using the Elvis operator is more DRY.

Spread

The spread operator, `*.`, is convenient when accessing a property or calling a method on a collection of items and collecting the results. It's essentially a shortcut for the collect GDK method, although it's limited to accessing one property or calling one method, for example:

```
def numbers = [1.41421356, 2.71828183, 3.14159265]
assert [1, 2, 3] == numbers*.intValue()
```

Spaceship

The spaceship operator `<=>` is useful when comparing values; for example, when implementing the compareTo method of the Comparable interface. For example, given a POGO where you want to sort by two properties, the spaceship operator makes the implementation very compact:

```
class Person implements Comparable<Person> {
    String firstName
    String lastName

    int compareTo(Person p) {
        lastName <=> p?.lastName ?: firstName <=> p?.firstName
    }

    String toString() { "$firstName $lastName" }
}

def zakJones = new Person(firstName: 'Zak', lastName: 'Jones')
def jedSmith = new Person(firstName: 'Jed', lastName: 'Smith')
def alJones = new Person(firstName: 'Al', lastName: 'Jones')

def persons = [zakJones, jedSmith, alJones]
assert [alJones, zakJones, jedSmith] == persons.sort(false)
```

because the operator returns –1 if the left is less than the right, 0 if they're equal, and 1 if the right is more than the left. So when the first expression (lastName <=> p?.last Name) is nonzero, its value is used as the return value and the sort is done by last Name. If the last names match, then the Elvis operator kicks in and the second expression (firstName <=> p?.firstName) is used to do a secondary sort by firstName.

You can also use the operator for one-off sorting regardless of whether the items are Comparable, for example:

```
assert [alJones, jedSmith, zakJones] == persons.sort(
    false, { a, b -> a?.firstName <=> b?.firstName })
```

which sorts just by firstName. Of course Groovy being Groovy, there's a shorter way of doing that:

```
assert [alJones, jedSmith, zakJones] == persons.sort(false, { it.firstName })
```

Field Access

If you have a need to bypass a getter method (or if there is none) and directly access a field, you can use the .@ operator. For example, this class uses some simple logic to return a default value if none is specified, but if you want to know if the value is unspecified, you still can:

```
class Thing {

    private static final String DEF_NAME = 'foo'

    String name

    String getName() { name == null ? DEF_NAME : name }
}
assert 'bar' == new Thing(name: 'bar').name
assert 'foo' == new Thing().name
assert null == new Thing().@name
```

Note, however, that this operator only works on the current class; if the field is in a subclass, the operator cannot access it, and you have to use standard reflection.

as

The as operator is very useful, because it can perform many type coercions. For example, there's no native syntax for a Set like there is for a List, but you can use as with List syntax to create a Set:

```
def things = ['a', 'b', 'b', 'c'] as Set
assert things.getClass().simpleName == 'HashSet'
assert things.size() == 3
```

in

The in operator is a convenient shortcut for the contains method in a collection:

```
assert 1 in [1, 2, 5]
assert !(3 in [1, 2, 5])
```

Method Reference

The `.&` operator lets you get a reference to a method and treat it like a closure. This might be useful if you're working with higher order methods where you pass a closure as a parameter and want the option to pass a method; the `.&` operator creates an instance of `org.codehaus.groovy.runtime.MethodClosure` that invokes your method when it's invoked.

```
class MathUtils {
    def add(x, y) { x + y }
}

def doMath(x, y, Closure c) {
    c(x, y)
}

def add = new MathUtils().&add
def multiply = { x, y -> x * y }

assert 8 == doMath(4, 2, multiply)
assert 6 == doMath(4, 2, add)
assert 2 == doMath(4, 2, { x, y -> x / y })
```

Overload Your Operators

Operator overloading is a powerful technique for compressing code, ideally in an intuitive way. It's important that if you add an operator overload that it make sense—be sure to think about how cryptic the code can get if you add an operator overload that isn't an appropriate choice.

The general approach for creating an operator overload is to implement the method that corresponds to the operator. The method must return this (or another instance) to work correctly. So, for example, if we have a `Person` class that has a collection of children:

```
class Person {
    String name
    List children = []
}
```

Adding a child to a `Person` instance is simple enough:

```
def parent = new Person(...)
def child = new Person(...)
parent.children.add child // or parent.children << child
```

But we can use the left-shift operator here to add a child:

```
class Person {
    String name
    List children = []
```

```
        def leftShift(Person child) {
            children << child
            this
        }
    }
```

and then the code becomes simply:

```
    def parent = new Person(...)
    def child = new Person(...)
    parent << child
```

The plus method would be another possibility (or you might implement both).

```
    class Person {
        String name
        List children = []

        def plus(Person child) {
            children << child
            this
        }
    }
```

and then you would use it like this:

```
    def parent = new Person(...)
    def child = new Person(...)
    parent += child
```

because parent += child is the equivalent of parent = parent + child. Note that internally we're still using << to add the child to the children list instead of switching to +=, because += creates a new List and copies the old list into it and then adds the new one. This is a lot more expensive than just adding to the current instance and should be avoided in general unless you have a reason to create a new list instance.

Table 1-1 shows the available overloadable operators and their corresponding implementation methods.

Table 1-1. Overloadable operators

Operator	Implementation method
a + b	a.plus(b)
a - b	a.minus(b)
a * b	a.multiply(b)
a ** b	a.power(b)
a / b	a.div(b)
a % b	a.mod(b)
a | b	a.or(b)

Operator	Implementation method
a & b	`a.and(b)`
a ^ b	`a.xor(b)`
a++ or ++a	`a.next()`
a-- or --a	`a.previous()`
a[b]	`a.getAt(b)`
a[b] = c	`a.putAt(b, c)`
a << b	`a.leftShift(b)`
a >> b	`a.rightShift(b)`
switch(a) { case(b) : }	`b.isCase(a)`
~a	`a.bitwiseNegate()`
-a	`a.negative()`
+a	`a.positive()`

Being Too Groovy

There's a natural tendency to embrace Groovy fully once it becomes apparent how much it has to offer over Java. Writing highly idiomatic Groovy code can lead to the code being hard to understand, though. I've written cryptic code with no comments that I've looked at months later and had to relearn how it works as if someone else had written it, because it was old enough that I didn't remember working on it, and I had sabotaged myself by writing the code in a way that made sense at the time but not when I came back to it.

The phrase I use for this is "be lazy but not sloppy." By this, I mean save yourself time (and typing) and take advantage of Groovy's cool features—but don't overdo it and make your code hard to work with and understand.

def Considered Harmful

One example of being "too groovy" is overusing the def keyword. Optional typing is very convenient, but specifying the type can help other readers of your code (and even yourself). Naming variables and methods well makes code more self-documenting, and the same goes for whether to type variables. For example, consider this relatively information-free line of code:

```
def foo = bar(5, true)
```

It's not at all clear what foo is or what you can do with it. If it's a string, call it a String (or whatever the type is).

I usually don't type both sides of an assignment, so because it's clear that strings is a List from the right side of the assignment, I'm okay with:

```
def strings = []
```
but when the right side is a method invocation, I'll type the left:
```
List<String> strings = someMethod('Hello', 'Groovy', 'World')
```
and I often add the generic type even though Groovy ignores it—again as a self-documentation practice and not because it has any other runtime effect. The same goes for the return type and parameter type(s) of methods; if it's void, I specify void some Method(...) instead of def someMethod(...), so the caller knows that there's nothing being returned.

each is a convenient way of looping, but I rarely use it, because it has almost no benefit over the for/in loop. For example, I would use:
```
for (string in strings) { ... }
```
instead of:
```
strings.each { string -> ... }
```
because they're equivalent, basically the same number of characters, and both are null-safe. And the for loop has the benefit that you can break out of it if there's a reason to stop looping, whereas each cannot, because returning from the closure that you pass to the each method returns from the closure, not each.

Of course, these are arguments about preferences—there's no right or wrong here. And I will certainly drop the type of a method parameter if it makes testing easier by letting me substitute a more convenient value that uses duck typing.

Closures Versus Methods

Another example of being "too groovy" is using a closure as a method where you don't use any features of the closure. If you don't set the delegate or use any other closure-specific feature, then there's no reason to use:
```
def foo = { <params> ->
  ...
}
```
instead of:
```
<return type> foo(<params>) {
  ...
}
```
and, in fact, using the method has the not-insignificant benefit of letting you specify the return type. Plus, things like AOP and method proxying that aren't Groovy-aware won't work at all with closures, because they're only treated like methods by Groovy—they're just public fields and are ignored by Java.

One real example of this is Grails services. Unlike controllers and taglibs, services are implemented with methods. A transactional service is implemented by Spring as a proxy that subclasses your service class and intercepts all method calls to start or join a trans-action as needed and manage error handling, automatic rollbacks, and so on. If you have a public closure in a service, it will be callable from Groovy just like a method, but it will not be transactional. The proxy only works with methods and completely ignores the closures, so you will introduce bugs that can be hard to track down by using closures here.

TypeChecked, CompileStatic, and invokedynamic

Groovy 2.0 and 2.1 add new features that make your code faster and provide more compiler checks. Groovy is a dynamic language and, as we've seen, this adds a tremen-dous amount of power and flexibility. But there are costs to this flexibility. One is that it's easier to introduce typos and mistakes into Groovy code than Java, because the compiler is more forgiving. For example, a one-character mistake such as:

```
int hc = someObject.hashcode()
```

will compile but fail with a `groovy.lang.MissingMethodException` at runtime (unless there is actually a `hashcode` method in the class). The compiler doesn't catch the mistake, because the code satisfies the Groovy grammar, but the compiler cannot know whether a `hashcode` method will be added to the metaclass before its first use in application code. And it can't assume that you meant to call the `hashCode` method.

Good testing should find errors like this, but Groovy now provides an option to make the compiler more aggressive: the `@TypeChecked` annotation. This can be applied at the class level or on individual methods, and the code within the scope of the annotation will be compiled more like Java than Groovy. You lose flexibility with this annotation but add earlier error checking.

`@CompileStatic` is the other new interesting annotation in 2.0. This adds the same checks as the `@TypeChecked` annotation and also compiles your Groovy code to nearly the same bytecode as that from the equivalent Java code. This means that you lose Groovy's metaprogramming support and some other dynamic features (although you retain many of the syntactic sugar features such as list and map comprehensions) but will see Java-like performance for the annotated code. Code that you would previously write in Java for maximum performance can now be written in Groovy.

Groovy 2.0 and 2.1 also have support for the new `invokedynamic` bytecode instruction that was added to support dynamic languages like Groovy and improve performance automatically. This differs from using `@CompileStatic` in that you don't make any changes to your code. Instead, you use a different compiler and runtime JAR. The "indy" version of Groovy takes advantage of the existence of the `invokedynamic` instruction in JDK 7 and later (with performance being much better in JDK 8).

See the Groovy 2.0 release notes (*http://groovy.codehaus.org/Groovy+2.0+release +notes*) and Groovy 2.1 release notes (*http://groovy.codehaus.org/Groovy+2.1+release +notes*) for more information about these and other new features.

CHAPTER 2

Grails Internals

The Grails Framework was initially discussed on the Groovy user mailing list in 2005. Ruby on Rails was becoming popular (having been released in 2004) and the idea of a JVM-based framework that used similar patterns and approaches seemed like a good one—where the dynamic power of the Groovy language and existing frameworks like Spring, Hibernate, Sitemesh, and several others could be combined into a powerful framework. Version 1.0 was released February 4, 2008, and version 2.0 on December 15, 2011. As of this writing, version 2.2 is the latest released version. Version 2.3 is being actively developed, and plans are being made for the 3.0 release.

Grails is a full-stack framework; meaning, it has support for all aspects of developing web applications. In addition, the framework is plugin-based, so developers can add on new functionality or replace the default implementation of a feature by installing one or more plugins into an application. In fact, newer versions of Grails often see functionality removed from the core and made available as a plugin. This includes Quartz (*http://grails.org/plugin/quartz*), Web Flow (*http://grails.org/plugin/webflow*), Jetty (*http://grails.org/plugin/jetty*), Tomcat (*http://grails.org/plugin/tomcat*), and Hibernate (*http://grails.org/plugin/hibernate*).

A typical Grails application leverages over 30 frameworks and libraries, with Grails wiring everything together and adding significant functionality of its own. Of course, Groovy (*http://groovy.codehaus.org/*) plays a huge role, providing dynamic language features, metaprogramming, and DSL support to make code and configuration more concise and expressive. The Spring Framework (*http://www.springsource.org/spring-framework*) provides a lot of core functionality, including a robust bean container, dependency injection, and support for transactions, database access, AOP, and proxies. In addition, the Grails web tier heavily uses Spring MVC. Hibernate (*http://hibernate.org/*) is no longer part of the core but it is a default plugin and is used in a large percentage of applications.

Some of the smaller libraries include cglib (*http://cglib.sourceforge.net/*) and Javassist (*http://www.csg.ci.i.u-tokyo.ac.jp/~chiba/javassist/*) for bytecode generation (for creating Java proxies at runtime); several Apache Commons libraries (*https:// commons.apache.org/*) including commons-collections (*https://commons.apache.org/ collections/*), commons-dbcp (*https://commons.apache.org/dbcp/*), and commons-lang (*https://commons.apache.org/lang/*); Ehcache (*http://ehcache.org/*) for object and data caching; log4j (*https://logging.apache.org/log4j/1.2/*) for logging support; SiteMesh (*http://wiki.sitemesh.org/display/sitemesh/Home*) in the web tier for page layout and templating; and Tomcat (*https://tomcat.apache.org/*) and H2 (*http://h2database.com/*) to provide an embedded web server and database in the development environment.

The idea of "convention over configuration" is a central philosophy. The idea is that, to the extent possible (and practical), the framework should do as much as possible for the developer, so you can be free to solve the real problems that the application was created to address instead of wasting time on plumbing code (and making it more fun to write your code). If you follow the convention patterns, which usually involve naming conventions and directory locations, along with simple instance and static variables in your classes, "magic" happens. Code is generated for you (often bytecode, so your classes aren't cluttered with computer-generated cruft) and behavior is added. The extra behaviors can come from methods added to your metaclasses, or by wrapping the Spring beans that represent your artifacts with proxies, or other artifact-specific approaches. But, in the end, a small amount of code results in a tremendous amount of functionality.

Note, however, that although it is often best to follow conventions, there are always ways to "go rogue" and use a different approach. If a feature of an underlying framework isn't exposed by Grails, or in general, if there isn't a "Grails way" to do something, then feel free to go around the framework and configure things yourself. But be sure that you know that there isn't a convenient Grails-based approach before going this route. Your application will be much easier to understand and maintain (especially important for new developers) if it follows standards.

Many of the conventions are implemented through the use of artifacts. Most application classes are of a particular artifact type, and most have a dedicated directory under the *grails-app* directory. These include controllers, domain classes, services, taglibs, and codecs (in the *utils* directory), and also *BootStrap.groovy*, *UrlMappings.groovy*, and filters classes in the *conf* directory. The exceptions are I18N message bundles in the *i18n* directory and GSPs in the *views* directory. Under the hood, Grails uses `org.code haus.groovy.grails.commons.ArtefactHandler` classes to manage the various types (e.g., `ControllerArtefactHandler` and `ServiceArtefactHandler`), and creates a `org.codehaus.groovy.grails.commons.GrailsClass` wrapper instance for each application artifact class to extract class properties and metadata, such as domain class constraints and the `allowedMethods` map in controllers (e.g., `DefaultGrailsTagLib Class` and `DefaultGrailsServiceClass`). Plugins can contribute new artifact types;

one example is the Quartz plugin (*http://grails.org/plugin/quartz*) that adds a `Job` artifact type.

Grails applications are web applications, so there is significant support for the web tier. This includes controllers to act as the server-side request handlers. JSPs are supported, but Groovy Server Pages (GSPs) are the preferred way of generating responses, because they support all of the same features but also Grails tags and even Groovy code. And, you are not restricted to only using GSPs and JSPs; you can render a response directly from a controller by writing to the response. One common idiom is the `render as XML` and `render as JSON` support, which conveniently serializes an object graph to XML or JSON. There is a DSL for routing application URLs to controller actions in `UrlMap pings.groovy`. Tomcat (or optionally Jetty) is available as a plugin to run an embedded web server in development mode, and creating a WAR file to deploy the application to a test or production server is as simple as running `grails war`.

Most web applications require data persistence, and Grails uses the GORM Framework for this. Originally tightly coupled to Hibernate, GORM was redesigned to be independent of its implementation (primarily to support NoSQL datastores) and now developers have the freedom to choose where to store their data. The Hibernate support was retrofitted to use the new approach, and there are now complete or partial implementations of GORM for MongoDB, Redis, Neo4j, Amazon SimpleDB, Riak, Gemfire, and JPA, and plans for supporting GORM for REST, Cassandra, as well as community-driven implementations. There is also an in-memory implementation that uses a `Con currentHashMap` store for use in unit testing.

Testing is critically important to the success of applications, and Grails has excellent support for writing and running tests. Unit and integration tests are supported by default, and plugins can add support for functional tests. JUnit (*https://github.com/junit-team/junit*) version 3 and 4 and Spock (*https://code.google.com/p/spock/*) are supported. AST transformations mix in significant functionality into unit tests, eliminating the need for base class hierarchies.

There is convenient support for "environments" in Grails—by default, `development`, `test`, and `production` (and it is easy to add your own). This makes it easy to define configuration settings across all environments, and environment-specific overrides, in `BootStrap.groovy`, `Config.groovy`, and `DataSource.groovy`. In addition, environments behave differently. In development mode, there is little or no caching and a reloading agent detects changed classes and reloads them on the fly, significantly increasing the time between server restarts. In the production environment, there is significant caching and no reloading by default (but GSP reloading can be enabled). The development environment is optimized for productivity, and the production environment is optimized for performance.

In addition, Grails provides many other useful features, including:

- Using services for transactions and to encapsulate business logic
- Using filters and interceptors to add behavior before or after requests
- Supporting internationalization (i18n) in controllers and GSPs based on Spring's core `MessageSource` concept
- Dependency management with Ivy (*https://ant.apache.org/ivy/*) using Maven repositories
- Convenient logging with Log4j, with a `log` variable added to all artifact classes by an AST transformation and a DSL to configure loggers and appenders

Grails is 100% open source; the code is hosted at GitHub (*https://github.com/grails/grails-core*). The development process is open, discussed on the mailing lists (*http://grails.org/Mailing+Lists*), and (at a high level) on the roadmap (*http://grails.org/Road map*). Anyone can contribute, from simply reporting an issue or requesting a feature in the bug tracker (*http://jira.grails.org/browse/GRAILS*), to contributing fixes and enhancements through pull requests and patches. Even the *grails.org* website is open source, and it is also hosted at GitHub (*https://github.com/grails-samples/grails-website*).

Installing Grails

Getting started using Grails is as simple as using Groovy. There are a few different ways to do this. The most direct is to download the latest ZIP distribution (*http://www.grails.org/download*), unpack the ZIP file to the location, set the `GRAILS_HOME` environment variable to point to your desired location, and add the *$GRAILS_HOME/bin* (or *%GRAILS_HOME%\bin* in Windows) directory to the `PATH` environment variable. That's all you need to do; run `grails --version` from a command prompt to verify that everything is working.

The GVM (Groovy enVironment Manager) tool described in Chapter 1 also works with Grails. It will install one or more versions of Grails and allows you to easily switch between installed versions if you have multiple projects using different versions of Grails. See the GVM site (*http://gvmtool.net/*) for usage information.

Creating an Application

Once Grails is installed, you can create an application and get it running and accepting requests in about one minute. Open a command prompt and cd into the directory where you want to project to exist and run:

```
$ grails create-app helloworld
```

If you've used earlier versions of Grails before 2.0, you'll be surprised at how little output there is from this command and others. A lot of the output isn't very interesting or useful, so it's mostly not shown. You can add the --verbose flag to see everything if you want.

A nte about the work directory

I encourage you to always edit *grails-app/conf/BuildConfig.groovy* when creating a new application (or plugin) and replace these three lines:

```
grails.project.class.dir = "target/classes"
grails.project.test.class.dir = "target/test-classes"
grails.project.test.reports.dir = "target/test-reports"
```

with this one:

```
grails.project.work.dir = 'target'
```

By default, Grails puts installed plugins, compiled classes, and other generated files in the project's work directory under the *.grails* directory in your home folder. By changing the work directory to be in the *target* folder in your application, I find that it keeps things better organized. Be sure to exclude the *target* directory from source control, because it's all generated code; you can use `grails integrate-with --git` to create a default *.gitignore* file if you haven't already. The biggest benefit of this configuration is that, if things start to seem strange and you see unexpected errors, you can just delete the *target* directory to force a full project rebuild.

Running the application

Once the `create-app` script finishes, `cd` into the *helloworld* directory (or whatever project name you used; Grails creates a new directory using the project name) and run the application with:

```
$ grails run-app
```

And that's it. You should see this message:

```
| Server running. Browse to http://localhost:8000/helloworld
```

and, if you view that address in a web browser, you can see the application's start page. Of course, there's not much that we can do with this application yet, but there's a significant amount of functionality available already.

The Grails Command Line

Grails uses Gant (*http://gant.codehaus.org/*), a Groovy wrapper around Ant (*https://ant.apache.org/*), as the technology behind its command-line scripts (although there are plans for 3.0 to replace Gant with Gradle (*http://www.gradle.org/*)). Grails includes over 50 scripts to perform various tasks, and these are documented in the reference documentation (*http://grails.org/doc/latest/*) in the Command Line group of the Quick Reference section in the right sidebar. Also, be sure to read the section in the Grails reference documentation on the command line (*http://grails.org/doc/latest/guide/commandLine.html*) for more general information, such as what switches are available and how to specify them.

You will find that you tend to use a core subset of these scripts on a regular basis. As we have seen, the `create-app` script is used to create a new application, and `create-plugin` creates new plugin projects. You can create artifact classes (domain classes, controllers, and so on) by hand, but it is far more convenient to use the scripts that do the work for you; these include `create-controller`, `create-domain-class`, `create-filters`, `create-script`, `create-service`, and `create-tag-lib` to create controllers, domain classes, filters, Gant scripts, services, and taglibs, respectively.

The `create` scripts result in basic starter classes but, for a more complete approach, use the `generate` scripts. `generate-controller` creates a full statically scaffolded CRUD controller for a specified domain class (along with a nearly complete unit test class), `generate-views` creates the GSPs that the generated controller uses to render responses, and `generate-all` creates all of the files that `generate-controller` and `generate-views` create. `generate-all` is the most convenient script to use, because it creates everything in one step. There is an "uber-generate" switch that will conveniently generate controllers, GSPs, and tests for all domain classes. It will not overwrite any existing files, but will prompt you about existing files in case you do want to regenerate them. Run `grails generate-all "*"` to generate everything with one command.

Artifacts are generated from templates that are included in your Grails installation. But these are just suggestions for the initial code and, if you want, you can customize them to include whatever standard code you like in generated classes. Run the `install-templates` script and edit the files in *src/templates* as needed. And you are not just limited to using the Grails bootstrap files. Check out Rob Fletcher's twitter-bootstrap-scaffolding (*https://github.com/robfletcher/twitter-bootstrap-scaffolding*) project, which uses Twitter Bootstrap (*http://twitter.github.com/bootstrap/*) for the scaffolded views.

Use the `compile` script to compile your Groovy and Java source to class files. This can be called directly, but it is usually called by other scripts for you, because most of the time, it is important to have up-to-date classes before performing another task.

Run your unit, integration, and functional tests with the `test-app` script. You can run all types in order, or any individual types.

Start the local server with `run-app`, which uses the embedded server (Tomcat by default, but Jetty if you prefer) to run your application as if it were an "exploded" WAR. You can also use the `run-war` script to build a full WAR file and deploy it to the embedded servlet container.

Once you are ready to deploy to a test server or even production, build a WAR file with the `war` script. This includes all of your compiled classes, JAR files, and static resources, and includes a generated *web.xml* file. Similarly, you can create an installable ZIP file for a plugin project with the `package-plugin` script.

When things get weird, and you see unexpected behavior of any type, run the `clean` script to delete generated class files and other resources. The next compile will be a full compile instead of an incremental compile. The dynamic nature of Groovy can confuse the compiler, and it is easy to get out of sync, so a full rebuild will often get you back on track. If you have dependency-related issues, or just want to see what your application's dependencies are, run the `dependency-report` script and open the generated HTML reports in a browser.

You can create missing test classes with the `create-unit-test` and `create-integration-test` scripts. Note that if you use the functional-test (*http://grails.org/plugin/functional-test*) plugin, do not run the `create-functional-tests` script if you are using an older (pre-2.0) version of the plugin. It will reset all of your *grails-app/conf* configuration files back to the default versions, and you will lose any changes.

There are also a few utility scripts that are very useful. Use `integrate-with` with its various flags to generate Eclipse/STS/GGTS project files, Intellij IDEA project files, a Textmate project file, an Ant build script, or a Git *.gitignore* file. `schema-export` hooks into the Hibernate DDL generation process to capture the SQL to create your tables, constraints, and foreign keys and write it to a file. This is convenient to ensure that the database will have the correct structure for your code, and is especially useful when mapping to an existing database. Use the `stats` script to write information about your application to the console, including how many artifacts of each type exist in your application and how many lines of code they have.

Finally, the script that I probably run more than any other is `console`. It launches a Groovy console (the same Swing application that the Groovy `groovyConsole` script launches) that is tightly integrated with your Grails application. Your application code and dependencies are included in its classpath, so you can run nearly any part of your application's functionality. The exception is that, because there won't be a web server running, you cannot call a controller or other HTTP-related feature. But you can access your database using GORM, your domain classes, or even SQL; you can call services or any other Spring beans; and, in general, use the console to prototype code and manually test features.

IDE Support

You are not required to use the command-line scripts when developing Grails applications and plugins; there are several IDEs and text editors with excellent support for Groovy and Grails.

The three best known IDEs for Grails development are Groovy/Grails Tool Suite (GGTS) (*http://grails.org/products/ggts*), IntelliJ IDEA (*https://www.jetbrains.com/idea/*), and NetBeans IDE (*http://netbeans.org/*). Each one supports creating applications and plugins, generating artifacts, and running Gant scripts all from the IDE. You can also easily launch your application from the IDE, with the option of starting in debug mode with breakpoints to diagnose issues. GGTS is an offshoot of the Spring-Source Tool Suite (STS) IDE that is based on Eclipse (*http://www.eclipse.org/*). It includes the Groovy-Eclipse (*http://groovy.codehaus.org/Eclipse+Plugin*) plugin for syntax highlighting and autocompletion of Groovy code, and robust support for Grails artifacts. IntelliJ is a commercial IDE with free support for Java and Groovy, although you must buy the Ultimate edition to get Grails support (*https://www.jetbrains.com/idea/features/groovy_grails.html*).

If you prefer a more lightweight development environment, there are several advanced text editors with support for Groovy and Grails development. TextMate (*http://macromates.com/*) is a popular one, although it is only available on the Mac. Sublime Text (*http://www.sublimetext.com/*) is a newer option and has most of the same features as TextMate but has the benefit of being cross-platform. Use the Grails package (*https://github.com/osoco/sublimetext-grails*) to add Grails and Groovy syntax highlighting and partial autocompletion. And, if you are a Vi/Vim (*http://www.vim.org/*) user, there are also resources to add Grails and Groovy support to this venerable text editor. See this two-part blog post (part 1 (*http://www.objectpartners.com/2012/02/21/using-vim-as-your-grails-ide-part-1-navigating-your-project/*) and part 2 (*http://www.objectpartners.com/2012/02/28/using-vim-as-your-grails-ide-part-2/*)) for tips to make Vim groovier.

Plugins

Notice that the start page lists the installed plugins; there are 23 by default. This includes 16 "core" plugins that form Grails itself:

- codecs
- controllers
- converters
- core
- dataSource
- domainClass
- filters
- groovyPages
- i18n

- `logging`
- `mimeTypes`
- `scaffolding`
- `services`
- `servlets`
- `urlMappings`
- `validation`

and seven that are optional and preinstalled for you.

- `cache`
- `database-migration`
- `hibernate`
- `jquery`
- `resources`
- `tomcat`
- `webxml`

 I usually refer to including a plugin in your application as "installing" it, but this isn't really what happens. There is an `install-plugin` script, but it's deprecated and will be removed. It doesn't really make much sense to install a Grails plugin; instead, we add a dependency on it as we would for a JAR dependency, in *BuildConfig.groovy*.

Optional Plugins

Each of the seven optional plugins are configured in the initial *BuildConfig.config* file that gets generated by the `create-app` script. They are included by default because many applications need their functionality, but any or all can be removed. These are all configured by default as suggestions, but if you don't need a plugin or aren't sure if you will need it in the future, remove it from *BuildConfig.groovy*. You can always add it back if you do need it.

The cache plugin

The `cache` plugin leverages the Spring Framework cache abstraction (*http://bit.ly/ Z5STH0*) added in Spring 3.1. It lets you easily annotate service methods to cache their return values, controller actions to cache their generated responses, and GSP fragments and rendered templates to cache their generated content. If you have any of these that are slow but are good caching candidates (i.e., given the same inputs you get the same output), you can use the plugin to store the data for future users rather than regenerating it each time. This can give you large performance boosts and increase scalability. The "core" plugin has an in-memory implementation but has extension plugins that add support for using libraries such as Ehcache (*http://ehcache.org/*) or Redis (*http://redis.io/*) for a more robust and configurable solution.

The database-migration plugin

The `database-migration` plugin adds integration with the Liquibase database refactoring tool (*http://www.liquibase.org/*). The plugin provides all of the features of Liquibase, and it is also tightly integrated with Grails. When you initially start an application, especially with "greenfield" projects where you design the database schema as you go, it's often convenient to let Grails and Hibernate drop and re-create the database tables every time you restart the application. But, eventually, things will stabilize and you will need a more formal change process, and Liquibase handles this very well. By generating scripts that are mostly database-agnostic (written in XML or the plugin's Groovy DSL) you can check new and updated domain classes into source control along with the scripts that make the necessary changes in the database. This lets you version the database like you do your code.

The hibernate plugin

The `hibernate` plugin adds support for using Hibernate (*http://hibernate.org/*) to access relational databases, usually with domain classes. Grails includes the H2 database (*http://h2database.com/html/main.html*), which is written in Java and supports in-memory as well as file-based databases, in addition to a traditional client-server configuration. This way, out of the box, your new application has support for a JDBC database for development and testing, which can easily be switched for a larger database like MySQL, PostgreSQL, or Oracle when needed. You'll see in the chapters on persistence that this plugin includes a Hibernate-backed implementation of GORM API. But, because GORM has several implementations, you can remove the `hibernate` plugin and replace it with one of those; use it alongside one or more of those; or, in unusual cases, even remove it completely if you have no need for database storage.

The jquery plugin

The `jquery` plugin doesn't do a lot really; it primarily makes the JQuery (*http://jquery.org/*) JavaScript library available to your application. Like any plugin, it is only downloaded once and is cached locally, so this makes it easier to use `jquery` in your applications by simply adding a line to *BuildConfig.groovy*. The plugin is also `resources`-aware, so it can easily participate in the 'resources` plugins' processing chain.

The resources plugin

The resources plugin and its dependent plugins (e.g., zipped-resources and cached-resources) add support for making static resources (e.g., CSS, JavaScript, and images) load faster. Features such as bundling files together, setting expires headers, and gzipping text files reduce the load on your servers, but, more important, make your pages load and render faster. Users quickly get frustrated with slow websites and are very likely not to return if performance is sluggish.

The tomcat plugin

The tomcat plugin adds an embedded version of the Tomcat servlet container (*https://tomcat.apache.org/*). This makes it easy to run your application in the development environment, because the plugin registers itself as the server to use in the run-app script. Jetty (*http://jetty.codehaus.org/jetty/*) was used as the embedded servlet container in earlier versions of Grails and it was tightly coupled. But, to make it easy to switch out, the interface between the container and Grails was made more pluggable to support using Tomcat, and it is straightforward to create plugins that add support for other containers such as Glassfish (*http://glassfish.java.net/*).

Note that the scope of the tomcat plugin in *BuildConfig.groovy* is build. This, along with the def scopes = [excludes: 'war'] configuration in the plugin's descriptor class, ensures that the plugin is only used for development and functional testing, but the jars are not included in the generated WAR files. This makes it possible to conveniently use Tomcat (or Jetty) while developing the application, but deploy to production into any servlet container.

The webxml plugin

There is no explicit dependency on the webxml plugin in *BuildConfig.groovy*, but it gets included because it is a dependency of the resources plugin. Grails transitively includes dependencies of dependencies for you, which greatly simplifies the configuration. You can't directly remove this plugin, because the resources plugin needs it to properly order its filters in the *web.xml* file, but, if you remove all plugins that depend on it (the spring-security-core plug-in also uses it), then Grails will remove it for you.

Core Plugins

Technically, you can remove some of the "core" plugins, but this isn't advised. They tend to have interdependencies and there isn't much benefit in removing them, even if the features they provide aren't needed by your application. But making Grails much more modular is an item on the development roadmap (*http://grails.org/Roadmap*); see the Application Profiles item. The current plan is to have several variants of Grails, from very small, lean configurations for specialized uses all the way to essentially what Grails is today.

The codecs plugin

The `codecs` plugin manages classes that can encode and decode between data types or formats. Grails ships with several codecs:

- `Base64Codec`
- `HexCodec`
- `HTMLCodec`
- `JavaScriptCodec`
- `MD5BytesCodec`
- `MD5Codec`
- `SHA1BytesCodec`
- `SHA1Codec`
- `SHA256BytesCodec`
- `SHA256Codec`
- `URLCodec`

It is simple to create your own by adding a Groovy class in the *grails-app/utils* folder. Additionally, the class name must end in `Codec`. The class can encode, decode, or both. To add support for encoding, add a static `encode` method or closure that takes a single argument; to support decoding, add a static `decode` method or closure that takes a single argument.

To use a codec, call the associated dynamic `encodeAs` and `decode` methods. For example, to html-escape a `String`, use `encodeAsHTML`; for example:

```
String hackXssAttempt = '<script>alert("hello")</script>'
assert hackXssAttempt.encodeAsHTML() ==
    '&lt;script&gt;alert(&quot;hello&quot;)&lt;/script&gt;'
```

Use the `decode` method to reverse the escaping:

```
assert '&lt;script&gt;alert(&quot;hello&quot;)&lt;/script&gt;'.decodeHTML() ==
    '<script>alert("hello")</script>'
```

Note that some codecs don't support decoding; for example, the digest-based codecs such as `MD5Codec`, `SHA1Codec`, and `SHA256Codec`.

As a simple example of a custom codec, consider this class. It converts camel-case strings to strings with underscores as separators, and also supports the reverse. Put this class in *grails-app/utils/com/yourcompany/UnderscoreCodec.groovy*, and you will have `encodeAsUnderscore` and `decodeUnderscore` methods:

```
package com.yourcompany

class UnderscoreCodec {

    static encode(o) {
        if (!o) return o

        def isLowerCase = { c -> Character.isLowerCase(c as char) }
        def isUpperCase = { c -> Character.isUpperCase(c as char) }

        def sb = new StringBuilder(o.toString())
        (1..sb.length()-2).each { int i ->
            if (isLowerCase(sb[i-1]) &&
                isUpperCase(sb[i]) &&
                isLowerCase(sb[i+1])) {

                sb.insert i++, '_'
            }
        }
        sb.toString()
    }

    static decode(o) {
        o?.toString()?.replaceAll '_', ''
    }
}
```

With that in place, you can use the codec like this:

```
assert 'FooAndBar'.encodeAsUnderscore() == 'Foo_And_Bar'
assert 'Foo_And_Bar'.decodeUnderscore() == 'FooAndBar'
```

 The *utils* folder is misunderstood by many developers. It is oddly named, considering that it is where codec classes go. It originally was expected that Grails would have multiple extension types like this, but that never happened. Some developers put utility classes here, but they should be in *src/groovy* or *src/java* along with the rest of your nonartifact code.

The controllers plugin

The `controllers` plugin configures most of the HTTP-related functionality in applications, and it is rare for an application to not have a web interface. Spring MVC backs the Grails controllers, but controller instances are not explicitly created as Spring MVC controllers. Instead, this plugin registers one controller as the `mainSimpleController` Spring bean (an instance of `org.codehaus.groovy.grails.web.servlet.mvc.Simple GrailsController`) and it handles all requests. It delegates to the `org.codehaus.groo vy.grails.web.servlet.mvc.MixedGrailsControllerHelper` helper class to find the controller class and method or closure that handles each request and calls it to handle the request. In addition, the plugin performs other configuration and registers several other Spring beans:

- Configures development mode reloading watch for controller classes in the *grails-app/controllers* directory
- Registers all controllers as Spring beans (by default as prototype scope) to support dependency injection
- Configures `org.springframework.web.servlet.mvc.method.annotation.Re` `questMappingHandlerMapping` and `org.springframework.web.serv` `let.mvc.method.annotation.RequestMappingHandlerAdapter` instances as Spring beans to support Spring MVC controllers written in Java or Groovy and annotated with `@Controller`
- Configures an `exceptionHandler` Spring bean to support error code URL mappings and add other exception handling logic during controller requests
- Configures a `multipartResolver` Spring bean (unless multipart file uploading is disabled)
- Configures a `viewNameTranslator` Spring bean
- Registers the `grails` servlet in *web.xml* to handle `*.dispatch` requests and forward internally to the appropriate handler
- Registers the `hiddenHttpMethod` filter in *web.xml* to support `REST` verbs beyond `GET` and `POST`
- Registers the `grailsWebRequest` filter in *web.xml* to create a new `GrailsWebRe` `quest` instance for each controller request
- Configures the AST transformations that mix in methods into controllers

The converters plugin

If you've ever used the convenient Grails `render data as XML` or `render data as` `JSON`, you've used this plugin. This is implemented by providing codecs and converters for converting objects to XML or JSON format and rendering to the servlet output writer. In addition, the plugin adds support for parsing requests in XML or JSON format into an XML DOM or JSON object depending on the request format.

The core plugin

The `core` plugin is mainly responsible for managing aspects of the Spring Framework integration with Grails.

One interesting thing that this plugin does is to override Groovy `MetaClass` resolution to ensure that `ExpandoMetaClass` is used instead of the default `MetaClassImpl`. This is needed to support convenient addition of methods and properties at runtime using syntax such as `Number.metaClass.bark = { -> "Woof!" }` to add a `bark()` method to all `Number` instances. In addition, it does the following:

- Watches *grails-app/conf/spring/resources.groovy* and *grails-app/conf/spring/resources.xml* for changes in development mode and reloads the beans defined there if you make changes
- Configures a Spring bean postprocessor that supports defining Spring bean properties in the `beans` property (*http://grails.org/doc/latest/guide/spring.html#propertyOverrideConfiguration*) in *Config.groovy*
- Configures a Spring bean postprocessor that supports setting Spring bean properties from the Grails configuration, using Spring's `${...}` syntax; because this is also `GString` syntax, be sure to use single quotes to avoid Groovy attempting to resolve the expressions before Spring can
- Configures Spring bean postprocessors that look for beans that implement the `GrailsApplicationAware`, `GrailsConfigurationAware`, and `PluginManagerAware` interfaces and calls the appropriate setter methods to inject those resources into the beans
- Configures the Spring bean builder to support annotated beans, for example `@Service` and `@Component`
- Configures a package scanner based on package names defined in *Config.groovy* to search for annotated Spring beans
- Registers a shutdown hook in development mode to shut down the Spring `ApplicationContext` when the application is stopped with Ctrl-C

The dataSource plugin

The `dataSource` plugin manages the creation and configuration of one or more `javax.sql.DataSource` instances based on the configuration in *grails-app/conf/DataSource.groovy*. Typically, an application will have just one `DataSource`, but you can configure as many as you like and also partition domain classes between them. The `DataSources` can be backed by a connection pool (the default) or retrieve connections for each call, and can configured as read-only or reference JNDI connection pools. The connection password can also be encrypted as long as the encryption codec is specified.

Each `DataSource` is registered with a suffix of `Unproxied`, and the actual Spring bean that is registered is an `org.springframework.jdbc.datasource.TransactionAwareDataSourceProxy` instance that wraps the real bean. This intercepts calls to the `getCon` nection method to return a new (or pooled) `Connection` only if there isn't an active one bound to the current transaction or Hibernate `Session`. This makes it easier to perform direct SQL queries and updates while using the active connection that Hibernate configures to make uncommitted changes visible to your queries.

In addition, a `TransactionManagerPostProcessor` bean postprocessor is registered to find Spring beans that implement the `TransactionManagerAware` interface and inject the `PlatformTransactionManager`.

This plugin is also responsible for registering the browser-based database console. This is a feature of the H2 database, but it works with any JDBC database for which you have a driver. It is enabled by default only in development, but you can configure which environments to include and also the URI from which the console is served. (by default `/dbconsole`).

Finally, the plugin deregisters JDBC drivers during shutdown or redeployment when the application is deployed as a WAR to avoid memory leaks.

The domainClass plugin

Grails domain classes are configured and managed by the `domainClass` plugin. It configures a watch for classes in the *grails-app/domain* directory in development mode to reconfigure based on updated properties and configurations.

Four Spring beans are registered for each domain class:

- A prototype-scoped bean to create new domain class instances; the name is the full class name
- A bean for the domain class artifact that wraps the actual class; the name is the full class name plus the suffix `DomainClass`
- A bean for the domain class `java.lang.Class`; the name is the full class name plus the suffix `PersistentClass`
- A `GrailsDomainClassValidator` bean that implements the Spring `org.spring framework.validation.Validator` interface and is the bridge between the validation rules specified in the domain class `constraints` block and the Spring validation workflow; the name is the full class name plus the suffix `Validator`

The domain class metaclass default constructor is overridden to return prototype instances from Spring. This is how dependency injection works in domain classes; by adding `def userService` as a field in a domain class, the bean is injected just like it would be in a controller, service, or any other artifact. Ordinarily, only beans retrieved from the `ApplicationContext` or dependency-injected get this behavior, but by using Groovy, it also works when using `new`.

There are a few other methods added to the metaclass:

- An `ident` method returns the domain class instance ID, regardless of its name.
- A static `create` method creates a new domain class instance (using the overridden metaclass constructor described above).
- The dynamic `addTo` and `removeFrom` collection methods add and remove instances in collections configured with `static hasMany = [ ... ]`.
- The dynamic `fooId` property retrieves the ID of a one-to-one or one-to-many property without loading the whole instance; for example, if a `Person` class has a `Manager manager` field, the `managerId` property would return the `Manager` foreign key value, without incurring the cost of lazy-loading the whole instance just to get its ID.

The filters plugin

The `filters` plugin configures Grails filters, which are a rare Grails artifact type that doesn't have its own folder under *grails-app*. Instead, they live in the *grails-app/conf* folder. Grails filters intercept controller requests, but not all requests. The name of the type is somewhat misleading, because it can cause confusion with servlet filters, which are classes that implement the `javax.servlet.Filter` interface and are registered in *web.xml*. If you have a need to intercept requests for requests that are not served by a controller, e.g., static resources or web service calls, use a servlet filter instead.

Grails filters are a convenient way to add interception logic across multiple controllers. There are three phases: before the controller action is called, after the controller is called, and after the view is rendered (or an exception occurs). You can stop the processing by returning `false` from the "before" handler, indicating that either the controller shouldn't be called because of some problem, or that the response has been handled directly by the filter.

Filters are indirect implementations of the Spring `org.springframework.web.serv let.HandlerInterceptor` interface. The plugin doesn't register one `HandlerIntercep tor` for each filters class but, instead, registers one composite interceptor (a `org.code haus.groovy.grails.plugins.web.filters.CompositeInterceptor` instance) that loops through each filters class at each phase.

A filters class can contain multiple filters, each potentially defining its own URIs or controllers and actions to which it applies, and the filters are called in the order defined in the class file. You can have multiple filters classes and they can optionally declare a `dependsOn` attribute to specify the order in which the sets of filters are run. So, for example, `FooFilters` can "depend on" `BarFilters`, which would result in each of the `BarFilters` filters being run in order, and then each of the `FooFilters` filters.

The groovyPages plugin

The `groovyPages` plugin provides support for GSPs and JSPs, including support for tag libraries (both traditional JSP tags and Grails taglibs).

Several taglibs are provided by default as part of Grails:

- `ApplicationTagLib`
- `CountryTagLib`
- `FormatTagLib`
- `FormTagLib`
- `JavascriptTagLib`
- `PluginTagLib`
- `RenderTagLib`
- `SitemeshTagLib`
- `ValidationTagLib`

Additionally, the plugin finds Groovy classes with names ending in `TagLib` in the *grails-app/taglib* directory and registers those as taglibs. It also configures a development-mode watch for changes in `taglib classes` and reloads them as needed.

The plugin creates several Spring beans:

- `gspTagLibraryLookup` finds all tags defined in Grails taglib classes.
- `jspTagLibraryResolver` resolves JSP taglibs by parsing *web.xml* and TLD files.
- `groovyPageResourceLoader` loads GSPs in development mode, and also when deployed as a WAR and either reloading or an external directory is configured.
- `groovyPageLocator` finds GSPs and caches precompiled GSPs when deployed as a WAR.
- `groovyPagesTemplateEngine` creates `org.codehaus.groovy.grails.web.pages.GroovyPageTemplate` instances for GSPs.
- `groovyPageRenderer` renders GSPs outside of the context of a web request; for example, from a service.
- `groovyPagesTemplateRenderer` does the work of rendering templates for the `render` tag defined in `RenderTagLib`; written in Java for performance.
- `groovyPageLayoutFinder` creates Sitemesh `Decorator` instances from Grails GSP layouts.
- `groovyPagesUriService` resolves URIs for controller actions.

- `jspViewResolver` creates Spring MVC `View` instances; these will be Grails `Groovy PageView` instances for GSPs and Spring `JstlView` instances for JSPs.
- `errorsViewStackTracePrinter` renders exception stack traces in the error page, trimmed of excess stack frames and including line numbers and source code to help identify the real problem.

The plugin adds support for viewing the source of a GSP in development mode. If you add `showSource` to the query string for a request, the generated Groovy source for the current GSP source will be rendered instead of the actual controller response.

The i18n plugin

The `i18n` plugin configures internationalization support in Grails. It looks for property files in the application's *grails-app/i18n* folder and configures the Spring `message Source` bean to resolve localized strings for the appropriate `Locale`.

The plugin also registers the Spring `localeChangeInterceptor` bean, which implements the `HandlerInterceptor` interface to intercept controller requests. It looks for the `lang` parameter and sets the `Locale` based on its value at the beginning of the request. This bean depends on the `localeResolver` bean that the plugin registers. This is a Spring `org.springframework.web.servlet.i18n.SessionLocaleResolver`, so once the locale is set, it will be remembered until the HTTP session times out or is invalidated.

The logging plugin

The `logging` plugin manages Log4j logging. It registers a listener in *web.xml* to initialize logging based on the Log4j DSL in *Config.groovy*, using `org.codehaus.groo vy.grails.plugins.log4j.Log4jConfig` to parse the DSL and create loggers and appenders. In development mode, the plugin reconfigures logging if *Config.groovy* is edited.

If the `grails.logging.jul.usebridge` property is set to `true` in *Config.groovy*, the plugin will configure a `org.slf4j.bridge.SLF4JBridgeHandler` to route JDK logging to Log4j. By default, this is enabled only in the development environment, because it is fairly slow.

Before Grails 2.0, the plugin would add a Commons Logging `log` property to the metaclass of every artifact. Grails 2 uses AST transformations extensively, so now this property is added directly to the class bytecode instead.

It is also possible to replace Log4j with its successor, Logback (*http://logback.qos.ch/*). If you install the `logback` (*http://grails.org/plugin/logback*) plugin and configure it as described in its documentation, your injected loggers will use Logback. In addition, you will be able to take advantage of Logback's increased performance and flexibility, and new features such as automatic compression of logfiles.

The mimeTypes plugin

The `mimeTypes` plugin registers the `mimeTypes` Spring bean, which is an array of `org.codehaus.groovy.grails.web.mime.MimeType` instances derived from the `grails.mime.types` property in *Config.groovy*.

These are used to infer the appropriate content type based on extension or `accept` request header. Checking the `accept` header is only enabled if the `grails.mime.use.ac cept.header` property in *Config.groovy* is `true`.

The plugin also configures the `grailsMimeUtility` bean that has utility methods for MIME types.

In addition, it adds mime type helper methods to the `HttpServletRequest` and `HttpServletResponse` metaclasses:

- `MimeType[] getMimeTypes()`
- `Object withFormat(Closure callable)`
- `String getFormat()`

The scaffolding plugin

The `scaffolding` plugin handles dynamic scaffolding. If a controller specifies a static `scaffolding` property, the plugin will use an instance of `org.codehaus.groo vy.grails.scaffolding.DefaultGrailsTemplateGenerator` to generate controller CRUD actions and GSPs in-memory at runtime. If the property value is `true`, the generator will look for a domain class with the same name as the controller minus `Con troller` (e.g., `BookController` would look for a `Book` domain class). Otherwise, the property value must be an existing domain class.

The services plugin

Transaction support in Grails service classes is configured by the `services` plugin. Services are transactional by default, so, without any configuration, the plugin will register the associated Spring bean using a Spring `TransactionProxyFactoryBean` to wrap the service instance in a transactional proxy. The proxy intercepts transactional methods and handles the logic for starting a transaction if one isn't running and is needed, joining an existing transaction, starting a new transaction, or throwing an exception if the method doesn't support running inside a transaction.

You can customize the proxy settings by using Spring's `org.springframework.trans action.annotation.Transactional` annotation. You can annotate at the class level and/or at the method level. The annotation supports specifying the propagation (the default being `Propagation.REQUIRED`; i.e., a transaction will be started if one isn't active, or the active transaction will be joined otherwise), the isolation level (which defaults to `Isolation.DEFAULT` to use the database default setting, often "read committed"), a timeout value (there is no default), and whether the transaction is read-only (the default is `false`). By default, runtime exceptions and errors trigger automatic rollbacks, but checked exceptions do not. You can specify which runtime exceptions and errors should not trigger rollbacks and which checked exceptions that should.

To disable transaction support for a service, you can use the `transactional` property:

```
static transactional = false
```

By default, services are singleton-scoped. But you can change the scope of the bean by setting the `scope` property to any value that Spring supports. One example would be to use `static scope = 'session'` and create something similar to a stateful session EJB. A new bean instance will be created on-demand the first time the bean is requested from the `ApplicationContext` and stored in the session. Because it is specific to a particular session, it can have state variables (which should be avoided with singletons because of thread-safety issues). When the session ends, the bean will be discarded and, if it supports a destroy method, it will be called to give you a chance to do whatever cleanup is needed.

You can also configure whether the service is lazily initialized. By default, this is set to `true`, but you can disable this and make initialization eager with the `lazyInit` property:

```
static lazyInit = false
```

If the service is transactional, its proxy uses a Spring `PlatformTransactionManager`. If you use multiple data sources, there will be a transaction manager configured for each one. The service can only use one transaction manager, so you can configure which one to use with the `datasource` property. This has no effect on which data source is used by individual domain classes, because this is configured for each domain class. It simply specifies which transaction manager will be active for the service method calls.

One implication of this is that, if you make changes to domain classes in multiple classes, only the changes that are made in the data source used by the service's transaction manager will be made transactionally. The other changes will not be transactional at all. You can configure an XA data source that will use two-phase commit across all data sources; the most convenient way to do this is to use the `atomikos` plugin (*http:// grails.org/plugin/atomikos*).

The servlets plugin

The `servlets` plugin adds helper methods to the `ServletContext`, `HttpSession`, `HttpServletRequest`, and `HttpServletResponse` metaclasses.

`ServletContext`, `HttpSession`, and `HttpServletRequest` each get `getProperty`, `set Property`, `getAt`, and `putAt` metaclass methods that allow getting and setting attributes using property syntax and subscript syntax. For example, you can access session attributes with `def foo = session.foo` or `def foo = session['foo']` instead of using the more verbose `def foo = session.getAttribute('foo')`. Setting attributes is similar: you can use `request.foo = 'bar'` or `request['foo'] = 'bar'` instead of `request.setAttribute('foo', 'bar')`.

The plugin adds an overload for the `<<` operator to the `HttpServletResponse` metaclass to write the value to the response writer. This lets you use syntax like `response << 'some content'` instead of `response.getWriter().write('some content')`.

A few additional methods are added to the `HttpServletRequest` metaclass:

- `boolean isRedirected()`
- `String getForwardURI()`
- `boolean isXhr()`
- `boolean isGet()`
- `boolean isPost()`
- `def find(Closure c)`
- `def findAll(Closure c)`
- `def each(Closure c)`

The accessor methods are more commonly used with property syntax—for example, `if (request.post) { ... }` or `if (request.xhr) { ... }`.

The `find` method loops through the request attributes and returns the first one the closure returns `true`, and the `findAll` method finds all matching attributes. The `each` method loops through all attributes and evaluates the closure for each one.

The `isXhr` method is used to check if the request was made using Ajax. Most JavaScript libraries add an `X-Requested-With` header with the value `XMLHttpRequest`, so that is used to make the determination. In addition, as of version 2.1.2 and 2.2, you can define a closure in *Config.groovy* under the `grails.web.xhr.identifier` key that can be used to further refine the logic.

The urlMappings plugin

URL mapping support is configured by the `urlMappings` plugin. It looks for Groovy classes in the *grails-app/conf* folder with names ending in `UrlMappings`.

The plugin registers the `grailsUrlMappingsHolder` Spring bean that contains `UrlMapping` instances that are constructed by parsing the `mappings` closure in the `UrlMappings` classes. It also creates the `grailsLinkGenerator` bean that builds links from controller and action names, URIs, or full URLs. And it creates the `grailsUrlConverter` bean to convert controller and action names to the appropriate syntax for URLs. By default, this uses a camel-case syntax (using `CamelCaseUrlConverter`) but you can configure hyphenation syntax using `HyphenatedUrlConverter` with the `grails.web.url.converter` attribute in *Config.groovy*:

```
grails.web.url.converter = 'hyphenated'
```

The plugin also registers elements in *web.xml*. All error code URL mappings are registered as `<error-page>` elements that are configured to be routed through the registered `ErrorHandlingServlet` for processing. Depending on the URL mappings, the error page can be rendered directly as a GSP or JSP, or through a controller action. It also registers `UrlMappingsFilter` as a filter to intercept requests and determine which controller and action to use to handle the request.

The validation plugin

The `validation` plugin adds validation-related metaclass methods to classes specified in the `grails.validateable.classes` property in *Config.groovy*:

- `boolean hasErrors()`
- `Errors getErrors()`
- `setErrors(Errors)`
- `void clearErrors()`
- `boolean validate()`

The plugin also uses a `ConstrainedPropertyBuilder` to parse the classes' con straints blocks.

Conventions

Grails is a convention-over-configuration framework, so let's take a look at the standard conventions used in the controller, service, and domain tiers.

Controller and View Conventions

The primary controller convention is that, by adding a Groovy class with a name ending in `Controller` under the *grails-app/controllers* folder, it automatically becomes a controller class in your application. This means that all public methods (and public closure fields, although methods are preferred) are controller actions that are called to handle web requests. And you don't even have to write any code; adding `static scaffold = true` or `static scaffold = SomeDomainClassName` to an empty controller class triggers the creation of dynamically scaffolded controller and GSPs at runtime.

Over 30 methods are mixed into controller classes with AST transformations. The majority are added from the org.codehaus.groovy.grails.plugins.web.api.Control lersApi class:

- Object bindData(Object target, Object args) (plus five variants)
- Object chain(Map args)
- String forward(Map params)
- String getActionName()
- String getActionUri()
- ApplicationContext getApplicationContext()
- Map getChainModel()
- String getControllerName()
- String getControllerUri()
- Errors getErrors()
- FlashScope getFlash()
- GrailsApplication getGrailsApplication()
- GrailsApplicationAttributes getGrailsAttributes()
- ModelAndView getModelAndView()
- GrailsParameterMap getParams()
- HttpServletRequest getRequest()
- HttpServletResponse getResponse()
- ServletContext getServletContext()
- HttpSession getSession()
- String getTemplateUri(String name)
- String getViewUri(String name)
- GrailsWebRequest getWebRequest()
- boolean hasErrors()
- void header(String headerName, Object headerValue)
- Object redirect(Map args)
- Object render(Object o)
- Object render(String txt)
- Object render(Map args)

- Object render(Closure c)
- Object render(Map args, Closure c)
- Object withForm(Closure callable)

Additionally, the void render(Converter converter) and void jsonHeader(Object value) methods are added from the org.codehaus.groovy.grails.plugins.convert ers.api.ConvertersControllersApi class, and the Object withFormat(Closure callable) method is added from the org.codehaus.groovy.grails.plu gins.web.api.ControllersMimeTypesApi class.

This is how properties like request, response, and params are available inside your controllers; they're not fields but, instead, are getter methods that Groovy allows you to access as if they were.

Another convention is that, if a controller action uses a GSP of the same name as the action name, you can omit it. This also depends on having the GSP in the correct folder. For example, given a controller such as:

```
class UserController {

    ...

    def list() {
        ...
        [count: count, users: users]
    }
}
```

the return value of a model Map (or none if no data is required by the GSP) is all that's required. Grails will look for *grails-app/views/user/list.gsp* and use it to generate the response. Because the folder name matches the logical controller name (i.e., class with Controller removed and with the first letter lowercased) and the GSP name matches the action name, it will be used. This is the equivalent of the more verbose:

```
def list() {
    ...
    render(view: 'list', model: [count: count, users: users])
}
```

Data binding conventions

You can manually get request parameter values from the params map, or call one of the overloaded bindData methods.

Layout conventions

Ordinarily, the GSP will use a layout, and a common way to specify which one to use is with a meta tag; for example:

```
<meta name='layout' content='main'>
```

This will look for *grails-app/views/layouts/main.gsp* and use that as the Sitemesh template. But, there are other options to determine which layout to use. One is with the static `layout` property in the controller class:

```
static layout = 'main'
```

In addition, you can specify the default layout globally in *Config.groovy*:

```
grails.sitemesh.default.layout = 'main'
```

These all require setting a value somewhere, but there are a few conventions that you can use that don't involve specifying any values. If no other rule determines a layout to use for a GSP, Grails will use *grails-app/views/layouts/application.gsp*, if it exists. In the previous example, if there were a GSP template *grails-app/views/layouts/user.gsp*, it would be used as the template for all GSPs used by the `UserController` actions unless overridden. And, in this example, you can also use the more fine-grained approach of creating a template for individual GSPs by creating *grails-app/views/layouts/user/list.gsp*.

URI conventions

If you have used other frameworks, you're probably used to configuring which URIs are handled by your controllers. You can do this in Grails, but, by default, a quasi-restful URI scheme is configured for you in *UrlMappings.groovy*:

```
class UrlMappings {

    static mappings = {
        "/$controller/$action?/$id?"{
            constraints {
                // apply constraints here
            }
        }

        ...
    }
}
```

This is a sensible default, and you can remove or reconfigure this default to use your own patterns and/or add additional mappings for specific cases. But most of the time, this default behavior plus some custom mappings is a good idea.

All of these conventions combined mean that, if you create a new controller class in the correct place with the correct name, put the controller's GSPs in the correct place with the correct names, and reference the applicable layouts (either by convention or using a `meta` tag), then serving your content "just works." After a few cycles of being aware of what you're doing, it becomes automatic (even more so with helper scripts such as `create-controller` and `generate-all`), and you can spend more time solving real application problems and less time messing with framework settings and configurations.

Service Conventions

Like controllers and most other artifact types, there is a naming convention for services. A Groovy class in your application becomes a Grails service if it is in the *grails-app/ services* folder and the class name ends in `Service`. In older versions of Grails, the `create-service` script generated a starter class with the property `static transac tional = true`, but this was removed because it's the default setting and, as such, is redundant. You should only specify the `transactional` attribute if all of the methods are nontransactional; for example, if the class has utility methods that don't write to the database.

In addition, services are automatically registered as Spring beans. By default, they're singletons, but it's a simple matter to change the bean scope by adding a `scope` property —for example, `static scope = 'session'`. The bean name is the class name with the first character lowercased.

The service becomes transactional if you have no `transactional` property (or if it's set to `true`) or if there is at least one Spring `@Transactional` annotation. Services get registered as Spring beans whether they're transactional or not, but if they are transactional, the actual bean instance will be a proxy around the real class instance. This way, all public method access can be intercepted, and a transaction can be started or joined, or an exception can be thrown if one isn't allowed, all based on metadata inferred from the Grails defaults or the `@Transactional` annotation values. Other than the optional addition of annotations, this is entirely automatic.

Domain Class Conventions

Domain classes are a rare artifact type where there is no naming convention—the class names can be any valid name. Domain classes are Groovy classes in the *grails-app/ domain* folder. Fields without a scope modifier (`public`, `private`, etc.) are automatically persistent. The class name maps to the backing database table name and field names map to column names, with a configurable naming convention that, by default, converts camel-case names to table and column names using underscores.

Like controllers, many methods are added to domain classes by AST transformations during compilation. There are over 20 instance methods, including:

- `Object attach()`
- `void clearErrors()`
- `void delete()`

- void delete(Map)
- void discard()
- Errors getErrors()
- Map getProperties()
- Boolean hasErrors()
- Serializable ident()
- boolean instanceOf(Class)
- boolean isAttached()
- Object lock()
- Object merge()
- Object merge(Map)
- Object mutex(Closure)
- Object refresh()
- Object save()
- Object save(Map)
- Object save(boolean)
- BindingResult setProperties(Object)
- String toString()
- boolean validate()
- boolean validate(boolean)
- boolean validate(List)
- boolean validate(Map)

and over 70 static methods, including:

- static Integer count()
- static Criteria createCriteria()
- static void deleteAll(Object[])
- static void deleteAll(Iterable)
- static List executeQuery(String)
- static List executeQuery(String, Collection)
- static List executeQuery(String, Map)

- static List executeQuery(String, Collection, Map)
- static List executeQuery(String, Map, Map)
- static Integer executeUpdate(String)
- static Integer executeUpdate(String, Map)
- static Integer executeUpdate(String, Collection)
- static Integer executeUpdate(String, Collection, Map)
- static Integer executeUpdate(String, Map, Map)
- static boolean exists(Serializable)
- static Object find(Object)
- static Object find(String)
- static Object find(Closure)
- static Object find(Object, Map)
- static Object find(String, Map)
- static Object find(String, Collection)
- static Object find(String, Collection, Map)
- static Object find(String, Map, Map)
- static List findAll()
- static List findAll(Object)
- static List findAll(String)
- static List findAll(Closure)
- static List findAll(Object, Map)
- static List findAll(String, Map)
- static List findAll(String, Collection)
- static List findAll(Map, Closure)
- static List findAll(String, Map, Map)
- static List findAll(String, Collection, Map)
- static List findAllWhere(Map)
- static List findAllWhere(Map, Map)
- static Object findOrCreateWhere(Map)
- static Object findOrSaveWhere(Map)
- static Object findWhere(Map)

- static Object findWhere(Map, Map)
- static Object first()
- static Object first(String)
- static Object first(Map)
- static Object get(Serializable)
- static List getAll()
- static Integer getCount()
- static PersistentEntity getGormPersistentEntity()
- static Map getValidationErrorsMap()
- static Map getValidationSkipMap()
- static Object last()
- static Object last(String)
- static Object last(Map)
- static List list()
- static List list(Map)
- static Object load(Serializable)
- static Object lock(Serializable)
- static Object merge(Object)
- static Object proxy(Serializable)
- static Object read(Serializable)
- static List saveAll(Iterable)
- static List saveAll(Object[])
- static DetachedCriteria where(Closure)
- static DetachedCriteria whereAny(Closure)
- static DetachedCriteria whereLazy(Closure)
- static Object withCriteria(Closure)
- static Object withCriteria(Map, Closure)
- static Object withDatastoreSession(Closure)
- static Object withNewSession(Closure)
- static Object withNewTransaction(Closure)
- static Object withSession(Closure)

- `static Object withTransaction(Closure)`
- `static Object withTransaction(TransactionDefinition, Closure)`

These methods are independent of the properties of the class. But, there are also dynamic methods added to the metaclass that are usually based on properties. Any persistent property can be included in a method starting with `findAllBy` or `findAllWhere`, for example, `findAllByFirstNameAndLastName`. Persistent collections that are mapped in the static `hasMany` block generate `addTo` and `removeFrom` methods; for example, `static hasMany = [children: Person]` adds the `addToChildren` and `removeFromChildren` methods.

Constraints can easily be added to domain classes by using the `constraints` DSL. Some of these are only run in application code, but many affect the table DDL without requiring any SQL coding on your part. Some examples include the `nullable` and `unique` constraints. These constraints come into play during validation, which is not separate from the domain classes but is instead triggered by the `validate` method, or by the `save` methods, which trigger validation and only attempt to save the instance if validation succeeded.

Further table DDL adjustments can be made with the `mapping` DSL, again without requiring any SQL. This includes customization of the table and column names, caching, field and collection laziness, and optimistic locking.

So, although a simple domain class such as:

```
class Person {
    String firstName
    String lastName
}
```

may seem like an anemic POGO, it's far from that. There is a tremendous amount of behavior added to the class by Grails.

More Information

This has been a rather detailed look at some of the internals of Grails. For a more comprehensive overview and introduction to Grails, see the Grails reference documentation (*http://grails.org/doc/latest/*)—in particular, the Getting Started section (*http://grails.org/doc/latest/guide/gettingStarted.html*). There are also more general books available. One that is somewhat dated but free is *Getting Started with Grails*, Second Edition (*http://www.infoq.com/minibooks/grails-getting-started*).

The most current book that covers Grails 2 is *The Definitive Guide to Grails 2*, and there is also *Grails in Action, Second Edition*, which covers Grails 2 but is only (as of this writing) available in an early access edition.

CHAPTER 3

Persistence

The persistence strategy in Grails is called Grails object relational mapping, or GORM. In earlier versions of Grails, this was a wrapper around Hibernate's ORM implementation, but has been abstracted to allow access to other data sources, including NoSQL datastores like MongoDB, Redis, and Neo4j. GORM for Hibernate has been retrofitted to follow the new GORM API, which provides a consistent developer experience regardless of the underlying storage implementation. See the grails-data-mapping project on GitHub (*https://github.com/SpringSource/grails-data-mapping*) for more detailed information.

But it is not merely a least-common-denominator approach where only the features that are common to all datastores are supported. Instead, there is a core set of functionality that all implementations must provide (mapping from domain classes to datastore storage, supporting dynamic finders and Criteria queries, and so on) but each provider also supports access to the underlying implementation to access noncore features directly.

This means that, for data that fits the relational model well, you can use Hibernate to manage persistence in a relational database; but, for less structured data or to support more dynamic schemas, you can use a NoSQL datastore. The Grails NoSQL plug-ins coexist well with Hibernate, so you are free to store all of your data in a relational database, all in one or more NoSQL datastores, or use a mix.

See the extensive GORM documentation in the Grails reference (*http://grails.org/doc/latest/guide/GORM.html*) for more information.

Data Mapping

The convention for mapping a Grails class to a datastore representation is to create a class under the *grails-app/domain* directory. These can be as simple as a class with one or more public fields; for example, this `Person` class:

```
package com.acme

class Person {
    String firstName
    String lastName
}
```

You can create domain classes by hand with your IDE or text editor, because they are just Groovy classes in the *grails-app/domain* directory (in the subdirectory corresponding to their package). However, the preferred way to create them is with the create-domain-class script (*http://bit.ly/15g7N18*), because it uses a standard template and automatically creates a corresponding test class:

```
$ grails create-domain-class person
```

You can see from the output that it creates a test class as well as the domain class (take this as a strong hint to remember to write tests!):

```
| Created file grails-app/domain/appname/Person.groovy
| Created file test/unit/appname/PersonTests.groovy
```

This example will create the class in the default artifact package because one is not specified but instead determined by the `grails.project.groupId` property in *Config.groovy*. You can specify the package to override this behavior:

```
$ grails create-domain-class com.mycompany.Book
```

The domain class is created from a template that you can customize. If you find yourself copying and pasting previous domain classes to save yourself the typing for commonly added features, or if you manually make these changes repeatedly, you can install the templates into your project and edit them:

```
$ grails install-templates
```

The template for domain classes is in *src/templates/artifacts/DomainClass.groovy*:

```
@artifact.package@class @artifact.name@ {

    static constraints = {
    }
}
```

If you have common code that you repeatedly add to new domain classes, you should update the template instead and save yourself the time. For example, you could make all new domain classes implement `Serializable` and add an empty `mapping` block:

```
@artifact.package@class @artifact.name@ implements Serializable {

    static constraints = {
    }

    static mapping = {
```

```
      }
   }
```

Nonpersistent Domain Classes

You may ask how to have nonpersistent domain classes in your application, and the short answer is that you can't. Of course, everything is possible, but Grails assumes that, if you are following the convention of putting a Groovy class in the *grails-app/domain* folder, you want the class to be persistent; you don't have to configure this, so there is no direct way to make it nonpersistent. But it is possible to have classes that model domain objects that do not map to a database table.

One way is to simply not invoke any GORM methods on domain classes that do not use the database. If you use Hibernate and have `dbCreate` set to `create-drop` or `up date`, you will end up with database tables for these, but you will be switching to using database migrations [e.g., by using the `database-migration` plugin (*http://grails.org/ plugin/database-migration*)] soon enough and, at that point, you can just choose to not create the tables.

The other way is to put them in *src/groovy* (or *src/java*). This has the benefit of being ignored by GORM, but it does partition your domain model into two different sections of your code.

The real issue here is a semantic one; the `domain` artifact type in Grails is for your persistent domain classes, and Grails does not have a well-defined concept of a general domain model, leaving that up to you.

Data Validation

GORM supports data validation with the `constraints` DSL. This is declared as a static closure in your domain class containing the various rules that define what is and is not valid data for each domain class. There are several built-in constraints (`blank`, `nulla ble`, `matches`, `creditCard`, and so on) and, for more complex validation checks, there is also support for custom validations. By default, all persistent properties are considered to be not-null, so there is an implicit `nullable: false` constraint.

Table 3-1 shows the built-in constraints; see the Grails reference documentation on internationalization (*http://grails.org/doc/latest/guide/i18n.html*) for information on how to use the i18n codes.

Table 3-1. GORM constraints

Name	Description	i18n code	Notes
blank (*http:// grails.org/doc/ latest/ref/ Constraints/ blank.html*)	Whether an empty String is allowed	className.propertyName.blank	
creditCard (*http:// grails.org/doc/ latest/ref/ Constraints/credit Card.html*)	Checks that a String is a valid credit card number	className.propertyName.creditCard.invalid	Uses the Apache Commons Credit CardVa lidator
email (*http:// grails.org/doc/ latest/ref/ Constraints/ email.html*)	Checks that a String is a valid email address	className.propertyName.email.invalid	Uses the Apache Commons EmailVa lidator
inList (*http:// grails.org/doc/ latest/ref/ Constraints/ inList.html*)	Checks that the value is in the specified list	className.propertyName.not.inList	Make sure the type of the list values matches the property type; consider using an Enum if possible
matches (*http:// grails.org/doc/ latest/ref/ Constraints/match es.html*)	Checks that a String matches a regular expression	className.propertyName.matches.invalid	
max (*http:// grails.org/doc/ latest/ref/ Constraints/ max.html*)	Checks that a Comparable property does not exceed the specified value	className.propertyName.max.exceeded	
maxSize (*http:// grails.org/doc/ latest/ref/ Constraints/ maxSize.html*)	Checks the maximum size of a String, Collection, or array	className.propertyName.maxSize.exceeded	

Name	Description	i18n code	Notes
min (*http:// grails.org/doc/ latest/ref/ Constraints/ min.html*)	Checks that a `Comparable` property does not exceed the specified value	`className.propertyName.max.exceeded`	
minSize (*http:// grails.org/doc/ latest/ref/ Constraints/ minSize.html*)	Checks the minimum size of a `String`, `Collection`, or array	`className.propertyName.maxSize.exceeded`	
notEqual (*http:// grails.org/doc/ latest/ref/ Constraints/notEqu al.html*)	Checks that the value is not equal to the specified value	`className.propertyName.notEqual`	
nullable (*http:// grails.org/doc/ latest/ref/ Constraints/nulla ble.html*)	Checks that the value is not null	`className.propertyName.nullable`	Defaults to `false`
range (*http:// grails.org/doc/ latest/ref/ Constraints/ range.html*)	Checks that a `Comparable` property is within the specified Groovy range	`className.propertyName.range.toosmall` or `className.propertyName.range.toobig`	
size (*http:// grails.org/doc/ latest/ref/ Constraints/ size.html*)	Restricts the size of a `String`, `Collection`, or array to the specified Groovy range	`className.propertyName.size.toosmall` or `className.propertyName.size.toobig`	
unique (*http:// grails.org/doc/ latest/ref/ Constraints/ unique.html*)	Checks that the value is unique	`className.propertyName.unique`	Can check one or multiple fields; executes a `select` query during validation
url (*http:// grails.org/doc/ latest/ref/ Constraints/url.html*)	Checks that the value is a valid URL	`className.propertyName.url.invalid`	Uses the Apache Commons `UrlVali dator`

In addition, there are two checks listed as constraints that are used to affect UI rendering but do not register validation errors: attributes (*http://grails.org/doc/latest/ref/Constraints/attributes.html*) and widget (*http://grails.org/doc/latest/ref/Constraints/widget.html*).

The syntax for specifying constraints is fairly straightforward; add the static con straints block, and inside it, list the various data validation rules:

```
class Thing {
    String cardNumber
    String color
    String email

    static constraints = {
        cardNumber creditCard: true, blank: false
        color inList: ['Red', 'Green', 'Blue']
        email unique: true, size: 5..100
    }
}
```

Let's take a closer look at the DSL to see how this works. To a new user, this syntax can seem a bit strange, but there is not really that much magic here. Each line is simply a method call. But, looking at the domain class, there are obviously no cardNumber, color, or email methods, just properties. It is more clear if we add in the optional parentheses:

```
static constraints = {
    cardNumber(creditCard: true, blank: false)
    color(inList: ['Red', 'Green', 'Blue'])
    email(unique: true, size: 5..100)
}
```

The first line is a call to a (nonexistent) cardNumber method, and the parameters are a single Map ([creditCard: true, blank: false]). This works because the Grails code that evaluates the constraints block registers an instance of org.codehaus.groo vy.grails.validation.ConstrainedPropertyBuilder as the delegate of the closure, and then invokes the closure. It runs because it is valid Groovy code, and missing meth- ods and properties get dispatched to the builder, which has the logic to convert the method calls and the Map values to constraint rules for the associated property (as long as there is a property corresponding to each method invocation). Each key/value pair in the parameter Map defines a constraint and its data. The constraints are implemented as classes implementing the Grails org.codehaus.groovy.grails.validation.Con straint interface; for example, NullableConstraint, MaxConstraint, and InListCon straint.

Custom Validation

Grails comes with many of the standard checks that you will need, but there will be cases where these checks are not sufficient. If you need to check a value in relation to another value, or do a more complicated check, you can create a custom validator. These are defined as closures with the `validator` name:

```
class User {
    String username
    String password

    static constraints = {
        username blank: false, unique: true
        password blank: false, size: 8..100, validator: { pwd, user ->
            if (user.username == pwd) {
                return 'user.password.matchesUsername'
            }
        }
    }
}
```

A custom validator can have from zero to three parameters. If it declares one, its value is the field value being validated (declaring none is the same, except that there is one parameter with default closure name `it`):

```
static constraints = {
    ...
    fieldName validator: { fieldValue ->
        // validate the field's value
    }
}
```

In all of these examples, the parameter names are just examples, and you can name them however you like; only the number of parameters is significant to GORM.

If a custom validator declares two parameters, then the first is the value and the second is the domain class instance being validated. This variant is useful if you need to access other persistent values in the instance, and also to access other class data such as dependency-injected fields. For example, it is a common practice to delegate business logic to services. By adding a dependency injection for a service, we can access it from the current instance:

```
class User {

    def userService

    String username
```

```
    String password

    static constraints = {
        ...
        password blank: false, size: 8..100, validator: { pwd, user ->
            return user.userService.validatePassword(pwd, user)
        }
    }
}
```

If the validator has three parameters, then the first is the value, the second is the instance, and the third is the Spring `Errors` instance. Use this approach when you need to directly call `rejectValue` or other `Errors` methods:

```
static constraints = {
    ...
    fieldName validator: { fieldValue, instance, errors ->
        ...
    }
}
```

Grails ignores any return value when using the three-parameter variant, because it is assumed that your validator works directly with the `Errors` instance.

 You can reuse custom validators by making them static properties of a utility class and referring to them from your domain classes:

```
class Validators {
    static passwordCheck = { pwd, user -> ... }
    static otherValidator = { value, obj, errors -> ... }
}
static constraints = {
    ...
    password blank: false, size: 8..100, validator: Validators.passwordCheck
}
```

If you need to access the database in a custom validator, be sure to wrap the calls in a `withNewSession` block. If you do not, you run the risk (only in Hibernate currently) of the query triggering a flush and causing unexpected problems.

Extreme Custom Validation

To really take matters into your own hands, you can completely bypass the standard validation approach and define your own validator class, or reuse an existing one (e.g., from a traditional Spring application). Each domain class artifact has an `org.code haus.groovy.grails.validation.GrailsDomainClassValidator`. This is registered as a Spring bean with a bean name that is the full class name with package and the suffix `Validator`, so the `com.myapp.User` domain class would have a corresponding `com.myapp.UserValidator` validator bean. Therefore, to define your own, register it in *grails-app/conf/spring/resources.groovy* with the correct name and it will replace the one that Grails registers by default:

```
import com.myapp.MyUserValidator

beans = {
    'com.myapp.UserValidator'(MyUserValidator)
}
```

Put this class in *src/groovy* or *src/java* and implement the Spring `org.springframe work.validation.Validator` interface. Grails validators support cascading to validate associated many-to-one fields; to participate in this, implement `org.codehaus.groo vy.grails.validation.CascadingValidator` instead. You will probably find that it is most convenient to subclass `org.codehaus.groovy.grails.validation.GrailsDo mainClassValidator` and override one or more of `validate(Object obj, Errors errors)`, `validate(Object obj, Errors errors, boolean cascade)`, and `postVa lidate(Object obj, Errors errors)`.

If you just implement one of the validator interfaces and do not subclass `GrailsDomain ClassValidator`, you will also need to wire up the validator to the domain class in *BootStrap.groovy*, because this will not be done automatically:

```
class BootStrap {

    def grailsApplication

    def init = { servletContext ->
      grailsApplication.getDomainClass('com.myapp.User').validator =
          grailsApplication.mainContext.getBean('com.myapp.UserValidator')
    }
}
```

Validation Plugins

There are also plugins available that offer custom validation. The `extra-validators` plugin (*http://grails.org/plugin/extra-validators*) has a validator for password confirmation, and one that checks postal codes for the UK, the US, and Canada.

The `constraints` plugin (*http://grails.org/plugin/constraints*) does a great job of formalizing the process for creating custom constraints. Each validator is defined as a closure in its own class and, by convention, the name of the class is used as the constraint type in the `constraints` block. For example, if you have custom logic to validate a zip code, you can create a `ZipCodeConstraint` class in *grails-app/utils* and the plugin will make it available as `zipCode`:

```
class Address {
    String line1
```

```
        String line2
        String state
        String zip

    static constraints = {
        ...
        zip zipCode: true
    }
}
```

See the plugin documentation for more examples of how to use the plugin.

Friendly Error Messages

When debugging, it is common to render the validation errors, but you have probably found that the default toString representation of the Errors object is not very useful. Here is a convenient way to add a getErrorStrings method to the MetaClass of all domain classes in *BootStrap.groovy*:

```
class BootStrap {

    def grailsApplication
    def messageSource

    def init = { servletContext ->

        for (dc in grailsApplication.domainClasses) {
            dc.metaClass.getErrorStrings = { Locale locale = Locale.getDefault() ->
                def stringsByField = [:].withDefault { [] }
                for (fieldErrors in delegate.errors) {
                    for (error in fieldErrors.allErrors) {
                        String message = messageSource.getMessage(error, locale)
                        stringsByField[error.field] << message
                    }
                }
                stringsByField
            }
        }
    }
}
```

It uses the messageSource bean to resolve the validation message from the appropriate *messages.properties* file for the specified Locale and returns a Map where the keys are field names and the values are a List of resolved validation messages. You can print all of the errors:

```
def person = new Person(...)
if (!person.save()) {
    log.debug "$person errors: $person.errorStrings"
}
```

or grab just the errors for a particular field:

```
def person = new Person(...)
if (!person.save()) {
   log.debug "$person username errors: $person.errorStrings.username"
}
```

Blanks Versus Nulls

In many cases, a blank string and null are equivalent—there is no value set. But HTTP
submissions from web browser POST requests send blank strings for inputs without a
value. This will not be the case with non-HTTP data, such as from other external clients
like web services or during testing, so converting blanks to nulls for the HTTP tier will
help simplify validation. While we're at it, we can also trim extra whitespace from submitted values.

To do this, create a filter in whatever package makes sense for your application, or add
this code to an existing filters class:

```
grails create-filters com.mycompany.myapplication.SiteFilters
```

The name of the filter is not important—it is just there so each one is distinct. In this
case, we want to filter all requests but ignore GET requests, because we are only
concerned with form submissions, so we check for GET or POST with the isPost()
metamethod added to HttpServletRequest:

```
package com.mycompany.myapplication

class SiteFilters {

   def filters = {
      blankToNullAndTrim(controller: '*', action: '*') {
         before = {
            if (request.post) {
               convertBlanksToNullsAndTrim(params)
            }
            true
         }
      }
   }

   private static void convertBlanksToNullsAndTrim(Map map) {
      def keys = [] + map.keySet() // copy to avoid
                               //ConcurrentModificationException
      for (name in keys) {
         def value = map[name]
         if (value instanceof String) {
            value = value.trim()
            if (value.length() == 0) {
               map[name] = null // don't remove - explicit set to null
            }
```

```
            else {
                map[name] = value // update if trimmed
            }
        }
        else if (value instanceof Map) {
            // recurse with empty nested param, e.g., "location":["id":""]
            convertBlanksToNullsAndTrim value
        }
    }
  }
}
```

If you use this approach, you can remove all of your blank:false constraints, because you will never have a blank string, only a null or a String with a nonzero length.

Transients

All typed public fields in a domain class are considered persistent. Any untyped fields (either typed as Object or declared with def) are ignored because GORM needs to know how to represent the values in the datastore. To indicate that a typed field should not be persisted, you can add it to the transients list:

```
class Video {
    String url
    Boolean viewed

    static transients = ['viewed']
}
```

Here, url is persistent, but viewed is not—it might just be used to set a temporary value during the request.

Typed getter and setter methods can be considered to represent persistent properties. A getter without a corresponding setter or a setter without a corresponding getter are fine; these utility methods will be ignored by GORM. But, if you create a matched pair of a getter and setter, they create a JavaBean property and are considered to be persistent. This is because Groovy fields without a scope modifier are converted by the Groovy compiler to a private field and a public getter/setter pair. GORM has no way of knowing that your getter/setter pair was created by you and not by the compiler. So, if you need these, just add their corresponding property name to the transients list:

```
class Person {
    String name
    private int shares

    int getShareCount() { shares }
    void setShareCount(int sc) { shares = sc }
```

```
    static transients = ['shareCount']
}
```

Mapping Collections

GORM uses mapped collections as its standard approach to mapping many-to-one and many-to-many relationships. For example, a Purchase has many OrderItems, so this would be modeled as:

```
class Purchase {
    Date purchaseDate
    static hasMany = [orderItems: OrderItem]
    // other properties
}
```

and:

```
class OrderItem {
    String itemId
    Integer quantity
    static belongsTo = [purchase: Purchase]
    // other properties
}
```

and will generate database tables (if you are using Hibernate, or the equivalent location in a NoSQL datastore) as described in the ER diagram in Figure 3-1.

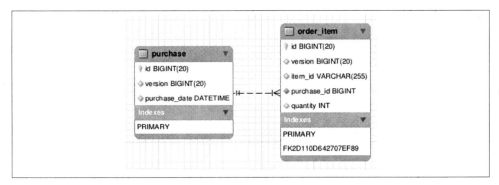

Figure 3-1. Purchase and OrderItem ER diagram

As modeled, this is a bidirectional relationship, and the belongsTo property ensures that Purchase deletes cascade to the OrderItem instances. To associate an OrderItem with a Purchase, call the method addToOrderItems, which is dynamically added to the metaclass by GORM:

```
def purchase = ...
purchase.addToOrderItems(new OrderItem(...))
purchase.save()
```

You could also use the simpler form:

```
class OrderItem {
    String itemId
    Integer quantity
    static belongsTo = Purchase
    // other properties
}
```

which would use a join table instead of a foreign key from the order_item table to the purchase table.

The underlying implementation of the persistent collections are dirty-aware Collection classes. So, when you add one new instance to a collection, GORM is aware of that change, and when the class is saved, the child object will be too.

Mapping a many-to-many relationship is similar. A common example is the User and Role relationship when modeling security:

```
class User {
    String username
    String password

    static hasMany = [roles: Role]
}
class Role {
    String name

    static hasMany = [users: User]
    static belongsTo = User
}
```

In this case, both classes end up with a mapped collection (the roles set in User and the users set in Role), and relating a User and a Role simply involves using the dynamic addTo method; in this case, user.addToRoles(role), because the User class is the "owning" side.

Querying

There are many ways to retrieve stored data using GORM, and for the most part, the same syntax is supported whether you use Hibernate or a NoSQL plugin. The get method retrieves a single instance by its ID and either returns the domain class instance for the specified table row or null if there isn't one. The read method is similar, but it also configures the instance to be partially read-only (currently only in Hibernate). It is only partial because you can modify the instance and push the changes to the database, but Hibernate will not automatically discover that the instance is modified using its dirty-checking process during a flush. load does not query the database, but instead returns a proxy for the requested instance. There is no data access until you access a class property, which triggers a lazy load of the data. This will throw an exception if there is not an associated row. The `lock` method is similar to `get`, but it also adds a pessimistic lock for the row. This is only valid in the context of a transaction, so it only makes sense in Hibernate or other datastores that support transactions and locking.

There are also methods that return multiple instances. The `list` method returns all instances if it is called with no arguments, but it supports a `Map` argument that can limit the number of instances to return and the offset, which is useful for pagination. `find Where` takes a `Map` and finds the first instance that matches the map values, and the `findAllWhere` method returns all matching instances.

Dynamic finders are a popular way to query. These are static methods that start with `findBy` (for a single result) or `findAllBy` (for all matching results), and the method name itself is parsed to build the actual query. These are dynamic methods, because it would be impractical to add them to the domain class bytecode using AST transformations along with the regular methods given the large number of combinations. As such, these can only be invoked from Groovy. One example is `Person.findAllByFirst NameAndAgeGreaterThan("Ralph", 70)`. Under the hood, this is converted to a Hibernate criteria query if you use Hibernate or a `org.grails.datastore.map ping.query.api.Criteria` query when using a NoSQL datastore, where the parameter names are extracted from the method name (`firstName` and `age`) along with other information to build the query such as `GreaterThan`. In earlier versions of Grails, you were limited to two expressions (e.g., `findByFirstNameAndLastName`), but this limitation was removed in version 2.0. This was an artificial limitation to keep method names from becoming very long.

Grails provides a wrapper for Hibernate criteria queries that has been generalized to NoSQL datastores. Dynamic finders support an impressive range of querying options, but by their nature (being a single method call), they cannot provide all of the necessary options for querying. You can use the criteria DSL to retrieve instances using a large number of filtering criteria. This example from the Grails reference documentation shows a somewhat complex but still very readable and intuitive example that would be impossible to represent with a dynamic finder:

```
def c = Account.createCriteria()
def results = c.list {
    like("holderFirstName", "Fred%")
    and {
        between("balance", 500, 1000)
        eq("branch", "London")
    }
    maxResults(10)
    order("holderLastName", "desc")
}
```

There is also a new querying option that was added in Grails 2.0: where queries. These look like criteria queries and, like dynamic finders and criteria DSL queries, they are converted to native criteria queries under the hood, but they take advantage of detached criteria—either a org.hibernate.criterion.DetachedCriteria if you use Hibernate or grails.gorm.DetachedCriteria if you use NoSQL. These have the benefit of having a syntax that is more expressive than the criteria DSL, in that the filtering criteria don't map as directly to the underlying implementation but instead use Java and Groovy syntax. As an example, consider this example from the Grails reference documentation:

```
def query = Person.where {
    (lastName != "Simpson" && firstName != "Fred") ||
    (firstName == "Bart" && age > 9)
}
def results = query.list(sort:"firstName")
```

The where method doesn't immediately execute the query like a regular criteria query, but instead just returns the DetachedCriteria instance. This lets you compose queries to reuse logic and only execute the query when you call find, get, list, count, or exists:

```
def query = Person.where {
    lastName == "Simpson"
}
def bartQuery = query.where {
    firstName == "Bart"
}
Person p = bartQuery.find()
```

Saving, Updating, and Deleting

You can use the save method to persist a single domain class instance. This returns null if there is a validation error, or the instance itself if it is successful. You can combine this with "Groovy truth" to verify that the save succeeded; for example:

```
def person = new Person(...)
if (person.save()) {
    // handle the success case
}
else {
    // handle the error case
}
```

Ruby on Rails has a similar method, but with a variant that will throw an exception if there is a validation error. save behaves like the Grails save method, whereas save! can throw an exception. This was mentioned on the Grails user mailing list as a useful addition, but unfortunately, Groovy cannot support that syntax yet. The solution that was implemented was to add a failOnError flag; for example:

```
def person = new Person(...)
try {
    person.save(failOnError: true)
    // handle the success case
}
catch (grails.validation.ValidationException e) {
    // handle the error case
}
```

This looks similar, but it behaves rather differently. If the instance had been previously retrieved from the database and updated instead of being created, it would become detached from the Hibernate session (or analogous datastore session), and that would require special handling if you update the data and try again. In addition, there is a nontrivial cost to throwing and catching an exception. Each one is not that bad, but this can add up and affect performance, especially in a Groovy-based application where there are so many additional stack frames. And, finally, there is a philosophical argument against this approach. Most of the time, you should expect validation problems, especially with user-submitted data. It is not at all exceptional that someone attempts to create an account with a username that is already taken, or users mistype their passwords (or are trying to hack into your site) or submit any other data that doesn't match your validation rules. Because it is so easy to use the "Groovy truth" approach, it doesn't make much sense to use the failOnError flag except in cases when you expect that the data is correct and want a failsafe (e.g., seed data for tests).

Updating data is similar to saving new instances, except that you make changes to an instance that you retrieve with a get call or a query. But you still call save, and the same rules apply:

```
def person = Person.get(params.id)
person.firstName = params.firstName
...
if (person.save()) {
    // handle the success case
}
else {
    // handle the error case
}
```

Deleting a single instance is simple because there is a delete method added to all domain classes:

```
def person = Person.get(params.id)
person.delete()
```

The where queries described previously are not limited to retrieving data; they can also perform bulk updates and deletes. Often, developers using GORM will do this by retrieving all of the needed instances with one of the supported query mechanisms, and updating or deleting them in a loop. This is inefficient, because you are doing work that can easily be done at the database, and you send a potentially large amount of data from the database to the server unnecessarily. Using a `where` query to do bulk updates and deletes is similar to what you would do in SQL or HQL. For example, to update one property, you can use something like:

```
def query = Person.where {
    lastName == 'Simpson'
}
int total = query.updateAll(lastName:"Bloggs")
```

Performing a bulk delete is similar:

```
def query = Person.where {
    lastName == 'Simpson'
}
int total = query.deleteAll()
```

These can both be written more compactly; for example:

```
int total = Person.where { lastName == 'Simpson' }.deleteAll()
```

If you use Hibernate and turn on SQL logging, you will see that the queries are very efficient. The `updateAll` method generates SQL similar to:

```
update person set last_name=? where last_name=?
```

and the `deleteAll` method generates:

```
delete from person where last_name=?
```

This is exactly the SQL that you would probably write yourself if you were unlucky enough not to have this available in GORM.

NoSQL Support

Because GORM is no longer coupled to Hibernate and is now an API, you can expect a significant amount of commonality between the various implementations. This means that, in general, you can use most of the same mappings and validations, persistence methods (e.g., `get`, `save`, `delete`, `count`), and even dynamic finders, criteria queries, and `where` queries. Some concepts aren't compatible across NoSQL implementations, such as transactions and locking, so you have to be somewhat aware of the underlying datastore. But, in general, your NoSQL domain classes and the code that uses them will look similar or identical to what you would have if you were using Hibernate.

There are several NoSQL plugins providing a GORM implementation currently available, with varying levels of usability. The more complete ones include the mongodb plugin (*http://grails.org/plugin/mongodb*), which adds support for the MongoDB document store (*http://www.mongodb.org/*); the redis-gorm plugin (*http://grails.org/plugin/redis-gorm*), which wraps the Redis key-value store (*http://redis.io/*); neo4j (*http://grails.org/plugin/neo4j*) for the Neo4j graph database (*http://www.neo4j.org/*); simpledb (*http://grails.org/plugin/simpledb*) for the Amazon SimpleDB datastore (*https://*

aws.amazon.com/simpledb/); and dynamodb (*http://grails.org/plugin/dynamodb*) for the Amazon DynamoDB datastore (*https://aws.amazon.com/dynamodb/*). These are documented in more detail here (*http://springsource.github.com/grails-data-mapping/*).

NoSQL implementations typically implement a large subset of the full GORM API, but they usually also add additional functionality, and they provide access to the underlying datastore itself so you can work with the native API directly. One example is the dynamic property support in the mongodb plugin. MongoDB documents do not have a fixed schema, so domain classes can store and retrieve additional unmapped properties as needed, as seen in this example from the plugin documentation:

```
def p = new Plant(name:"Pineapple")
p['color'] = 'Yellow'
p['hasLeaves'] = true
p.save()

p = Plant.findByName("Pineapple")

println p['color']
println p['hasLeaves']
```

There is also support for 2d geospatial indexes (*http://docs.mongodb.org/manual/core/geospatial-indexes/*) to query by location.

CHAPTER 4
Spring

Grails is a metaframework in that it ties together several other frameworks, and none is more pervasive in Grails than the Spring Framework. Grails uses a significant amount of Spring core functionality and optional modules including managing artifacts and many classes as Spring beans (using Spring's dependency injection to manage the graph of dependencies), its datastore integration features (by default using its Hibernate integration), support for proxies and AOP to enable transparent transactions (and caching and security via plugins), internationalization, resource management, and a lot more.

In addition, there are many Spring extensions (both official and third party) that are readily usable in a Grails application. Many are already exposed via plugins (e.g., Spring Security), but if not, you can use an extension like you would in any Spring-based application. You can use annotated bean classes or the newer Java configuration, or copy bean definitions into *grails-app/conf/spring/resources.xml* (this isn't created by default so you need to create it yourself) or convert them to Groovy syntax in *resources.groovy*. Register any dependencies in *BuildConfig.groovy*, and you're ready to go.

Inversion of Control and Dependency Injection

One of the central ideas of Spring that Grails uses heavily is Inversion of Control (IoC), also known as Dependency Injection (DI). This reverses the direction of managing object dependencies from the older style of creating them directly or pulling them in from a repository (e.g., JNDI) to a style where beans don't know how to retrieve their dependencies, but have setter methods and constructors that are used to push dependencies in. This obviously changes everything and opens up many possibilities for much more dynamic and loosely coupled code, and fits the Grails model very well.

In older versions of Spring dependency injection, you would use XML configuration files, but now it's as simple as using the `@Autowired` annotation. In Grails, it's even simpler; any Spring bean written in Groovy (this includes all of the standard artifacts such as controllers, services, and taglibs) can inject the userService bean by adding the line:

```
def userService
```

as a class-scope field. You can specify the type of the field if you want (this can help IDE autocompletion), but it's not necessary.

This seems quite magical but, like most things in Grails (and Groovy), it's actually very simple. It makes a lot more sense if you recall that fields in Groovy classes that don't have a scope modifier are, by default, public, and the Groovy compiler converts them to a private field and a getter and setter (unless you have already created the getter or setter—it won't replace yours). This means that this field is actually implemented as if you had this code:

```
private Object userService

void setUserService(Object userService) {
    this.userService = userService
}

Object getUserService() {
    return userService
}
```

For our purposes, the getter isn't very useful, but the setter is. That's because, by default, Grails creates its beans with autowiring enabled, and is set to "by name" mode. So, as Spring is building its ApplicationContext and wiring together the various dependencies, if it sees a setter whose property name matches a bean name, it will call the setter to inject that bean. So, even though Spring doesn't know anything about Groovy, because it sees the public setter that the Groovy compiler created, it injects the userService bean into your bean as if you had created the setter for that purpose.

Therefore, it should be clear why adding def beanName inside a method doesn't work: it's just a local variable and not a candidate for dependency injection.

Complex Dependency Configuration Using Spring SpEL

In general, setting bean dependencies in *resources.groovy* is done with either other beans or properties that are numbers, strings, Booleans, etc. But you can use Spring Expression Language (SpEL) in property value strings to access other beans' properties and even call their methods. For example, if the Bar class has a name property (or getName method), you can access it to configure the foo bean:

```
beans = {
    bar(Bar)

    foo(Foo) {
        name = '#{bar.name}'
```

```
    }
}
```

Or, if you want to leave the logic for how to resolve the property in the Foo class, you
can call a method instead:

```
beans = {
    bar(Bar)

    foo(Foo) {
        name = '#{bar.resourceName()}'
    }
}
```

For more information, see the relevant section in the Spring documentation, Expression
support for defining bean definitions (*http://bit.ly/17dRoqd*).

Manually Injecting Dependencies at Runtime

If you manually instantiate classes that aren't Spring beans, but would like to conveniently inject Spring bean dependencies into them (e.g., classes in *src/groovy* and *src/
java*), you can do this if you have access to the Spring ApplicationContext. This is
simple if you dependency-inject the grailsApplication bean into the artifact class
(e.g., a controller or a service) that is creating the instance:

```
def grailsApplication
```

and then you can autowire properties by name with this:

```
import org.springframework.beans.factory.config.AutowireCapableBeanFactory
...

def instance = new XXX(...)

def ctx = grailsApplication.mainContext
ctx.beanFactory.autowireBeanProperties(instance,
    AutowireCapableBeanFactory.AUTOWIRE_BY_NAME, false)
```

Just as in Spring bean classes or Grails artifact classes, any public property or setter
method that corresponds to a bean name in the ApplicationContext will be set with
that bean.

Bean Scopes

By default, Spring beans are singletons: only one instance is created, and each time you
get the bean from the ApplicationContext (either directly or via dependency injection), you'll get the same instance. This is a sensible default, because beans often have
no mutable state, so they're safe to share between collaborators and between threads.
They can have state, in particular injected dependencies, but as long as this state is

initialized early and not changed, it's not a thread-safety concern. Spring manages creating the instances and wiring dependencies, but without the problems associated with traditional singletons. Of course there are plenty of reasons why a particular bean cannot be a singleton, so beans can have a "scope."

To receive a new instance from the `ApplicationContext` each time, set the scope of the bean to `prototype`. It will still have dependencies injected like singleton beans, but now it can have mutable state, because each caller gets its own copy. Grails controllers are an example of prototype beans; this is to support a rarely used feature inspired by Rails controllers where the controller itself is used as the GSP model when none is specified. Often, when a GSP is used to render a response, the last statement of a controller action is a `Map` containing the model data to use in the GSP; if you don't return anything (and don't call `redirect`, `forward`, or `chain`), then the controller's fields are used as the model data.

Another supported scope is `session`. You could use this for shopping carts and other similar patterns, much like a stateful EJB session bean. The first time the bean is requested from the `ApplicationContext`, it is created and stored in the HTTP session, and subsequent requests return this instance until the session times out or is explicitly invalidated. Separate sessions each get their own instance. A similar scope is `request`; these are created per request instead of per session, so they're much shorter lived.

You can also define your own scope by implementing the `org.springframe work.beans.factory.config.Scope` interface and registering it in the `BeanFactory`:

```
ctx.beanFactory.registerScope 'myScope', new MyScope()
```

You can use this in a controller or service class with the `scope` property; for example:

```
static scope = 'myScope' // or session/prototype/etc.
```

For Spring beans that you manually wire in *resources.groovy*, add the property in the bean definition:

```
myBean(MyBeanClass) { bean ->
    bean.scope = 'myScope' // or session/prototype/etc.
}
```

Transactional Services

If you follow the convention for Grails services and create a Groovy class in the *grails-app/services* folder whose name ends in `Service`, the class will automatically be registered as a service for you. This means that, by default, it is registered as a Spring bean (whose bean name is the class name with a lowercase first letter), the bean scope is `singleton`, and all public methods will be transactional. That makes the class a great place to put business logic, especially if it involves database persistence.

You can specify the bean scope of a service with the static `scope` property; this can be any valid value supported by Spring and the most common are `singleton` and `proto type`, and to a lesser extent `request` and `session`. The default scope (if none is specified) is `singleton`.

By default, all public methods in a service are transactional. Older versions of Grails included the line `static transactional = true` in generated services, but that has been removed, because it's redundant. You should only set the `transactional` attribute if you're disabling transactions—for cases where the service manages business logic but doesn't write to the database.

The transaction isolation is set to `Isolation.DEFAULT`; that is, the default settings for your database are used instead of explicitly using read-commited, serializable, etc. The propagation level is `Propagation.REQUIRED`, which means that, if a transaction was already active before calling a service method, it will be joined and not committed after successfully invoking the method, because it was already started; however, if one isn't active, it will create one and commit it after invoking the method. There is no timeout configured, the transaction won't be read-only, and the `Exception` types that trigger an automatic rollback are the defaults; runtime exceptions and errors trigger rollback and checked exceptions (even though Groovy doesn't make you catch or rethrow checked exceptions) do not cause a rollback. This last point can be confusing for developers without much experience with Spring or JEE transactions. The logic is that in Java, because you must either catch a checked exception or declare it in the `throws` clause, you have the opportunity to handle the exception and will decide if the exception merits an explicit rollback. But because you don't have to catch runtime exceptions or errors, it's assumed that the transaction should be automatically rolled back for you, to keep state from being inconsistent. Because Spring doesn't know about Groovy's exception handling rules, the Java rules apply.

@Transactional

You're not limited to the default transaction settings or forced to use complex configurations to customize services' transaction behaviors. Customizing is simple; use the `org.springframework.transaction.annotation.Transactional` annotation. If you have even one `@Transactional` annotation, Grails assumes that you're taking the configuration into your own hands and doesn't configure the default transaction settings for the class. You can put the annotation at the class level, and/or on individual methods, and you can combine class-scope and method-scope annotations to configure default settings at the class level, but configure overrides for individual methods.

In this example, `someMethod` will be transactional, inheriting the settings from the class annotation, but `someOtherMethod` requires that an existing transaction be active:

```
package com.mycompany

import org.springframework.transaction.annotation.Propagation
import org.springframework.transaction.annotation.Transactional

@Transactional
class SomeService {

    def someMethod() {
        ...
    }

    @Transactional(propagation=Propagation.MANDATORY)
    def someOtherMethod() {
        ...
    }
}
```

Another approach is to omit the annotation at the class level to support nontransactional methods and to annotate methods directly. In this example, someMethod is not transactional (but won't trigger an exception if it is called during a transaction), someOther Method has the default settings, and yetAnotherMethod requires that a transaction be active already:

```
package com.mycompany

import org.springframework.transaction.annotation.Propagation
import org.springframework.transaction.annotation.Transactional

class SomeOtherService {

    def someMethod() {
        ...
    }

    @Transactional
    def someOtherMethod() {
        ...
    }

    @Transactional(propagation=Propagation.MANDATORY)
    def yetAnotherMethod() {
        ...
    }
}
```

Transaction Proxies

Whether you use the default Grails configuration or annotations, the transaction management is implemented by Spring with a proxy. Spring uses the CGLIB library to create a subclass of your service, where each proxied method (all public methods when not using annotations or if the class is annotated, annotated public methods otherwise) is intercepted by the proxy to start or join a transaction (or throw an exception if one isn't allowed) and then call your implementation code. You can see that this is the case by printing the class name of your injected service, (e.g., `println userService.get Class().name`); it should look something like this:

```
com.foo.bar.UserService$$EnhancerByCGLIB$$32cb6433
```

We can see that the proxy is a runtime-generated subclass of the real bean class by printing its superclass:

```
println userService.getClass().superclass.name
```

which should print:

```
com.foo.bar.UserService
```

Digging further, we can list all of the interfaces implemented by the proxy:

```
for (iface in ctx.mathService.getClass().interfaces) {
    println iface.name
}
```

which should print:

```
org.springframework.aop.SpringProxy
org.springframework.aop.framework.Advised
net.sf.cglib.proxy.Factory
```

Unintentionally bypassing the bean proxy

Be careful when calling annotated methods within a service when the annotation settings are different. Because you're "underneath" the proxy, it's a direct method call, and any checks that the proxy would have done will be bypassed. For example, if you want to store auditing data in the database, but don't want a failure there to roll back the transaction, you can do that work in a new transaction by setting the propagation to `Propagation.REQUIRES_NEW`:

```
@Transactional
void someMethod(...) {

    // do some work ...

    storeAuditData(...)
}

@Transactional(propagation=Propagation.REQUIRES_NEW)
void storeAuditData(...) {
    //
}
```

Unfortunately, though, the call to `storeAuditData` won't trigger the creation of a second transaction, because it's a direct call. You can fix this by calling the proxy's method, and that involves getting access to the Spring bean that represents this service. You can't just add a dependency injection (`def fooService`), because that would be circular; instead, if you add a dependency injection for the `grailsApplication` bean, you can access the `ApplicationContext` easily from there and get the service from it:

```
def grailsApplication

@Transactional
void someMethod(...) {

    // do some work ...

    def myProxy = grailsApplication.mainContext.fooService
    myProxy.storeAuditData(...)
}

@Transactional(propagation=Propagation.REQUIRES_NEW)
void storeAuditData(...) {
    //
}
```

Another more traditional option is to implement the `org.springframework.con text.ApplicationContextAware` interface, but that involves more plumbing code.

An even more automatic fix would be to wire up a `getMyProxy()` method (and therefore a `myProxy` property) into the metaclass of all services in *BootStrap.groovy*:

```
class BootStrap {

    def grailsApplication

    def init = { servletContext ->

        for (sc in grailsApplication.serviceClasses) {
            sc.clazz.metaClass.getMyProxy = { ->
                grailsApplication.mainContext.getBean(sc.propertyName)
            }
        }
    }
}
```

or in the `doWithDynamicMethods` callback in a plugin:

```
def doWithDynamicMethods = { ctx ->
    for (sc in application.serviceClasses) {
        sc.clazz.metaClass.getMyProxy = { ->
            application.mainContext.getBean(sc.propertyName)
        }
    }
}
```

and then this call would have the expected effect:

```
@Transactional
void someMethod(...) {

    // do some work ...

    myProxy.storeAuditData(...)
}

@Transactional(propagation=Propagation.REQUIRES_NEW)
void storeAuditData(...) {
    //
}
```

Transaction Utility Methods

For complex workflows, it can be helpful to have access to information about the current transaction. Ironically, although services are the best place in Grails to do transactional work, the static `withTransaction` method that's available in all domain classes is more useful in this regard, because the method signature has an `org.springframework.transaction.TransactionStatus` variable. But there's no direct way to access information about the current transaction in a service. That's easy to fix though—we can add some transaction utility methods to service metaclasses; for example, in *BootStrap.groovy*:

```
import org.springframework.transaction.interceptor.TransactionAspectSupport
import org.springframework.transaction.support.TransactionSynchronizationManager

class BootStrap {

    def grailsApplication

    def init = { servletContext ->
        for (sc in grailsApplication.serviceClasses) {
            def metaClass = sc.clazz.metaClass

            // returns boolean
            metaClass.isTransactionActive = { ->
                TransactionSynchronizationManager.isSynchronizationActive()
            }

            // returns TransactionStatus
            metaClass.getCurrentTransactionStatus = { ->
                if (!delegate.isTransactionActive()) {
                    return null
                }
                TransactionAspectSupport.currentTransactionStatus()
            }

            // void, throws NoTransactionException
            metaClass.setRollbackOnly = { ->
```

```
        TransactionAspectSupport.currentTransactionStatus().setRollbackOnly()
      }

      // returns boolean
      metaClass.isRollbackOnly = { ->
        if (!delegate.isTransactionActive()) {
          return false
        }
        delegate.getCurrentTransactionStatus().isRollbackOnly()
      }
    }
  }
}
```

Now you can force the transaction to roll back by calling `setRollbackOnly()` and, in a workflow that has multiple steps, you can call `isRollbackOnly()` early in each method before doing expensive work that will only be rolled back, to see if that work makes sense to do.

Bean Life Cycles and Interfaces

In addition to wiring up dependencies between beans, the `ApplicationContext` is responsible for managing the beans' life cycles. Two important hooks are the initialization and destruction phases. When you register your own Spring beans in *resources.groovy*, you can use the `org.codehaus.groovy.grails.commons.spring.BeanConfiguration` instance (typically a `org.codehaus.groovy.grails.commons.spring.DefaultBeanConfiguration`) that is the argument of the bean definition closure to set the `initMethod` and/or the `destroyMethod` names; for example:

```
authenticationManager(com.mycompany.myapp.LdapAuthenticationManager) { bean ->
    serverUrl = '...'
    password = '...'
    bean.initMethod = 'init'
    bean.destroyMethod = 'destroy'
}
```

Most of the time, however, the beans that you create are automatically registered for you by Grails. In that case, you can implement the `org.springframework.beans.factory.InitializingBean` interface and its `afterPropertiesSet` method to do initialization work after all dependencies and other properties have been set, and the `org.springframework.beans.factory.DisposableBean` interface and its `destroy` method to do work during a clean shutdown; for example:

```
package com.mycompany.myapp

import org.springframework.beans.factory.DisposableBean
import org.springframework.beans.factory.InitializingBean

class LdapAuthenticationManager implements InitializingBean, DisposableBean {
```

```
    ...

    void afterPropertiesSet() {
        // initialization work
    }

    void destroy() {
        // shutdown work
    }
}
```

 Whether you use initMethod or InitializingBean.afterProperties
Set, because Spring is unaware of the various Grails life cycle phases,
you are somewhat limited in what you can do in the initialization phases. In particular, because plugins won't have initialized yet, you cannot
use GORM methods. If you find you cannot do some initialization work
because of this, you can inject your bean in *BootStrap.groovy* and do the
work there, because by the time bootstrap classes are called, everything
has been configured and is ready to use.

In earlier versions of Grails, the log field was added using runtime
metaprogramming, but in Grails 2.0 and higher, it's injected with an
AST transformation (compile-time metaprogramming), so you can use
logging in either callback method.

Bean Postprocessors

Bean (and BeanFactory and BeanDefinitionRegistry) postprocessors provide a powerful approach to customizing Spring beans. They're particularly useful to reconfigure
beans contributed by third-party JARs or plugins where you can't (or shouldn't) edit the
code. Instead, you can hook into the construction process and customize one or more
beans at runtime, changing or adding properties, the bean implementation class, and
other attributes and settings.

The most common interface to use is org.springframework.beans.factory.con
fig.BeanPostProcessor, which has two methods, postProcessBeforeInitializa
tion and postProcessAfterInitialization. You can do what you want with each, but
typically postProcessBeforeInitialization works with class metadata like annotations, because the instance has been created but it isn't fully initialized yet. It's common
to return a proxy for the real instance from postProcessAfterInitialization, although you can also just reconfigure the initialized instance with updated properties.

You can also create an org.springframework.beans.factory.config.BeanFactory
PostProcessor, which has one method, postProcessBeanFactory. This takes a single

argument: a `ConfigurableListableBeanFactory` that you can use to customize a `Bean Definition` from its `getBeanDefinition` method, or loop through all of the beans using the names from the `getBeanDefinitionNames` method. Your postprocessor will be called after the bean factory is partially initialized but before beans have been instantiated. This gives you a chance to modify the `BeanDefinition` instances that will be used to define the actual beans. You can add, remove, or change bean properties and even the class that will be instantiated.

The `org.springframework.beans.factory.support.BeanDefinitionRegistryPost Processor` interface extends `BeanFactoryPostProcessor` and has one method, `post ProcessBeanDefinitionRegistry`, where you can add or remove `BeanDefinition` instances in the `BeanDefinitionRegistry`.

To add a postprocessor, implement whichever interface(s) you want in a class in *src/ groovy* or *src/java* and register it as a bean (using any name you want, because it's not particularly relevant) in *resources.groovy*. Spring will see that it implements one of the interfaces and will use it as a postprocessor, calling the methods at the appropriate points in the construction of the `ApplicationContext`:

```
import com.mycompany.myapp.MyPostProcessor
beans = {
    myPostProcessor(MyPostProcessor)
}
```

 The `cloud-foundry` (*http://grails.org/plugin/cloud-foundry*) and `hero ku` (*http://grails.org/plugin/heroku*) plugins both provide runtime reconfiguration of the JDBC `DataSource`, NoSQL connection information, and so on, using this approach. This keeps your application highly decoupled from the hosting location, because a bean postprocessor detects the environment variables that Cloud Foundry and Heroku make available, and transparently reconfigures the appropriate Spring beans for you. You can see the source of the shared base class that each plugin extends to provide provider-specific settings discovery here (*http:// bit.ly/136sBaT*).

A Groovier Way

You can also customize a `BeanDefinition` in the `doWithSpring` closure in a plugin. The `delegate` of the closure is the active `grails.spring.BeanBuilder` that Grails uses to register beans in the `ApplicationContext` that are defined by the builder's DSL. You can use the `getBeanDefinition` method to retrieve a previously defined bean definition (typically an `org.springframework.beans.factory.support.GenericBeanDefini tion`) and modify its attributes:

```
def doWithSpring = {
   def beanDef = getBeanDefinition('someBeanName')
   beanDef.beanClass = NewClass
   beanDef.propertyValues.add('order',
   application.config.plugin?.rendering?.order ?: [])
}
```

Note that because this runs during your plugin's initialization, plugin loading order is important; the only bean definitions that will be available are those configured by plugins that have already initialized. You can use the `loadAfter` plugin descriptor attribute to configure this.

Bean Aliases

Spring allows bean aliases where an alternate name is registered in addition to the real name of a bean. You can use this when you have multiple implementations of a bean and choose one via configuration at startup—for example, per-environment or some other rule. This is partially broken in Grails before 2.1 in that, before version 2.1, you could register aliases but only to beans in the same plugin or *resources.groovy*. As of version 2.1 though, all aliases work regardless of the location of the alias and bean definitions.

This works the same way in a plugin's `doWithSpring` as in *resources.groovy*, because in both cases, the closure's delegate is the `BeanBuilder`. You can access the `RuntimeSpring Configuration` with the `getSpringConfig` method and call `addAlias` on that; for example:

```
import grails.util.Environment

beans = {

   String realBeanName

   switch (Environment.current) {
      case Environment.TEST:
         realBeanName = 'testCardProcessingService'
         break
      case Environment.PRODUCTION:
         realBeanName = 'productionCardProcessingService'
         break
      default: // Environment.DEVELOPMENT, custom envs
         realBeanName = 'mockCardProcessingService'
         break
   }

   springConfig.addAlias 'cardProcessingService', realBeanName
}
```

Now, when a controller or other artifact that supports dependency injection injects the `cardProcessingService` bean, it will get the correct one depending on the current running environment. This has the benefit of centralizing the logic and not polluting the application code with logic to determine in each case which bean to use.

 The cache plugin registers the alias `cacheOperationSource` for the bean that Spring autoregisters as `org.springframework.cache.annota tion.AnnotationCacheOperationSource#0`, which cannot be used with Grails dependency injection using the standard `def beanName` pattern.

Internationalization

Grails has first-class support for internationalization with the *.properties* files in the *grails-app/i18n* folder. All generated controllers, GSPs, and layouts are fully internationalized with no hardcoded strings; instead, strings are resolved from the message bundles defined in the *.properties* files using the `message` (*http://grails.org/doc/ latest/ref/Tags/message.html*) tag and the current `Locale`. In addition, domain class validation errors are internationalized the same way, using the i18n message bundles. This can make the code harder to read (especially if the message codes are cryptic or not intuitive), but it makes displaying your site in another language much simpler, because you just need to ensure that all English messages have corresponding translated messages for your supported languages.

This is all enabled under the hood by the use of the `messageSource` bean, an implementation of the `org.springframework.context.MessageSource` interface. In a Grails application, this will be a `PluginAwareResourceBundleMessageSource` that supports loading messages from the application as well as from installed plugins and supports reloading in the development environment. You can work directly with the `message Source` bean using dependency injection like with any Spring bean: `def message Source`. Often it's easier to use the `message` tag because tags can conveniently be called in controllers. But, in services or other classes, where it's impractical to call a taglib, just use the `messageSource` bean.

Resources

Spring has an abstraction for low-level resources with its `org.springframe work.core.io.Resource` and `org.springframework.core.io.ResourceLoader` interfaces. There are several concrete `Resource` implementations, including `UrlResource`, `ClassPathResource`, `FileSystemResource`, `ServletContextResource`, `InputStream`

Resource, and `ByteArrayResource`. It rarely matters what the concrete class is though, because you can use the methods `exists()`, `getInputStream()`, `getURL()`, and so on.

For example, consider a configuration file that you put in the *web-app/WEB-INF* folder, *data.xml*. This is safe from public viewing, because the container blocks access to all files in *WEB-INF*. So how do you read the contents of the file at runtime? A naive approach that works in development mode is:

```
new File('web-app/WEB-INF/data.xml').text
```

This won't work in a deployed WAR for two reasons. One is that there is no *web-app* folder, and the other is that the WAR may not be expanded onto the filesystem depending on which container you use, so there may be no `File` access at all even if you "fix" the path. But you certainly wouldn't want to have brittle logic that computes the file path depending on how the application is running.

This method in `ResourceLoader` looks promising:

```
Resource getResource(String location);
```

So how do we access a `ResourceLoader` in Grails? The `ApplicationContext` implements the interface and will usually be the most convenient way to manage resources. Getting access to the `ApplicationContext` can be done a few different ways; the most convenient is to add a dependency injection for the `grailsApplication` bean (`def grailsApplication`) because `grailsApplication.mainContext` resolves to the `ApplicationContext`; you can also implement `ApplicationContextAware`.

Then it's as simple as executing:

```
String xml = ctx.getResource('WEB-INF/data.xml').inputStream.text
```

and there's no dependence on any particular environment or logic to compute various paths to the file, depending on how the application is being run, because Spring abstracts that away. If you run:

```
println ctx.getResource('WEB-INF/data.xml').getClass().name
```

you'll see that the implementation class is `org.springframework.web.context.support.ServletContextResource`, and running:

```
ctx.getResource('WEB-INF/data.xml').file.path
```

will print something like:

```
/path/to/appname/web-app/WEB-INF/data.xml
```

when running under `run-app` and:

```
/usr/local/apache-tomcat-7.0.29/webapps/appname/WEB-INF/data.xml
```

when running as a WAR deployed to Tomcat (assuming Tomcat is configured to explode WARs).

Resource Dependency Injection

A more automatic approach would be to use dependency injection to let Spring inject the resource into one of your beans, rather than explicitly pulling it like we have been. If you move the file from the *WEB-INF* folder to either *grails-app/conf* or *src/java*, it will be copied into the classpath, so we can access it as a classpath resource. Consider this simple class:

```
package com.mycompany.myapp

import org.springframework.core.io.Resource

class FooManager {

    Resource xmlFile

    // class methods
}
```

If we wire this class up as a bean in *resources.groovy*, for example:

```
import com.mycompany.myapp.FooManager

beans = {

    fooManager(FooManager) {
        xmlFile = 'classpath:data.xml'
    }
}
```

then the resource will be discovered and injected into the bean. Now it will be an instance of `org.springframework.core.io.ClassPathResource`, and accessing the content of the file is as simple as:

```
String xml = xmlFile.inputStream.text
```

inside any of the methods in `FooManager`. You can even go further and specify the type as a `File`:

```
package com.mycompany.myapp

class FooManager {

    File xmlFile

    // class methods
}
```

and then the content will be available as:

```
String xml = xmlFile.text
```

ResourceLocator

As of Grails 2.0, there is also another option for finding resources: the `org.code` `haus.groovy.grails.core.io.ResourceLocator` interface and its implementations. This has two primary methods: `Resource findResourceForURI(String uri)` and `Resource findResourceForClassName(String className)`. The advantage of using `ResourceLocator` over the Spring option is that `ResourceLocator` implementations are Grails classes and are aware of the structure of application and plugin paths and can also access contents of binary plugins.

To use this, get a reference to the `grailsResourceLocator` bean, typically using dependency injection (e.g., `def grailsResourceLocator`). Then you can conveniently access files when running locally using `run-app` or when deployed as a WAR (e.g., getting the content of a JavaScript file provided by the JQuery plugin, without having to know anything about where the actual file is located):

```
def resource = grailsResourceLocator.findResourceForURI
    ('js/jquery/jquery-1.8.3.min.js')
String jqueryJs = resource.inputStream.text
```

or an application file you have placed in the *WEB-INF* folder:

```
def resource = grailsResourceLocator.findResourceForURI('WEB-INF/someDataFile.xml')
```

Data Binding and Validation

Data binding and validation help make integrating HTTP request data with domain classes much easier in Grails. Much of the core implementation is handled by Spring, with Grails adding a layer on top to make the integration more direct and add in special handling.

Data Binding

Spring provides several implementations of JavaBean `PropertyEditors` to convert `Strings` (typically from web requests) to numbers, dates, or anything that has a string form that can be converted. These are used by the `org.codehaus.groo` `vy.grails.web.binding.GrailsDataBinder`, which extends the underlying Spring data binding implementation to add Grails-specific hooks, such as working with the `params` map in controllers, being aware of the `constraints` property in domain classes, and guarding against changing properties such as `metaClass`, `id`, and `version`.

Spring and Grails register several property editors, and you can register your own by registering a `CustomEditorConfigurer` bean (a bean postprocessor), giving it a list of `PropertyEditorRegistrar` instances referencing your editors. This is somewhat cumbersome though, but in Grails 2.3 the data binding implementation will be heavily refactored to retain the binding features, but add several new ones and significantly simplify the process for adding custom binding approaches.

Validation

In traditional Spring applications, it is common to create validators for the app's DAOs, and Spring has an `org.springframework.validation.Validator` interface to standardize the behavior. But there are no concrete implementations of the interface, because validation is very domain-specific. Although you're probably unaware of it, Grails creates an instance of `Validator` for each domain class; if you loop through the `ApplicationContext` beans, you'll see that for a `com.foo.bar.Person` domain class there will be a `com.foo.bar.PersonValidator` bean (an instance of `org.codehaus.groovy.grails.orm.hibernate.validation.HibernateDomainClassValidator`, if you're using Hibernate) along with a `com.foo.bar.Person` bean (a "prototype" bean that is used in the overridden constructor to create instances and support bean autowiring), a `com.foo.bar.PersonPersistentClass` bean, and a `com.foo.bar.PersonDomainClass` bean.

Validation problems are represented by the `org.springframework.validation.Errors` interface, typically a `grails.validation.ValidationErrors` instance, which extends a Spring implementation that provides most of the functionality. An `Errors` instance is wired into all domain classes as the `errors` property, making it very convenient to access after performing validation checks (either directly with the `validate` method or indirectly with the `save` method). It will contain information about what went wrong, including the original invalid values and error codes for displayable messages. This gets coupled with the Spring and Grails support for i18n message bundles (under the *grails-app/i18n* directory) to allow you to display human-readable validation messages and also support localized versions as needed.

Database Persistence

Typically, we use GORM and Hibernate to manage database persistence in a Grails application, although many apps now use NoSQL datastores in addition to or instead of relational databases. Under the hood, the Hibernate integration is managed by Spring, from the `org.springframework.orm.hibernate3.LocalSessionFactoryBean` factory bean (in Grails, it's the `org.codehaus.groovy.grails.orm.hibernate.ConfigurableLocalSessionFactoryBean` subclass) that's used to configure `org.hibernate.SessionFactory` instances to the `org.springframework.orm.hibernate3.HibernateTransactionManager` implementation of the `org.springframework.transaction.PlatformTransactionManager` interface that abstracts away the implementation details of transaction management (this is also a Grails-specific subclass, `org.codehaus.groovy.grails.orm.hibernate.GrailsHibernateTransactionManager`).

Thread-Local Holders

One significant feature of the Spring/Hibernate integration is the seamless access of active persistence objects. It would be cumbersome to explicitly open a Hibernate `Ses sion` or start a transaction and have to pass one or more related objects from method to method, so Spring stores various objects (the active transaction, the current Hibernate session, and so on) in `ThreadLocal` scope, because web requests are handled per thread. So it's easy for code that's aware of this pattern to access the current transaction or Hibernate session (or just know if one is active) by using the `org.springframe work.transaction.support.TransactionSynchronizationManager` and `org.spring framework.orm.hibernate3.SessionFactoryUtils` helper classes.

This is further helped by the `org.codehaus.groovy.grails.orm.hibernate.sup port.GrailsOpenSessionInViewInterceptor` instance, which implements the `org.springframework.web.context.request.WebRequestInterceptor` interface that Grails registers to intercept all controller requests. This interface has callbacks for doing work before a controller action starts, after it does its work, and after the view is rendered. This should sound familiar if you've used filters before, because they are also managed by a `WebRequestInterceptor`. The `GrailsOpenSessionInViewInterceptor` opens a `Session` at the start of all controller requests and registers it in thread-local scope (in an `org.springframework.orm.hibernate3.SessionHolder` keyed by the owning `SessionFactory`). Then, after the request, it flushes and closes the `Session`.

So, for the entire duration of the request, there is always an active `Session` available. This is important for a few reasons. The Hibernate implementation of GORM uses an `org.springframework.orm.hibernate3.HibernateTemplate` under the hood to exe-cute most queries. Criteria queries are relatively thin wrappers around the Hibernate Criteria feature, and where queries, dynamic finders, and other GORM methods are converted to Criteria queries or call an applicable Hibernate `Session` method. `Hiber nateTemplate` uses `SessionFactoryUtils.getSession()` to find or create a `Session`. If one is active, it uses it and doesn't close it, because that's the responsibility of whatever code opened it (most likely, `GrailsOpenSessionInViewInterceptor`). If one isn't, it creates one and closes it when finished. This is why lazy-loaded collections and entities fail to load when a query executes in a new thread; the instances retrieved become disconnected when the session closes. But, when the query runs in the request's thread, the session is still active after the query, so lazy loading works. The plugins that enable asynchronous processing (Quartz, GPars, and Executor) all implement patterns similar to `OpenSessionInView`, because they support running in new threads.

JdbcTemplate

It is usually most convenient to use `groovy.sql.Sql` when executing SQL queries in Groovy, but Spring has a utility class with many of the same features, `JdbcTemplate`.

You give it a reference to a `DataSource` (typically, in the constructor) and it handles most of the gory details of getting a `Connection`, `Statement`, and `ResultSet` for you (and closing them when it is finished), and has smart error handling which converts checked `SQLExceptions` into a rich hierarchy of unchecked exceptions. The code ends up being a bit more verbose than using `groovy.sql.Sql` but far more compact than the equivalent direct JDBC code:

```
import misc.Person
import org.springframework.jdbc.core.RowMapper
import org.springframework.jdbc.core.JdbcTemplate
import java.sql.ResultSet
import java.sql.SQLException

def dataSource = ctx.dataSource

def template = new JdbcTemplate(dataSource)

long id = ...

Person person = template.queryForObject(
    "select first_name, initial, last_name from person where id = ?",
    [id] as Object[],
    new RowMapper<Person>() {
        Person mapRow(ResultSet rs, int rowNum) throws SQLException {
            def p = new Person(firstName: rs.getString('first_name'),
                               initial: rs.getString('initial'),
                               lastName: rs.getString('last_name'))
            p.id = id
            p
        }
    }
)
```

Other Database Support

Although they're less often used (especially in Grails), Spring does have support for JDO with the `org.springframework.orm.jdo.JdoTemplate` and `org.springframework.orm.jdo.support.JdoDaoSupport` classes, JPA with the `org.springframework.orm.jpa.JpaTemplate` and `org.springframework.orm.jpa.support.JpaDaoSupport` classes, and iBATIS (2.x) SQL Maps.

Spring MVC

Nearly all Grails applications have a web frontend, and most of the time, this is implemented with controllers. These are core artifacts in the *grails-app/controllers* folder. There are several convenient conventions associated with controllers; classes in the *controllers* folder are automatically registered as controllers, public closures and methods are automatically registered as actions, simply returning a `Map` from an action renders the GSP corresponding to that controller and that action, using the `Map` as the data model in the view, and the `"/$controller/$action?/$id?"` { ... } URL mapping entry (added by default in the generated *UrlMappings.groovy* file) ensures that actions are automatically available externally using a REST-like URL scheme.

Your classes in *grails-app/controllers* don't implement the Spring `Controller` interface (directly or via something funky like an AST transformation) and don't extend a `Controller` base class; instead, Grails uses one facade `Controller` to handle all requests: `org.codehaus.groovy.grails.web.servlet.mvc.SimpleGrailsController`. This is registered as the `mainSimpleController` bean. This delegates most of the work to the `grailsControllerHelper` bean, an instance of `MixedGrailsControllerHelper` which finds the action method or closure and invokes it, returning an `org.springframe work.web.servlet.ModelAndView` that you may be familiar with if you've worked with Spring MVC in a traditional Spring application.

In addition, Grails invokes interceptors before and after controller actions. These come from various sources, including explicitly created `HandlerInterceptor` classes such as `GrailsOpenSessionInViewInterceptor` (via an `org.springframework.web.serv let.handler.WebRequestHandlerInterceptorAdapter` adapter) and `org.code haus.groovy.grails.web.i18n.ParamsAwareLocaleChangeInterceptor` (which extends Spring's `org.springframework.web.servlet.i18n.LocaleChangeIntercep tor`), but also Grails filters and controller interceptors (`beforeInterceptor` and `after Interceptor` closures defined in controller classes).

Filters

Filters in Grails are somewhat misleadingly named, because it seems like they're Servlet filters, but they're implemented with a `HandlerInterceptor` (indirectly), so they only work with controller requests. For each filter class, Grails creates an adapter instance of `org.codehaus.groovy.grails.plugins.web.filters.FilterToHandlerAdapter` to integrate it into the filters list. `FilterToHandlerAdapter` implements the `HandlerIn terceptor` interface and extracts information from the DSL that developers use to define the filtering rules in an *XXXFilters.groovy* file (the patterns for which URIs, controllers, and actions apply; the `before`, `after`, and `afterView` closures; and so on) to use when the various interface methods are called. This way, we can take advantage of the filter conventions so there's less plumbing work involved while still taking advantage of the Spring integration.

Controller interceptors look a lot like filters (although there are only the before and after phases, no "after view") but they're not implemented with a `HandlerIntercep tor`. Because they only apply to the controller where they're defined, the logic is applied per request, in `AbstractGrailsControllerHelper`.

If you need to intercept more than just controller requests, you can create a class that implements `javax.servlet.Filter` (or extend an existing base class like `org.springframework.web.filter.OncePerRe questFilter`) and add it to *web.xml* like in any application. This can be done in plugins in the `doWithWebDescriptor` block, or in an application by running the `install-templates` script and editing *src/templates/war/web.xml*.

Using Spring MVC Controllers

It's been possible to use Spring MVC controllers in Grails since version 1.2; before that, it was possible with the `springmvc` plugin (*http://grails.org/plugin/springmvc*). The process is fairly straightforward; create your controller classes in the *src/java* or *src/groovy* folder and add an `org.springframework.stereotype.Controller` annotation. Grails doesn't autodiscover the annotated classes though; you need to add the relevant packages to the `grails.spring.bean.packages` list property in *Config.groovy*; for example:

```
grails.spring.bean.packages = ['com.mycompany.myapp.billing',
                               'com.mycompany.myapp.card.api']
```

When you create the classes, use the same techniques that you would in a traditional Spring application; for example, annotating an action method with `org.springframe work.web.bind.annotation.RequestMapping`:

```
@RequestMapping("/mvc/hello.dispatch")
public ModelMap handleRequest() {
   return new ModelMap()
      .addAttribute("text", "some text")
      .addAttribute("cost", 42)
      .addAttribute("config",
         grailsApplication.getConfig().flatten()));
}
```

One unfortunate aspect of the integration is that all `RequestMapping` URI values must end in `.dispatch`. You can make this more natural by adding entries in *UrlMap-pings.groovy*; for example:

```
class UrlMappings {

   static mappings = {

      ...

      "/mvc/hello"(uri:"/mvc/hello.dispatch")

      "/mvc/other"(uri:"/mvc/other.dispatch")
   }
}
```

These controller classes will become standard Spring beans, so they're candidates for dependency injection. Use the `org.springframework.beans.factory.annota tion.Autowired` annotation on fields in Groovy classes:

```
@Autowired
def grailsApplication
```

and on setters in Java:

```
private GrailsApplication grailsApplication;

@Autowired
public void setGrailsApplication(GrailsApplication app) {
    grailsApplication = app;
}
```

You can also use the `javax.inject.Inject` annotation; for example, using constructor injection:

```
private GrailsApplication grailsApplication;

@Inject
public FooController(GrailsApplication app) {
    grailsApplication = app;
}
```

Remoting

Spring has support for remoting using several protocols. The Grails `remoting` plugin (*http://grails.org/plugin/remoting*) implements this support for remote method invocation (RMI), Hessian (Caucho's lightweight binary HTTP-based protocol), Burlap (another protocol from Caucho, which uses XML), and Spring's HTTP invoker (implemented by Java serialization via HTTP).

The plugin makes it simple to provide remote access to a Grails service. The service must implement an interface, because it will be used to create a proxy that clients use to make the remote calls. For example, consider this simple interface (in this case, a Groovy version in *src/groovy*, but it can also be written in Java or from a JAR file):

```
package test.remoting

interface Math {
    int add(int i1, int i2)
    int multiply(int i1, int i2)
}
```

Creating the remoted service only requires two things: you have to implement the interface, and you have to add a static `expose` property containing a list of one or more protocol names to expose (any of `burlap`, `hessian`, `httpinvoker`, and `rmi`). This service (in *grails-app/services* like any Grails service) exposes all four protocols:

```
package test

import test.remoting.Math

class MathService implements Math {

    static expose = ['hessian', 'rmi', 'httpinvoker', 'burlap']

    int add(int i1, int i2) {
        i1 + i2
    }

    int multiply(int i1, int i2) {
        i1 * i2
    }
}
```

The plugin adds a servlet (an `org.springframework.web.servlet.DispatcherServ` `let`) for each protocol and an `org.springframework.web.servlet.HandlerMapping` to route to them, and registers a proxy (using an `org.springframework.aop.frame` `work.ProxyFactoryBean` and an `org.springframework.aop.target.HotSwappable` `TargetSource`) in the `ApplicationContext` for each remoted service (in this example, `MathServiceProxy` and `MathServiceTargetSource` beans). In addition, for each exposed protocol, it registers an `org.springframework.remoting.support.RemoteEx` `porter` subclass (e.g., an `org.springframework.remoting.caucho.HessianServi` `ceExporter` for the Hessian protocol) bean (in this example, `burlap.MathService`, `hessian.MathService`, `httpinvoker.MathService`, and `rmi.MathService`).

Client Access

The most convenient way for clients to connect to your exposed services is to use Spring's client support for the various protocols, and Grails applications using the remoting plugin can create services that connect to remoted services just as easily as exporting the remoted services in the server application. All that's involved is creating a service with the same name as the remote service (the package can be different) and adding a `remote` property defining connection information.

The service shouldn't implement the interface that the remote service exposes, but it must be available in the classpath; it would be a good idea to create a third Java/Groovy project containing all of your remoted interfaces and any custom classes used in method calls and adding the generated JAR file to the dependencies of the server and client applications. This is because the plugin just uses the service as a container for the `remote` property and replaces it in the `ApplicationContext` with a proxy (an `org.springfra` `mework.remoting.support.RemoteAccessor` subclass such as an `org.springframe` `work.remoting.caucho.BurlapProxyFactoryBean` for the Burlap protocol) bean that does implement the interface and makes the remote calls for you.

The `remote` property is a `Map` and specifies the interface to implement (under the `iface` key) and the remote protocol to use (under the `protocol` key); the protocol value can be one of the four supported values that are valid in the `expose` list in the remoted service class. In addition, you must specify the connection information. If you specify the full URL string under the `url` key it will be used; otherwise, the `host`, `port`, and `webcon text` values are used to build a URL. `host` defaults to `localhost` if not specified, "port" defaults to 1199 when using RMI or 8080 otherwise, and `webcontext` defaults to the root context.

For example, this service will create a proxy client using Hessian:

```
package client

class MathService {
    static remote = [
        protocol: 'hessian',
        iface: test.remoting.Math,
        host: 'my.server.com',
        port: 8888,
        webcontext: 'remote'
    ]
}
```

This service will create a proxy client using Burlap:

```
package client

class MathService {
    static remote = [
        protocol: 'burlap',
        iface: test.remoting.Math,
        host: 'my.server.com',
        port: 8888,
        webcontext: 'remote'
    ]
}
```

This service will create a proxy client using HttpInvoker:

```
package client

class MathService {
    static remote = [
        protocol: 'httpinvoker',
        iface: test.remoting.Math,
        host: 'my.server.com',
        port: 8888,
        webcontext: 'remote'
    ]
}
```

Finally, this service will create a proxy client using RMI:

```
package client

class MathService {
    static remote = [
        protocol: 'rmi',
        iface: test.remoting.Math,
        host: 'my.server.com',
        port: 10199,
        webcontext: 'remote'
    ]
}
```

JMS

Using the Java Message Service (JMS) is a common way to add synchronous and asynchronous messaging to an application, to make the application components more loosely coupled and reliable. Spring adds support for sending and receiving messages by using JMS topics and queues. It is common to use the `org.springframe work.jms.core.JmsTemplate` helper class, which has features similar to the `JdbcTem plate` JDBC helper. It manages connecting to the JMS `ConnectionFactory`, provides helper methods to abstract away the rather cumbersome JMS API, and also converts checked `JMSExceptions` to a hierarchy of runtime exceptions.

EJBs

Enterprise JavaBeans (EJBs) are rarely used in Grails applications, because Spring and Grails provide lightweight replacements for most of the useful features of EJB; for example, Hibernate and GORM (and now NoSQL support) instead of Entity beans, Grails services instead of stateless and stateful session beans, and the `jms` plugin (*http:// grails.org/plugin/jms*) to use JMS instead of message-driven beans. But, if you have existing EJBs that provide useful services, there's no need to rewrite them unless you also need the benefits of deploying on a lightweight container instead of a full application server, and Spring has several integration hooks to make EJB access transparent to your code.

JMX

There are plenty of highend monitoring solutions for web applications, but JMX remains as a simple and straightforward solution for monitoring and configuring aspects of an application using tools like JConsole (which is included with all JDK installs). Spring offers integration with JMX through various helper classes such as `org.spring framework.jmx.export.MBeanExporter` and others.

It shouldn't be much of a surprise that there's a Grails plugin to make using JMX even easier: the jmx plugin (*http://grails.org/plugin/jmx*) significantly reduces the amount of configuration you need to do.

It creates a javax.management.MBeanServer by using the Spring org.springframe work.jmx.support.MBeanServerFactoryBean factory bean, and automatically registers a Log4j and an org.hibernate.jmx.StatisticsService MBean (the latter only if the Hibernate plugin is installed). In addition, it exposes any Grails service that declares static expose = ['jmx'] and any Spring beans listed in the grails.jmx.export Beans attribute in *Config.groovy* as MBeans. All public setters and getters are exposed except for any that you exclude using the plugin's configuration.

See the jmx plugin documentation (*http://grails.org/plugin/jmx*) for more details.

Email

Many applications need to send email, and the JavaMail API provides a robust implementation of this. It's not the easiest API to use, but luckily, the Spring support for sending email using JavaMail makes it a lot more straightforward, and the Grails mail plugin (*http://grails.org/plugin/mail*) makes it painless to send plain-text and HTML emails, add attachments, and even use GSP templates.

See the mail plugin documentation (*http://bit.ly/YKmsig*) for more details.

Cache Abstraction

The cache abstraction feature was added to Spring in version 3.1, so applications using Grails 2.0 or higher can use it. This is an API for caching method calls, typically those that are slow or resource-intensive but that return the same result given the same parameter values.

This has been implemented in Grails in plugins; there is a "core" cache plugin (*http://grails.org/plugin/cache*) that provides an in-memory implementation, and extension plugins including cache-ehcache (*http://grails.org/plugin/cache-ehcache*) and cache-redis (*http://grails.org/plugin/cache-redis*) that use Ehcache and Redis, respectively, to implement the caching logic.

Method call caching is supported in Spring beans (typically Grails services) by using the Spring org.springframework.cache.annotation.Cacheable, org.springframe work.cache.annotation.CachePut, and org.springframework.cache.annota tion.CacheEvict annotations.

The core plugin also has annotations with the same names in the expectation that we can add additional parameters above what Spring supports in the future. The plugins also add web-tier caching for controller actions (for annotated controller methods, but not closures) and GSPs, using the `<cache:block>` and `<cache:render>` tags.

See the documentation for the caching plugins (*http://grails-plugins.github.com/grails-cache/*) for more details about how to use them in your applications.

CHAPTER 5

Hibernate

Hibernate is a powerful and popular object-relational mapping (ORM) library and it forms the basis of the standard persistence layer in Grails. Hibernate addresses the "impedence mismatch" between object-oriented code and the relational database storage model. It also tries (and largely succeeds) in providing a mostly transparent persistent API where developers don't need to consider the implementation details of storing and retrieving data because that's handled under the hood.

Mapping Domain Classes

In general, you map a domain class to each table, although it's common to partition tables into one or more classes (a domain class with components) and it's also possible to map a domain class to multiple tables with a database view. Class properties map to database columns (which may be a foreign key to another table represented by its own domain class in a one-to-one or many-to-one relationship) or collections representing a one-to-many relationship with another domain class. Arrays of simple types are also supported, as are maps.

Traditionally, Hibernate applications used XML files (typically with a *.hbm.xml* file extension) to define the mapping between the code and the database. When annotations were added to Java in version 1.5, Hibernate added a more intuitive annotation-based mapping approach that keeps the metadata together with the code. Under the hood, however, Hibernate creates a metamodel of the domain classes (using the `org.hiber nate.cfg.HbmBinder` for HBM files and `org.hibernate.cfg.annotations.Entity Binder` for annotations) that's independent of its source.

You could create an entire Hibernate data model yourself programmatically using these APIs directly, but that would defeat the purpose. But, that's what GORM does for you —it determines the data to be used to create the same metamodel objects (`Persistent Class`, `Table`, `PrimaryKey`, and so on) that `HbmBinder` and `EntityBinder` do, but from your application's domain classes instead of POJOs. This is done by `org.codehaus.groo vy.grails.orm.hibernate.cfg.GrailsDomainBinder`, if you're interested in the implementation details.

The simplest domain class is just a POGO with zero or more public fields:

```
class Person {
    String firstName
    String lastName
}
```

By default, all properties are considered persistent and are mapped to the appropriate column type in the table (e.g., `String` → VARCHAR, `Long` → BIGINT). If you have properties that aren't persistent (e.g., ones used for calculated or temporary values), you can exclude them from processing by adding them to the `transients` list:

```
class Person {
    String firstName
    String lastName
    int clickCount
    private boolean clicked // private, so not considered persistent

    static transients = ['clickCount']
}
```

 Nullability and primitive data types (`int`, `long`, `boolean`, etc.) do not mix, so in most cases, be sure to use the nonprimitive versions of these types (`Boolean`, `Integer`, `Long`, etc.). Primitive types are valid types for persistent properties but are impractical for validation. Because they get assigned a default value by the constructor (numbers default to zero and boolean to `false`), it makes it impossible to know whether the values were intentionally set to the default or they weren't set at all. Use nonprimitive types instead so that unset values are `null` and you can report that as an error if the property is required.

In addition, if a database column is nullable but the associated domain class field is primitive, you would see a `NullPointerException` when loading instances from the database, due to autoboxing from `null`. It wouldn't be reasonable to simply assume null numbers are zero and null booleans are `false`; null means that the value is not set and zero and `false` are valid values. Fortunately, Hibernate won't allow a primitive field to have a nullable column, but this makes the metadata and the database inconsistent.

You can create getter or setter methods, but if you create a matching pair, they'll be interpreted as a property and considered persistent, so you need to add the corresponding property name to the `transients` list:

```
class Person {
    String firstName
    String lastName
    int clickCount

    // ok, not considered a property
    void setSomething(boolean something) { ... }

    // ok, not considered a property
    int getSomethingElse() { ... }

    // considered a property
    String getFullName() { ... }
    void setFullName(String name) { ... }

    static transients = ['clickCount', 'fullName']
}
```

 Like any Groovy class, you can create setter and/or getter methods for
public properties; however, be careful when doing this in domain
classes, because you can trick Hibernate into thinking your instances
have been modified when they haven't. Hibernate caches persistent
property data to compare with the current state when flushing to determine if an instance is dirty. If you change the value when it's set (e.g.,
converting to uppercase, or setting a default value when the persistent
value is null), then it will be seen as different from when it was retrieved
and persisted. Hibernate calls the getter methods (either yours or the
autogenerated ones that the Groovy compiler creates) to do the checks,
so returning a value that's different from what was set will also indicate
a modification.

Dialects

Dialects are an important aspect of Hibernate and help to make your code database-
independent. SQL for querying, inserting, and updating (DML statements) tends to be
fairly standardized, but there are plenty of extensions. SQL for creating and altering
tables, columns, indexes, and other database structures often is not standardized well
at all. These differences are all managed by choosing an org.hibernate.dialect.Dia
lect for the database that you're using. There are several standard implementations
provided with Hibernate (MySQL5InnoDBDialect, Oracle10gDialect, PostgreSQLDia
lect, H2Dialect, and so on), and there are also third-party implementations; you can
also create your own by subclassing Dialect or one of the concrete implementations.

Dialect implementations are responsible for generating the correct SQL for the active
database. This helps to keep the Hibernate API clean, because there is rarely a need to

do something differently based on which database is active. In particular, you usually don't need different code for accessing the database in integration tests, even if you use the in-memory H2 database. You're also more free to switch database implementations; for example, if you outgrow MySQL or PostgreSQL (or find yourself with too much cash), you can easily switch to Oracle.

Dialect Autodetection

You don't have to specify the dialect to use, because Grails will attempt to infer it for you. You can bypass autodetection by setting the `dialect` attribute in the `dataSource` section of *grails-app/conf/DataSource.groovy* for each environment. If you don't, Grails registers a `dialectDetector` Spring bean that uses a connection from the datasource to inspect the database metadata. This works well in general, but it's still a good idea to specify the dialect explicitly:

```
environments {
   development {
      dataSource {
         dbCreate = 'validate'
         url = 'jdbc:mysql://servername:port/dbname'
         driverClassName = 'com.mysql.jdbc.Driver'
         username = ...
         password = ...
         dialect = org.hibernate.dialect.MySQL5InnoDBDialect
      }
   }
   ...
}
```

In particular, you should specify the dialect if you're using MySQL. The `dialectDetec` `tor` bean will correctly detect that you're using MySQL but it will choose `MySQLDia` `lect`, which doesn't specify the table engine in `CREATE TABLE` statements. This will result in using nontransactional MyISAM tables if you haven't changed the default engine type in *my.cnf* (although MySQL has changed the default to InnoDB in 5.5). Because you most likely want InnoDB tables to have support for transactions and foreign keys, you should specify an InnoDB dialect; use `MySQLInnoDBDialect` for older versions and `MySQL5InnoDBDialect` for version 5 and higher.

Dialect Customization

Because specifying the dialect to use is as simple as adding a property to *Data-Source.groovy*, it's very easy to customize a dialect in Grails. For example, to always use UTF-8 in your MySQL tables to properly support Unicode (the default is `latin1`), add `DEFAULT CHARSET=utf8` to your `CREATE TABLE` statements by overriding `getTableTy` `peString()` in a class in *src/groovy* or *src/java*:

```
package com.mycompany

import org.hibernate.dialect.MySQL5InnoDBDialect

class MyDialect extends MySQL5InnoDBDialect {

    @Override
    String getTableTypeString() {
        super.getTableTypeString() + ' DEFAULT CHARSET=utf8'
    }
}
```

To use the boolean type instead of bit(1), which lets you use true and false literals when you work directly with SQL and changes the values from values that don't display on a console to 0 and 1, add a call to registerColumnType in the constructor:

```
package com.mycompany

import java.sql.Types

import org.hibernate.dialect.MySQL5InnoDBDialect

class MyDialect extends MySQL5InnoDBDialect {

    MyDialect() {
        registerColumnType Types.BIT, 'boolean'
    }
}
```

When you use Oracle or PostgreSQL, Hibernate defaults to using a sequence for primary key generation, because autoincrement columns aren't supported. It only creates one sequence for all tables though; you can customize this in a custom dialect that overrides the getNativeIdentifierGeneratorClass method to return a SequenceGenerator that creates a sequence for each table. In this example, the naming convention is simple: it just prefixes the table name with seq_ to generate the sequence name, but you're free to use your own approach. Also, be sure to change the base class to whatever Oracle dialect you're using, and if you're using PostgreSQL, the same approach will work, just extend PostgreSQLDialect. MyDialect is based on code from *http://communi ty.jboss.org/wiki/CustomSequences*:

```
package com.mycompany

import org.hibernate.dialect.Dialect
import org.hibernate.dialect.Oracle10gDialect
import org.hibernate.id.PersistentIdentifierGenerator
import org.hibernate.id.SequenceGenerator
import org.hibernate.type.Type

class MyDialect extends Oracle10gDialect {

    @Override
```

```
Class<?> getNativeIdentifierGeneratorClass() {
    TableNameSequenceGenerator
}

static class TableNameSequenceGenerator extends SequenceGenerator {
    @Override
    void configure(Type type, Properties params, Dialect dialect) {
        if (!params.getProperty(SEQUENCE)) {
            String tableName = params.getProperty(
                PersistentIdentifierGenerator.TABLE)
            if (tableName) {
                params.setProperty SEQUENCE, "seq_" + tableName
            }
        }
        super.configure type, params, dialect
    }
}
}
```

Hibernate Without GORM

If you haven't used Hibernate outside of Grails before, it can be a helpful exercise to create a basic Hibernate application to get an appreciation of how things work and what Grails provides. We can cheat a bit and do this inside a Grails application so we don't need to configure all of the JAR dependencies. Create a Grails application from your IDE or the command line:

```
$ grails create-app pure_hibernate
$ cd pure_hibernate
```

hibernate.cfg.xml

Use the `create-hibernate-cfg-xml` script to create a *hibernate.cfg.xml* file that we'll use to register persistent classes:

```
$ grails create-hibernate-cfg-xml
```

and rename it to *hibernate_pure.cfg.xml* so GORM doesn't automatically load it (it will be in *grails-app/conf/hibernate*).

Update the contents to look like this:

```
<?xml version='1.0' encoding='UTF-8'?>
<!DOCTYPE hibernate-configuration PUBLIC
    '-//Hibernate/Hibernate Configuration DTD 3.0//EN'
    'http://hibernate.sourceforge.net/hibernate-configuration-3.0.dtd'>

<hibernate-configuration>

    <session-factory>
```

```
<property name='hibernate.connection.driver_class'>org.h2.Driver</property>
<property name='hibernate.connection.url'>
jdbc:h2:mem:hibernateDb;MVCC=TRUE
</property>
<property name='hibernate.connection.username'>sa</property>

<property name='show_sql'>true</property>
<property name='format_sql'>true</property>
<property name='use_sql_comments'>true</property>
<property name='hbm2ddl.auto'>create-drop</property>

<property name='dialect'>org.hibernate.dialect.H2Dialect</property>

<mapping resource='pure/Author.hbm.xml' />
<mapping class='pure.Book' />

</session-factory>

</hibernate-configuration>
```

Note that we have to configure database connectivity because we don't have access to the `DataSource` created from *DataSource.groovy*. The example is for an in-memory H2 database but feel free to change to a different supported database.

See the Hibernate documentation (*http://bit.ly/10XQT1w*) for more details about what properties are available.

HibernateUtil

You'll need a utility class that configures Hibernate and makes the `SessionFactory` available; create *src/groovy/hibernate/HibernateUtil.groovy*:

```
package hibernate

import org.hibernate.SessionFactory
import org.hibernate.cfg.Configuration

class HibernateUtil {

    static final SessionFactory sessionFactory
    static {
        sessionFactory = new Configuration()
            .configure('/hibernate_pure.cfg.xml')
            .buildSessionFactory()
    }

    static void shutdown() {
        sessionFactory.close()
    }
}
```

Author

Create a simple POGO that will represent an author in *src/groovy/pure/Author.groovy* (not in *grails-app/domain*):

```
package pure

class Author {
    Long id
    String name
}
```

Note that, unlike when using GORM, we have to define the id field (and version, if we want to enable optimistic locking).

We'll map this class using XML, so we need an *Author.hbm.xml* file in the pure package; non-Java source in *src/java*, *grails-app/conf*, and *grails-app/conf/hibernate* are copied to the classpath, so create *grails-app/conf/hibernate/pure/Author.hbm.xml* with this content:

```
<?xml version='1.0'?>
<!DOCTYPE hibernate-mapping PUBLIC
    '-//Hibernate/Hibernate Mapping DTD//EN'
    'http://hibernate.sourceforge.net/hibernate-mapping-3.0.dtd'>

<hibernate-mapping>

    <class name='pure.Author' table='author'>

        <id name='id' column='id'>
            <generator class='native' />
        </id>

        <property name='name' column='name' />

    </class>

</hibernate-mapping>
```

Book

Create another POGO to represent a book in *src/groovy/pure/Book.groovy*:

```
package pure

import javax.persistence.CascadeType
import javax.persistence.Column
import javax.persistence.Entity
import javax.persistence.GeneratedValue
import javax.persistence.Id
import javax.persistence.JoinColumn
import javax.persistence.ManyToOne
```

```
import javax.persistence.Table

@Entity
@Table(name='book')
class Book {

    @Id @GeneratedValue
    @Column
    Long id

    @Column
    String title

    @ManyToOne(cascade=CascadeType.ALL)
    @JoinColumn(name='author_id')
    Author author
}
```

This class uses JPA annotations, so there's no need for an XML mapping file. It is up to you whether to use annotated classes or regular POGOs/POJOs that are mapped with *hbm.xml* files. If you are integrating legacy code in a Grails applicaiton, you can continue to use the files you have. If you create new classes, you can use whichever approach works best for you.

Note that XML-mapped files are added to the Hibernate *cfg.xml* file using a `mapping` element with the `resource` attribute set, and annotated classes use the `class` attribute.

Experimenting with the APIs

Now we can test the configuration and mappings. Start up a console with `grails con sole` and execute this (using the Script → Run menu item) to create some authors:

```
import pure.Author
import hibernate.HibernateUtil

import org.hibernate.Session
import org.hibernate.Transaction

Session session = HibernateUtil.sessionFactory.openSession()
Transaction tx = session.beginTransaction()

Author author = new Author(name: 'Hunter S. Thompson')
session.save author

author = new Author(name: 'Douglas Adams')
session.save author

author = new Author(name: 'Tom Robbins')
session.save author
```

```
tx.commit()
session.close()
```

This should be successful, and you should see the generated SQL for the inserts into the author table in the output.

Next, create some books referencing the authors you just created:

```
import pure.Author
import pure.Book
import hibernate.HibernateUtil

import org.hibernate.Session
import org.hibernate.Transaction

Session session = HibernateUtil.sessionFactory.openSession()
Transaction tx = session.beginTransaction()

Author author = session.get(Author, 1L)
Book book = new Book(title: 'Fear and Loathing in Las Vegas', author: author)
session.save book

author = session.get(Author, 2L)
book = new Book(title: "The Hitchhiker's Guide to the Galaxy", author: author)
session.save book

author = session.get(Author, 3L)
book = new Book(title: 'Still Life with Woodpecker', author: author)
session.save book

tx.commit()
session.close()
```

This should also be successful and generate the SQL to load the Author instances and insert the records in the book table.

We can search with HQL to retrieve the instances:

```
import pure.Author
import pure.Book
import hibernate.HibernateUtil

import org.hibernate.Session
import org.hibernate.Transaction

Session session = HibernateUtil.sessionFactory.openSession()
Transaction tx = session.beginTransaction()

List authors = session.createQuery('from Author a order by a.name desc').list()
println "Author count: ${authors.size()}"
for (Author author in authors) {
    println "   Author: $author.name"
}
```

```
List books = session.createQuery('from Book b order by b.title asc').list()
println "Book count: ${books.size()}"
for (Book book in books) {
    println "   Book: $book.title"
}

tx.commit()
session.close()
```

Finally, close the `SessionFactory`:

```
import hibernate.HibernateUtil
```

```
HibernateUtil.shutdown()
```

This is a fairly simple example, but it does point out how much extra work you have to do when you bypass GORM. Most of the configuration in the XML file and the annotations is done automatically by GORM for you. And the persistence code is polluted with the calls to access a `Session` and start and commit a transaction. There are no convenience methods defined on the classes (e.g., `save`, `list`, etc.) so we need to call `Session` methods for those. This can be made easier with the Spring `HibernateTemplate`, but it's still a lot more work than just using GORM.

This also shows that, although it's more work to bypass GORM and use Hibernate directly, if you have existing Hibernate classes and code or if you need to access a feature that isn't exposed in GORM, you can do that easily.

The Session

The Hibernate session is the central access point for persistence with Hibernate. Grails developers rarely interact with it directly, but GORM does to an extent and the `HibernateTemplate` class that is used for querying uses it extensively. The session uses a JDBC `Connection` that it opens on demand (so simply creating a `Session` doesn't connect to the database, only when it's needed). It also maintains a first-level cache for instances and mapped collections. A `Session` is retrieved from a `SessionFactory`, which also manages the second-level caches.

All persistence is managed by the session. It has methods to retrieve individual instances (`get` and `load`), create new or update existing instances (`save`, `saveOrUpdate`, `update`, and `persist`), delete instances (`delete`), and update previously retrieved instances with current data (`merge` and `refresh`). For more extensive queries, there are the query methods `createCriteria` (for Criteria queries), `createQuery` (for HQL select and update queries), and `createSQLQuery` (for raw SQL queries).

withSession

Accessing the current session in older version of Grails was somewhat convoluted; you had to get access to the `sessionFactory` bean (typically with dependency injection) and call its `getCurrentSession()` method. This is still valid, but it's far more convenient to use the static `withSession` method that is added to all domain classes via metaprogramming:

```
Book.withSession { session ->
    session.flush()
    session.clear()
}
```

If you need access to a `Session` method that isn't exposed by GORM, this is a convenient way to access it.

withNewSession

`withSession` accesses the currently active session, but there are times when you need a separate session to do work; you can use the `withNewSession` method for this:

```
Book.withNewSession { session ->
    // do work
}
```

GORM custom validators are one use case for `withNewSession`. Because Hibernate flushes queued updates before executing queries, if you need to access the database to validate one or more domain class properties, you can do the work in a new session to avoid an untimely flush.

Open Session in View

The open session in view (OSIV) pattern is common when using Hibernate, and Grails implements it with the `org.codehaus.groovy.grails.orm.hibernate.sup port.GrailsOpenSessionInViewInterceptor` class (which extends the `org.spring framework.orm.hibernate3.support.OpenSessionInViewInterceptor` Spring class). This interceptor opens a Hibernate session at the beginning of each request, and flushes and closes it after it's finished.

This is primarily there for lazy-loaded one-to-many collections and many-to-one relationships. If there wasn't an open session, after loading the instance, it would immediately become disconnected. This is because GORM uses an `org.springframe work.orm.hibernate3.HibernateTemplate` to do the querying and it has logic to use an existing session using `SessionFactoryUtils.getSession()` or create one if none is active. When it gets an active session, it doesn't close it because it didn't open it, but if it has to create one, then it will close it. This disconnects all loaded instances, so trying

to access a collection would throw an exception. Because the `OpenSessionInViewIn`
`terceptor` opens a session and registers it in a `ThreadLocal` (via `SessionFactoryU`
`tils`), this keeps the session active, and the collections and relationships can be resolved.

By default, Hibernate automatically pushes changes in persistent instances during a
flush. The OSIV interceptor flushes at the end of the HTTP request, so any "dirty"
instances have their changes pushed to the database even if you don't call `save()`. This
surprises people who think they're just temporarily updating values—for example, to
pass to the view to be rendered—but the changes end up being persisted (as long as
there are no validation errors).

To get around this, you can use the `read()` method to load an existing instance if you
only want to modify it temporarily, such as for rendering in the GSP, but don't want
changes autopersisted because `read()` disables dirty checking. Another option is to call
`discard()` on modified instances; this disconnects the instance from the session and
no changes will be pushed to the database.

Disabling OSIV

Although it's not recommended, if you need to you can disable the OSIV interceptor(s)
(one is created for each `DataSource`). Make sure you know what you're doing though
if you decide to make this change.

The easiest way to do this is to create a no-op implementation of the `WebRequestInter`
`ceptor` interface:

```
package com.yourcompany.yourapp

import org.springframework.ui.ModelMap
import org.springframework.web.context.request.WebRequest
import org.springframework.web.context.request.WebRequestInterceptor

class NoopOpenSessionInViewInterceptor implements WebRequestInterceptor {
    void preHandle(WebRequest request) {}
    void postHandle(WebRequest request, ModelMap model) {}
    void afterCompletion(WebRequest request, Exception e) {}
}
```

and register an instance of your class as the `openSessionInViewInterceptor` Spring
bean in *grails-app/conf/spring/resources.groovy*:

```
import com.yourcompany.yourapp.NoopOpenSessionInViewInterceptor

beans = {
    openSessionInViewInterceptor(NoopOpenSessionInViewInterceptor)
}
```

If you use multiple datasources, you will need to create one bean for each datasource; just add the datasource name as the bean name suffix. So, for example, if you had a second `dataSource_lookup` datasource, you would register two bean overrides:

```
import com.yourcompany.yourapp.NoopOpenSessionInViewInterceptor

beans = {
    openSessionInViewInterceptor(NoopOpenSessionInViewInterceptor)
    openSessionInViewInterceptor_lookup(NoopOpenSessionInViewInterceptor)
}
```

Custom User Types

Hibernate has built-in support for many Java types:

- Numbers:
  - Integer and int
  - Long and long
  - Short and short
  - Float and float
  - Double and double
- The date/time classes:
  - java.util.Date
  - java.sql.Date
  - java.sql.Time
  - java.sql.Timestamp
  - java.util.Calendar
- String
- byte and Byte
- boolean and Boolean
- byte[]
- java.lang.Class
- java.util.Locale
- java.util.TimeZone
- java.util.Currency
- Any class that implements Serializable

These should suffice for most data that you store in a database, but there are times when you need to be able to customize how a type is stored. For example, you may have a class with multiple fields that should map to multiple columns in a table, but it's not a candidate to be a full domain class or even a component. Or, perhaps you need to store a supported data type, but in a nonstandard way. The solution is to create a class that implements org.hibernate.usertype.UserType (or one of the more advanced custom type interfaces) and register it as the type handler in your domain class.

For example, if you have a need for storing an encrypted string, you could manage it explicitly in the domain class, encrypting it when you set the value and decrypting it when you access it. But this pollutes the class with storage implementation details that aren't relevant to the real function of the domain class. Delegating this responsibility to a helper keeps things more modular.

The most important methods in the interface are nullSafeGet and nullSafeSet. These manage the low-level details of using JDBC to convert the data type(s) from the database into the Java data type(s) and vice versa. For example, consider this UserType implementation that encrypts a String (e.g., to store a credit card number, but not a password, because passwords should never be decryptable):

```
package com.yourcompany

import java.sql.PreparedStatement
import java.sql.ResultSet
import java.sql.Types

import org.hibernate.usertype.UserType

class EncryptedString implements UserType {

   Object nullSafeGet(ResultSet rs, String[] names, Object owner) {
      String value = rs.getString(names[0])
      value == null ? null : CryptoUtils.decrypt(value)
   }

   void nullSafeSet(PreparedStatement st, Object value, int index) {
      if (value) {
         st.setString index, CryptoUtils.encrypt(value.toString())
      }
      else {
         st.setNull index, Types.VARCHAR
      }
   }

   Class<String> returnedClass() { String }

   int[] sqlTypes() { [Types.VARCHAR] as int[] }

   Object assemble(Serializable cached, Object owner) { cached.toString() }
```

```
    Object deepCopy(Object value) { value.toString() }

    Serializable disassemble(Object value) { value.toString() }

    boolean equals(Object x, Object y) { x == y }

    int hashCode(Object x) { x.hashCode() }

    boolean isMutable() { true }

    Object replace(Object original, Object target, Object owner) { original }
}
```

nullSafeGet and nullSafeSet use the standard data marshalling approach as most other implementations, and handling null values appropriately (note that, unlike most other user type classes, there is no logging, because we do not want to risk exposing information). But, instead of doing the encryption and decryption inline, they delegate to a utility method that handles the implementation details.

You would use this in a domain class by specifying the type for the field in the mapping block; for example:

```
package com.yourcompany

class CreditCard implements Serializable {

    String number
    Long userId
    String cardholderName
    Integer expirationMonth
    Integer expirationYear
    CreditCardType type

    static mapping = {
        number type: EncryptedString
    }
}
```

This is a somewhat contrived example, because you wouldn't really want to handle the logic for encrypting credit card data or other highly sensitive information. Instead of defining your own custom data types for use cases like this, consider using the jasypt-encryption plugin (*http://grails.org/plugin/jasypt-encryption*), which uses the Jasypt library (*http://www.jasypt.org/*). It has excellent support for strong encryption, and many built-in custom types for persisting encrypted data in GORM domain classes.

See the Hibernate documentation (*http://bit.ly/YpMgvy*) for additional information and examples. Also, you can see examples of some fairly advanced user types in the Jasypt encryption project (*http://www.jasypt.org/*), for example, in this package (*http://bit.ly/XCl8vS*).

Optimistic and Pessimistic Locking

Hibernate supports pessimistic locking with `Session.lock()`. There several supported variants, but `LockMode.PESSIMISTIC_WRITE` is commonly used (this is what the corresponding GORM methods use) and will execute a `select ... for update` query (as long as the dialect and database support it) that will result in the row being exclusively locked. This is a safe way of guarding access to data, but the lock must occur during a transaction and will typically only be released when the transaction commits or rolls back. This creates the potential for performance issues and risk of lock contention.

The alternative is optimistic locking, which doesn't use database locking at all but instead attempts to determine that concurrent edits have occurred. The approach Hibernate uses for this is to add a column that maintains the current version of each row. This is usually a sequential number but can also be a `timestamp`, although that will add the low but nonzero chance of failing to detect a collision if two updates occur at the same millisecond on a fast machine.

If two users retrieve a row with version N and both modify and save the row with different edits, the second user's changes will revert the first user's changes. Like software commits into a version control system, they need to merge their changes instead. To detect that this has occurred, the generated update SQL will look like `update <table name> set <col1>=?, <col2>=?, ... where id=? and version=?`. It's sufficient to only specify the primary key for the update, but by also including the version value from when the record was retrieved, if the version has changed between the time the record was retrieved and now, the update won't occur (the row count for the update will be 0), and this indicates that a concurrent modification happened. This will result in the dreaded `StaleObjectStateException`, and the second edit should be done again after reloading the record with the other user's changes.

Grails defaults to enabling optimistic locking for all domain classes, and in general this shouldn't be changed. But, if you need to, for example, when mapping to a legacy database or for tables that aren't updated and therefore have no risk of concurrent edits, you can disable it with `version false`:

```
class ZipCode {
   String value
   static mapping = {
      version false
   }
}
```

If you have a rare application that doesn't use optimistic locking in any domain classes (or where it's more common to disable it than not), you can change the default and disable it in *Config.groovy*:

```
grails.gorm.default.mapping = {
   version false
}
```

Any domain classes that do use optimistic locking can reenable it in the `mapping` block:

```
static mapping = {
   version true
}
```

Accessing the Session's Connection

The various object-oriented querying approaches provided by Hibernate are sufficient in most cases, but when you need to execute a SQL query or update, it is possible. The `Session` class has a `connection()` method that can be used to get the current JDBC `Connection` associated with the session, but it's now deprecated and scheduled for removal in Hibernate 4.0. The replacement approach is to use the `doWork` method with an implementation of the `Work` interface. Using the `groovy.sql.Sql` class makes working with JDBC significantly easier:

```
import groovy.sql.Sql
import java.sql.Connection
import org.hibernate.jdbc.Work

Author.withSession { s ->
   s.doWork new Work() {
      void execute(Connection c) {
         String sqlString = ...
         new Sql(c).eachRow sqlString, {
            ...
         }
      }
   }
}
```

schema-export

Whether you're creating a new database as part of a greenfield application or mapping to an existing legacy database, you must ensure that the database has the correct structure and that Hibernate maps to it correctly. The `schema-export` script (*http://bit.ly/ 15gaeRo*) is very convenient for verifying your domain class mappings.

If you run the script without any arguments it will generate the DDL that Hibernate would use to create a new database:

```
$ grails schema-export
```

By default, the output is written to a file in *target/ddl.sql* but you can specify a file path:

```
$ grails schema-export /path/to/file
```

You can also execute the drop and create statements to create your database schema with the `export` parameter:

```
$ grails schema-export export
```

and like any Gant script, you can run it in any environment to use the database settings for the specified environment:

```
$ grails prod schema-export export
$ grails -Dgrails.env=staging schema-export export
```

The script is also multiple-datasource aware; specify the datasource to use with the `datasource` parameter:

```
$ grails schema-export export -datasource=lookup
```

SQL Logging

There are two ways to see the generated SQL that Hibernate executes for your queries. The simpler way is to add `logSql=true` to the `dataSource` section for any environment (or the top-level section so it applies to all environments) in *DataSource.groovy*:

```
dataSource {
    dbCreate = ...
    url = ...
    logSql = true
}
```

This works but is limited, because it just writes to `stdout`. So, for example, if you deploy to Tomcat, your *catalina.out* file will become huge fairly quickly.

The better option is to use Log4j logging. Hibernate logs SQL statements using the `org.hibernate.SQL` logger at the debug level. `PreparedStatement` setters are logged by the `BasicBinder` class at the trace level. So you can enable one or both of these in the `log4j` section for each environment in *Config.groovy*:

```
log4j = {
    error 'org.codehaus.groovy.grails',
          'org.springframework',
          'org.hibernate',
          'net.sf.ehcache.hibernate'

    debug 'org.hibernate.SQL'
    trace 'org.hibernate.type.descriptor.sql.BasicBinder'
}
```

Note that the type logging can be verbose and should only be enabled when you're having issues.

This isn't much better than dumping everything to `stdout`, because it actually does exactly that. By default, Grails configures `stdout` appender, so all of the logging will go there. But now that we're using Log4j, we have more options. For example, we can partition the log messages into multiple logfiles, such as one for SQL logging and one for everything else (and both configured as rolling loggers with a maximum file size to keep the logfile(s) from becoming gigantic):

```
log4j = {

    appenders {

        rollingFile name: 'logfile', maxFileSize: '512KB', maxBackupIndex: 10,
            file: (System.getProperty('catalina.base') ?: 'target') +
                    '/logs/application.log',
            layout: pattern(conversionPattern:
                            '%d{dd MMM yyyy HH:mm:ss} %p [%c] - <%m>%n')

        rollingFile name: 'fileSQL', maxFileSize: '512KB', maxBackupIndex: 10,
            file: (System.getProperty('catalina.base') ?: 'target') +
                    '/logs/sql.log',
            layout: pattern(conversionPattern:
                            '%-27d{dd/MMM/yyyy HH:mm:ss Z} %-10r [%t] - %m%n')

    }

    error 'org.codehaus.groovy.grails',
            'org.springframework',
            'org.hibernate',
            'net.sf.ehcache.hibernate'

    debug additivity: false, fileSQL: 'org.hibernate.SQL'
    trace additivity: false, fileSQL:
                            'org.hibernate.type.descriptor.sql.BasicBinder'

    root {
        warn 'logfile'
    }
}
```

This configuration is also somewhat environment-aware for the file location. When using run-app, the catalina.base system property isn't set, so the files get written to the *target/logs/* directory. If you deploy to Tomcat, then catalina.base will be available, and files will get written to Tomcat's *logs* directory along with the other logfiles.

Using either approach, you can turn on SQL formatting and/or SQL comments with Hibernate properties in *DataSource.groovy*. To enable SQL formatting (to pretty-print the SQL on multiple lines with indentation), add format_sql=true, and to enable SQL comments (so you can know what triggered a query), add use_sql_comments=true, both in the hibernate section:

```
hibernate {
    cache.use_second_level_cache = ...
    cache.use_query_cache = ...
```

```
        cache.region.factory_class = ...
        format_sql = true
        use_sql_comments = true
    }
```

Along these lines, there are a few plugins that can help with SQL query monitoring. The `grails-melody` plugin (*http://grails.org/plugin/grails-melody*) integrates the JavaMelody (*https://code.google.com/p/javamelody/*) library, the `newrelic` plugin (*http://grails.org/plugin/newrelic*) integrates New Relic (*https://newrelic.com/*), and the Mini Profiler (*http://grails.org/plugin/miniprofiler*) plugin is a newer pure Grails plugin.

Proxies

Hibernate proxies are a convenient way to support lazy loading. For example, in this simple domain class, the `author` property is lazy-loaded:

```
class Book {
    String title
    Author author
}
```

and, in this class, the `books` property (a `Set` of `Book` instances) is lazy-loaded:

```
class Author {
    String name
    static hasMany = [books: Book]
}
```

This means that when you retrieve a `Book`, it will load the regular properties (in this case just `title`), but the `author` property will actually be an instance of a dynamically generated (using Javassist (*http://www.jboss.org/javassist*)) subclass of your `Author` class. This proxy instance will have the `id` set, and any method call (or property access, which would call the corresponding getter method) other than `getId` will trigger a database call to load the `Author` data.

The `books` collection in the `Author` class will behave similarly. It's not loaded initially along with the other data (`name`, in this case), but the collection (a lazy-aware instance of `PersistentSet`, or `PersistentList` if you configured the property as a `List`) will populate itself from the database as soon as you access its contents or call a method that depends on the data in the collection (e.g., `size()`).

This can be a significant performance booster, because you don't need to worry about loading lots of data just to access a few properties of an instance. If everything were eager, it would be possible to load the entire database into memory depending on the mappings between domain classes.

The `load()` method (described in "load()" on page 156) is another Hibernate feature that uses proxies.

equals, hashCode, and compareTo

One thing to be aware of when using proxies is that you need to implement `equals` (or `compareTo`, if you implement `Comparable`) and `hashCode` in domain classes that will be stored in collections. If you don't, nonproxy instances and proxy instances with the same data will not be considered the same, because the default implementation of `equals` only returns `true` if the instances are the same (`==`, in the Java sense).

This isn't a severe problem, because nonproxied objects in the Hibernate session will be used instead of creating proxy instances. For example, if an instance would be a proxy in general (e.g., when using the `load()` method, or instances in a unidirectional collection), but it's already in the cache as as an unproxied instance, then that unproxied instance be returned.

Where it is problematic is when mixing detached or nonpersistent instances with persistent instances. For example, if you store a `Book` instance in the HTTP session (in general, not a good idea), it will be detached from the Hibernate session that loaded it. If you then were to add it to a `books` collection of an `Author` that already contains the corresponding persistent instance, it will be added again if you have no `hashCode` and `equals` methods:

```
def book = session[bookKeyName]
def author = Author.get(authorId)
author.addToBooks(book)
author.save()
```

This will fail at the `save()` call for various reasons, but would have been a no-op with proper `hashCode` and `equals` methods.

Grails doesn't implement any of these methods for you, because there's no sensible default implementation; you certainly don't want to include every property. Because the implementation depends on business rules, you need to implement the methods yourself just like you would in a non-Grails application.

The Commons Lang project has two convenience classes to help implementing `hashCode` and `equals` methods, `HashCodeBuilder` and `EqualsBuilder`:

```
import org.apache.commons.lang.builder.EqualsBuilder
import org.apache.commons.lang.builder.HashCodeBuilder

...

@Override
boolean equals(other) {
    if (is(other)) {
        return true
    }

    if (!(other instanceof Book)) {
```

```
        return false
    }

    new EqualsBuilder()
       .append(title, other.title)
       .append(author, other.author)
       .isEquals()
}

@Override
int hashCode() {
    new HashCodeBuilder()
       .append(title)
       .append(author)
       .toHashCode()
}
```

You can also use the `@EqualsAndHashCode` annotation in Groovy classes, which uses an AST transformation to add an implementation of the `hashCode` and `equals` methods into the bytecode of the annotated class:

```
import groovy.transform.EqualsAndHashCode

@EqualsAndHashCode(includes='title,author')
class Book {
    String title
    String author
}
```

Caching

The default second level cache provider in Grails is Ehcache, and it's a good default; it should handle your needs in most applications. You can (and should) customize the caching behavior per cache and set default values. You don't have to do anything (other than enabling caching in *DataSource.groovy* with the `hibernate.cache.use_sec ond_level_cache` setting), but it's a good idea to look at the caching requirements on a case-by-case basis and tune as needed.

Customizing the behavior is simple—just create an *ehcache.xml* file in the root of your classpath. Files in *grails-app/conf* and non-Java files in *src/java* are copied to the classpath, so either is a good choice. See *http://ehcache.org/ehcache.xml* for a well-commented example file that has a lot of useful information to get you started. This is the same file as the *ehcache-failsafe.xml* that's in the Ehcache JAR, which provides the default values if Ehcache doesn't find an *ehcache.xml* file.

```
<defaultCache
    maxElementsInMemory="10000"
    eternal="false"
    timeToIdleSeconds="120"
```

```
        timeToLiveSeconds="120"
        overflowToDisk="true"
        maxElementsOnDisk="10000000"
        diskPersistent="false"
        diskExpiryThreadIntervalSeconds="120"
        memoryStoreEvictionPolicy="LRU"
    />
```

Examples

Create these domain classes:

```
package caching

class Book {

    String title

    static mapping = {
        cache true
    }
}
```
```
package caching

class Author {

    String name

    static hasMany = [books: Book]

    static mapping = {
        cache true
        books cache: true
    }
}
```

Make sure that these settings are configued in *DataSource.groovy*:

```
hibernate {
    cache.use_second_level_cache = true
    cache.use_query_cache = true
    format_sql = true
    use_sql_comments = true
}
```

The settings are fairly self-explanatory: cache.use_second_level_cache enables second-level caching overall, cache.use_query_cache enables the query cache (but doesn't automatically cache any queries), format_sql pretty-prints the SQL on multiple lines to make it easier to read, and use_sql_comments adds comments to the SQL so you can see what triggered that query. There will also likely be other settings in this block (e.g., cache.region.factory_class).

Run a Grails console (`grails console` from the command line or via your IDE).

Enable statistics gathering by running:

```
def statistics = ctx.sessionFactory.statistics
statistics.statisticsEnabled = true
```

For the rest of the examples, be sure to include the imports for the domain classes:

```
import caching.Book
import caching.Author
```

Create a new book:

```
new Book(title: 'book 1').save()
```

Retrieve the instance you created by its ID using `get()` and you'll see the expected SQL (essentially just `select * from book where id=1` with the variables fully enumerated and with random names for uniqueness):

```
println Book.get(1)
```

Rerun this, and it will print the instance out again, but this time note that there's no SQL in the output. This is because the instance was loaded from the second level cache, because `get()` always uses the instance cache, and domain-level caching is enabled for this class by the `cache true` mapping entry.

Retrieve the instance by using a dynamic finder:

```
println Book.findAllByTitle('book 1', [cache: true])
```

and you'll see the expected SQL (essentially `select * from book where title=?`). If you rerun that command, you won't see any SQL this time. This is because the IDs of instances in cached queries are stored in the query cache, and query caching is enabled for the query by [`cache: true`]. The IDs aren't enough to avoid the SQL query to get the instance data, but the instances are cached in the instance cache, so there's no database access required at all for the second and subsequent queries.

You can peek into the query cache with this code snippet:

```
ctx.sessionFactory.queryCache.region.toMap().each { k, v ->
    println "Cache entry: key=$k\nvalue=$v"
}
```

The map keys are `org.hibernate.cache.QueryKey` instances (the significant data in this case being the query SQL and the query parameters), and the values are `Array List` instances where the first item is the timestamp of when the data was cached and the remaining items are the IDs of the instances.

We can do similar queries for an `Author`. Create an instance:

```
new Author(name: 'author 1').save()
```

and retrieve this one with a finder first instead of `get`:

```
println Author.findAllByName('author 1', [cache: true])
```

The SQL is as expected. Now, if we retrieve the instance using `get()`, there's no SQL:

```
println Author.get(1)
```

because as with the book examples, the query cache stores the ID and puts the instance in the instance cache. Rerun the finder or the `get()` call and neither will go to the database.

We enabled collection caching of the `books` collection in the `Author` class (with the `books cache: true` entry in the `mapping` block) and can see that by adding the book to the author's collection:

```
Author.get(1).addToBooks(Book.load(1)).save()
```

and reloading the instance and retrieving the books collection:

```
Author.withTransaction {
    println Author.get(1).books
}
```

We need to use `withTransaction` or something similar to keep the instance connected to the Hibernate session that loaded it so the `Book` collection can load (it's lazy-loaded because we didn't override the default).

Run that again, and you won't see any SQL. The behavior is similar to the query cache; the collection IDs are cached in the collection cache, and the instances are cached in the `Book` instance cache.

The cache region name for a domain class is the full class name, so you can also peek at the instance caches for domain classes using code like this:

```
ctx.sessionFactory.getSecondLevelCacheRegion(Book.name).toMap().each { k, v ->
    println "Cache entry: key=$k\nvalue=$v"
}
```

where `Book.name` is a shortcut for `Book.class.getName()`; replace it with the names of other domain classes that use caching.

The cache region name for a cached collection is the containing class's full name plus the collection field name, so you would inspect the `Author` books collection cache with:

```
def region = ctx.sessionFactory.getSecondLevelCacheRegion(Author.name + '.books')
region.toMap().each { k, v ->
    println "Cache entry: key=$k\nvalue=$v"
}
```

Note that the caches may be empty or not have all of the data you expect depending on when you triggered storing the data and the cache expiration duration (which defaults to 120 seconds).

Caching API

You can use Hibernate's caching API to inspect and manipulate the various caches. These methods are available from the `SessionFactory`; call the `getCache()` method to get the `org.hibernate.Cache` instance that manages the various caches.

evicting

Use the `Cache.evictEntityRegion(Class)` method to remove all cached instances for the specified domain class, or `Cache.evictEntity(Class, Serializable)` to remove a single instance by its ID.

Use the `Cache.evictCollectionRegion(String)` to remove all cached mapped collections for a domain class. For example, given an `Author` class with a `books` collection (`static hasMany = [books: Book]`), you would call:

```
sessionFactory.cache.evictCollectionRegion(Author.name + '.books')
```

because the region name for a cached collection is the containing class's full name plus the collection field name.

`evictCollectionRegion` removes all cached collections in the class; to remove just one instance's collection, use `evictCollection` and the `Author` ID:

```
sessionFactory.cache.evictCollection(Author.name + '.books', 123L)
```

 Be careful when calling API methods that take a domain class ID. GORM does some type conversions for you (e.g., the `get` method will accept a `String` or any numeric type and convert it to the actual ID type, typically Long), but this isn't the case elsewhere. If your domain class ID type is `Long` (the default, if you haven't overridden it), then be sure to pass long values, such as `Cache.evictEntity(Book, 123L)` and not `Cache.evictEntity(Book, 123)`, where 123 is an `int` and won't result in an exception, but won't evict anything either.

Accessing caches

You can access the various caches from the `SessionFactory`. To get the `org.hiber nate.cache.Region` instance for a particular second-level cache, use `SessionFacto ry.getSecondLevelCacheRegion(String)`.

The parameter is the full domain class name: `def region = sessionFactory.getSe condLevelCacheRegion("com.foo.bar.Book")` or `def region = sessionFacto ry.getSecondLevelCacheRegion(Book.name)`.

You can get a `Map` of all of the second-level cache regions with `SessionFactory.getAll SecondLevelCacheRegions`. The keys are `Strings`, and are the full domain class name for class caches or the full class name plus the collection field name for collection caches, and the values are `Region` instances.

The query cache (an `org.hibernate.cache.QueryCache` instance) is available from the `SessionFactory.getQueryCache()` method, and the timestamps cache that maintains the last updated time for various tables to coordinate query timeouts (an `org.hiber nate.cache.UpdateTimestampsCache` instance) is available from the `SessionFacto ry.getUpdateTimestampsCache()` method.

Query Caching Considered Harmful?

Query caching seems like a good idea, and it is in many cases, but it's not guaranteed to help performance and can actually hurt performance. Alex Miller's blog post "Hibernate query cache considered harmful?" (*http://tech.puredanger.com/2009/07/10/hibernate-query-cache/*) points out some interesting issues of which you should be aware.

The primary issue with the query cache is that Hibernate has to be fairly pessimistic when managing it. It's computationally complex to determine if a cached query result would be affected by saving, updating, or deleting a domain class instance. And, even if that were implemented, a database trigger could affect data in unexpected ways. So, Hibernate just assumes that a change could affect cached results and purges them. This means that read-only and read-mostly domain classes might be good candidates for query caching, but others that write to the database often will constantly be clearing all cached queries that have instances of that type. You can see that it wouldn't take many writes to completely defeat the savings from caching, and even make queries slower than always going directly to the database.

In general, you can enable query caching by setting the `hiber nate.cache.use_query_cache` property in *grails-app/conf/DataSource.groovy* to `true`, but this doesn't automatically enable the cache for individual queries. You need to execute each query with caching enabled, and it's slightly different for each approach. For example, to cache a dynamic finder, the syntax is:

```
Book.findAllByTitle(title, [cache: true])
```

The syntax for a criteria query is:

```
Book.withCriteria {
    eq 'title', title
    cache true
}
```

and for HQL queries with `executeQuery`, it's:

```
Book.executeQuery('from Book b where b.title=:title',
                  [title: title], [cache: true])
```

In the first few Grails 2.0.x releases, query caching was enabled by default for all queries; this is configured by the `grails.hibernate.cache.queries` option in *grails-app/conf/ Config.groovy*. Given the performance risks of always using query caching, I recommend you disable this property by setting it to `false` and explicitly cache individual queries only for cases where you're comfortable that there will be a performance benefit. The default was changed to `false` in later versions.

Note that the query cache stores IDs, not whole instances. This means that you will save the cost of executing the query in the database, but Hibernate will use the cached IDs to load individual instances for the query result. If you've also enabled second-level caching for your query-cached domain classes, you will further minimize database access. For example, with second-level caching disabled, the finder example above will generate SQL similar to `select * from book where title=?` for the first call and SQL similar to `select * from book where id=?` for the second. Caching instances in the instance cache makes the second database call unnecessary.

HQL

Dynamic finders, criteria queries, and the new `where` queries in Grails 2.0 tend to be the most popular approaches to querying in Grails, but I find HQL to be more readable and intuitive, having done a lot of SQL work in the past. One argument for criteria queries and against HQL is in the case where you dynamically build up the query, such as when presenting a search screen for your users where most of the fields are optional. But we'll see that given how GORM integrates HQL querying, even that becomes nearly as clean with HQL and criteria.

The `find` (*http://bit.ly/XN719q*), `findAll` (*http://bit.ly/YKnx9M*), and `executeQuery` (*http://bit.ly/11hmjkP*) static GORM methods all support HQL, but I tend to use `exe cuteQuery` (and `executeUpdate` (*http://bit.ly/17BB8lV*) for update and delete operations).

`executeQuery` always returns a `List` of results, even if you specify a limit of one result. In fact, the `List` is a regular `java.util.ArrayList`; it's not a Hibernate-specific `List` implementation like the one used to model ordered collections in domain classes (`PersistentList`) so you're free to modify the contents.

Note that like `withTransaction`, `withSession`, and `withNewSession`, the `execute Query` and `executeUpdate` methods can be called on any arbitrary domain class, because the methods are independent of the class on which they're defined.

executeQuery

There are five variants of `executeQuery`; if the query isn't parameterized, then you can just execute a query for the HQL string:

```
def roles = Role.executeQuery('select r from Role r order by r.name')
```

If the query is parameterized, you can use ? characters like in SQL queries and provide a List of parameter values:

```
String loginName = ...
def users = User.executeQuery(
    'from User u where u.username=? or u.email=?',
    [loginName, loginName])
```

or you can use named parameters (which are significantly more readable) and provide a Map of parameter values keyed by the names specified in the query:

```
String loginName = ...
def users = User.executeQuery(
    'from User u where u.username=:login or u.email=:login',
    [login: loginName])
```

Note here that, because the named parameter is repeated, it only occurs once in the parameter map.

Both parameter styles support a Map of parameters to customize the results or behavior of the query:

max

Limits the maximum number of records to return (typically for pagination)

offset

Specifies the offset position into the results (typically for pagination)

readOnly

If true, will return results that are not dirty-checked and whose snapshots of persistent state are not maintained

fetchSize

Specifies the fetch size for the underlying JDBC query

timeout

Specifies the timeout for the underlying JDBC query

flushMode

Overrides the current session flush mode

cache

If true, will use the query cache

Query Syntax

The syntax of HQL queries is similar to that of SQL (select … from … where …). Most of the same constructs from SQL are supported in HQL, with the significant difference being that you work with class and property names, never table or column names. Also, it's rare to explicitly join in HQL (although there are reasons to in certain cases), because Hibernate knows the relationships between your classes and uses those to create joins in the generated SQL.

When selecting all elements from a query, the `select` keyword is often optional, so `select u from User u ...` and `from User u ...` are equivalent. A case where it is required is when you have a join but only want to return one of the joined types, such as `select u from User u, Role r where ....`

These examples presume that there is a `User` domain class; it should be in a package, but there's rarely a need to include the full class name with package, because GORM defaults to autoimporting all classes. If you have two domain classes with the same name in different packages, this will fail, so you must disable autoimport in the `mapping` block:

```
static mapping = {
    autoImport false
}
```

and then use the full class name, such as `from com.yourcompany.User u ....` You can shorten this to `from $User.name u ...` if the HQL string is a `GString`, because `User.name` is the equivalent of `User.class.getName()`.

Report Queries

Most queries return domain class instances, but it's possible to return specified properties. This type of query is commonly referred to as a "report query," because it's often used when generating reports instead of the more common case where you're updating data or using it to render HTML responses.

Single properties

If you select a single property, the return type will be a `List` of that type; for example:

```
def firstNames = Author.executeQuery('select a.firstName from Author a')
```

will return a list of strings.

Multiple properties

If you select multiple properties, the return type will be a `List` of `Object[]` arrays; for example:

```
def names = Author.executeQuery('select a.name, a.age from Author a')
```

will return a list of `Object[]` where the first array element is a string with the name, and the second array element is the age (an integer or whatever numeric type the age property has).

new list

You can return a List of List instances by using the new list construct:

```
def names = Author.executeQuery(
    'select new list(a.name, a.age) from Author a where ...')
```

You can also build object instances as long as the specified class has a constructor that is compatible with the query (the class can be a POJO or a POGO, it doesn't need to be a domain class). These queries will return a List of instances of the specified class:

```
def names = Author.executeQuery(
    'select new Address(a.street, a.city, a.state, a.zip) from Author a where ..,')
```

This example would require a constructor similar to:

```
Author(String street, String city, String state, String zip) {
    ...
}
```

and, if Author is a domain class, you must additionally add a default constructor:

```
Author() {}
```

because the compiler only adds a default constructor if there are no constructors in your code, and the default constructor is required by Hibernate.

And, finally, you can return a List of Map instances by using the new map construct; the map keys will be the alias names defined in the HQL:

```
def names = Author.executeQuery(
    'select new map(a.name as fullName, a.age as age) from Author a where ...')
```

Aggregate Functions

Several aggregate functions on class properties are supported:

- avg(...)
- sum(...)
- min(...)
- max(...)
- count(*)
- count(...)
- count(distinct ...)
- count(all ...)

Expressions

There are many expressions supported in HQL `where` clauses:

- Mathematical operators: +,-, *,/
- Binary comparison operators: =, >=, <=, <>, !=, `like`
- `and`, `or`, `not`
- `in`, `not in`, `between`, `is null`, `is not null`, `is empty`, `is not empty`, `member of`, `not member of`
- Date and time functions: `current_date()`, `current_time()`, `current_time stamp()`, `second(...)`, `minute(...)`, `hour(...)`, `day(...)`, `month(...)`, `year(...)`
- EJB-QL 3.0 functions: `substring()`, `trim()`, `lower()`, `upper()`, `length()`, `locate()`, `abs()`, `sqrt()`, `bit_length()`, `mod()`
- Collection functions: `size()`, `minelement()`, `maxelement()`, `minindex()`, `maxindex()`, `elements()`

Collections

You can work with collections directly like you would in Groovy code, and also use joins to include collections in the `select` or `where` clause; for example:

```
def newAuthors = Author.executeQuery(
    "select a from Author a where a.books is empty")

def prolificAuthors = Author.executeQuery(
    "select a from Author a where size(a.books) > 10")

def grailsAuthors = Author.executeQuery(
    "select a from Author a join a.books as book " +
    "where lower(book.title) like '%grails%'")

Book book = ...
def author = Author.executeQuery(
    "select a from Author a where :book in elements(a.books)", [book: book])
```

Collections Performance

As we saw in Chapter 3, GORM uses mapped collections to map many-to-one and many-to-many relationships. Unfortunately, although this is convenient, it isn't the best approach for performance. This is because the `hasMany` declaration adds a `Set` property containing the `OrderItem` instances. A `Set` guarantees uniqueness, and to enforce this, Hibernate has to load all of the other instances from the database to check whether the new instance is already there (or equivalent to one based on `hashCode` and `equals` checks). The collection defaults to being lazy-loaded, but accessing its contents triggers a full load from the database.

The problem is the same if you change the collection type to `List`:

```
class Purchase {
    Date purchaseDate
    List orderItems
    // other properties
    static hasMany = [orderItems: OrderItem]
}
```

because the `List` order must be maintained, so again all of the existing instances will be loaded. If you enable SQL logging as described above, you will see all the unexpected database activity.

The persistent collection instances are dirty-aware Hibernate classes so Hibernate can detect when an instance is added to or removed from a collection and make the corresponding changes in the database. But by inverting the ownership (in traditional Hibernate applications, collections are usually "inverse" collections that don't drive persistence), we've added these extra collection maintentance costs.

In addition, even though we're just attempting to store a new `OrderItem` instance, because the collection is a property of the `Purchase` class, the version of the `Purchase` will be incremented. This means that concurrent changes run a fairly high risk of an optimistic locking exception for the `Purchase`.

Mapping a many-to-many relationship is similar, because both sides have a `hasMany` property representing the mapped collection.

Changing the type to a Hibernate `Bag` (which has no uniqueness or order guarantees) would seem to be a solution:

```
class Purchase {
    Date purchaseDate
    Collection orderItems
    static hasMany = [orderItems: OrderItem]
    // other properties
}
```

but this still has issues; see my "Hibernate Bags in Grails 2.0" blog post (*http://burtbeck with.com/blog/?p=1029*) for more details about bags.

The Solution

I described this issue at SpringOne/2GX in 2010; you can watch the talk online (*http://www.infoq.com/presentations/GORM-Performance*), and you can also see this discussed in my blog post (*http://burtbeckwith.com/blog/?p=169*) that addresses these issues and has sample code and a PDF of an earlier presentation.

Once you have determined that the number of elements in a mapped collection will be a performance concern (there is no standard number for this, it depends on your use cases), you can address the issue by simply not using mapped collections. You will lose some convenience, but it is relatively easy to regain a lot of it.

The solution for the `OrderItem`/`Purchase` many-to-one mapping is to remove the `hasMany` in `Purchase`, replace the `belongsTo` in `OrderItem` with a reference to the owning `Purchase`—for example, `Purchase purchase`. This will result in the same database structure (unless you were using a join table, which is rare in many-to-one), because there is still a foreign key from the `order_item` table to the `purchase` table. Saving an `OrderItem` instance changes, from adding it to the `orderItems` collection in `Purchase` to setting the `purchase` reference in the `OrderItem` and saving it directly. This will be more efficient and is arguably more intuitive.

One thing that is lost in this approach is a convenient way to get all of the `OrderItem` instances associated with a `Purchase`, but that's easy to get back: add a method in the `Purchase` class that returns `OrderItem.findAllByPurchase(this)`. You also lose cascaded deletes if you had specified the `dependsOn` property, but it's simple enough to delete a `Purchase` in a transactional service method that deletes the associated `OrderItem` instances first.

The fix for many-to-many is more involved, but not too bad. Ordinarily, Grails developers don't think much about the join table that links the two "many" tables, because it's transparent in the code. But you can map a domain class to that table, and it just needs two properties: foreign keys for each of the other tables. If the primary key is defined as `composite` and composed of these two foreign keys, the table structure will be the same as what Grails was using; this makes data migration a no-op. There is a bit more work involved, because Hibernate requires that the join table domain class implement `Serializable` and have well-defined `equals` and `hashCode` methods. You can see an example of this in the previously referenced presentation, and if you're using the `spring-security-core` plugin, you already have an example in your application, because the `UserRole` class uses exactly this approach.

Session.createFilter()

`Session.createFilter()` is a useful method for working with collections. Because working with collections is a double-edged sword (they help performance by being lazily loaded and not incurring database access until they're explicitly accessed, but fully initialize when loading), it is convenient to use `createFilter` to access a subset of a collection. For example, you can use it to determine the number of elements in a collection without initializing the collection. This would make a convenient utility method:

```
class Branch {
    String name
    static hasMany = [visits: Visit]

    int getVisitCount() {
        visits == null ? 0 : withSession {
            it.createFilter(visits, 'select count(*)').uniqueResult()
        }
    }
}
```

You can also use it to retrieve some of the items in a mapped collection without loading the whole collection. It's easy to retrieve a page of the collection (this makes more sense if the collection is a List) with Session.createFilter() (you can also use a query, either criteria or HQL, but that's more involved):

```
class Branch {
    String name
    List visits
    static hasMany = [visits: Visit]

    List<Visit> getVisitsByPage(int pageSize, int pageNumber) {
        Branch.withSession { session ->
            session.createFilter(visits, '')
                    .setMaxResults(pageSize)
                    .setFirstResult(pageSize * pageNumber)
                    .list()
        }
    }
}
```

Custom Configurations

GORM exposes a lot of configuration options in the mapping block of domain classes, but not everything that's configurable in Hibernate is available as a GORM option. In those cases, you can make the changes with a custom Configuration class. By default, Grails uses an instance of GrailsAnnotationConfiguration (*http://bit.ly/138x2hE*), and your best bet is to subclass that to retain its functionality.

One common approach is to override the secondPassCompile() method, because at that point, the metadata will have been configured and you can customize it as needed. It's also possible to customize the generated DDL statements used to create or update the database (depending on your dbCreate setting) by overriding generateSchema CreationScript(), generateDropSchemaScript(), and generateSchemaUpdate Script(). You can customize the Settings instance that's used to configure much of

Hibernate by overriding the `buildSettings(Properties)` method. Any of the public or protected methods in the class are candidates for overriding; it's a good idea to browse the source of the class to understand where the various hooks are.

To create your own version, subclass `GrailsAnnotationConfiguration` (either in *src/ java* or *src/groovy*) and register it in the `dataSource` block(s) for whichever environments should use it (register it in the global section if all environments share one):

```
dataSource {
    pooled = true
    driverClassName = '...'
    username = '...'
    password = '...'
    configClass = 'com.yourcompany.yourapp.YourConfigurationClassName'
}
```

As an example, let's look at how to specify the names of the foreign keys for many-to-one relationships. Given a simple trio of classes to model a music collection:

```
package music

class Artist {
    String name
}

package music

class Album {
    Artist artist
    String name
}

package music

class Track {
    Album album
    String name
}
```

we'll have two foreign keys; one for the album → artist relationship and one for the track → album. If you create these domain classes and run `grails schema-export`, you'll see that the generated DDL contains statements like these:

```
alter table album add constraint FK5897E6F2551B863
foreign key (artist_id) references artist;

alter table track add constraint FK697F14B63AA2231
foreign key (album_id) references album;
```

When debugging database issues, cryptic names like FK5897E6F2551B863 and FK697F14B63AA2231 are next to useless. You can specify the names in *hbm.xml* files or in the corresponding annotations, but it's not an option with GORM. But that's simple to remedy:

```
package programming.grails

import org.apache.commons.collections.map.MultiKeyMap
import org.codehaus.groovy.grails.orm.hibernate.cfg.GrailsAnnotationConfiguration
import org.hibernate.MappingException
import org.hibernate.cfg.Settings
import org.hibernate.dialect.Dialect
import org.hibernate.mapping.ForeignKey
import org.hibernate.mapping.PersistentClass
import org.hibernate.mapping.RootClass

class MyConfiguration extends GrailsAnnotationConfiguration {

    private boolean alreadyProcessed
    private MultiKeyMap fkNames = new MultiKeyMap()

    MyConfiguration() {
        fkNames.put 'music.Track', 'music.Album', 'FK_TRACK_ALBUM'
        fkNames.put 'music.Album', 'music.Artist', 'FK_ALBUM_ARTIST'
    }

    protected void secondPassCompile() throws MappingException {
        super.secondPassCompile()

        if (alreadyProcessed) return

        def rootClasses = classes.values().findAll { it instanceof RootClass }) {
        for (RootClass rc in rootClasses) {
            for (ForeignKey fk in rc.table.foreignKeyIterator) {
                String fkName = fkNames.get(rc.className, fk.referencedEntityName)
                if (fkName) fk.name = fkName
            }
        }

        alreadyProcessed = true
    }
}
```

Here we store the foreign key names in a MultiKeyMap using the two class names as a key, and loop through the ForeignKey instances looking for matches. If we find one, we update the name.

Mapping Views and Subselect Classes

It is typical to have a one-to-one mapping between tables and domain classes, especially in greenfield projects where the developers are able to design the database. But you are not restricted to getting all of the data for a domain class from a single table, and you don't need to map every column in a table.

Database views are a convenient way to aggregate data within a table or across multiple tables, and treat it like a physical table. Mapping a domain class to a view isn't directly supported but it's not much work to configure.

Consider this simple data model:

```
package programming.grails

class Organization {
   String name
  // other unrelated fields
}
```

```
package programming.grails

class AuthUser {
  String username
  String password
  Organization organization
  // other unrelated fields
}
```

where a user in the system has a username and a password to authenticate, and is associated with an organziation. It would be convenient to map a domain class that represents an active user in the system but doesn't know about the password field because it's only needed when authenticating, and has access to the organization's name but not the other unrelated data:

```
package programming.grails

class UserInfo {
   String name
   String orgName
}
```

But, if you create this domain class as it stands, Hibernate will expect a `user_info` table; there's no mapping between the class and the tables that it needs to refer to. That mapping can come from a view (this syntax is an example and won't work for all databases):

```
CREATE OR REPLACE VIEW v_user_info AS
SELECT u.name, u.id, u.version, o.name org_name
FROM auth_user u, organization o
WHERE u.organization_id = o.id
```

Now we can add a `mapping` block to tell GORM that the "table" for the domain class is this view:

```
package programming.grails

class UserInfo {
    String name
    String orgName

    static mapping = {
        table 'v_user_info'
    }
}
```

It wouldn't make much sense to use this domain class to update data, but because the view query includes the user ID, you can execute finders and `get()` calls if you have the user's ID.

Subselect Domain Classes

Ordinarily, you map all columns from a table in the corresponding domain class, but this isn't always desirable. If there are columns that aren't needed (e.g., large VARCHAR columns), or that are only needed for certain queries, you can map just the required fields. Of course, if you don't map every column, and one or more of the omitted columns doesn't allow `null` values, you won't be able to insert or update rows, but there are options for that.

Looking back at the `AuthUser` class above, if there were a requirement that the user data be available but you need to ignore the `password` column (because it's only needed for authentication), we could create a second `Person` domain class that has all of the `AuthUser` fields except `password`:

```
package programming.grails

class Person {
    String name
    Organization organization
}
```

A view is an option for restricting the available fields, but there's an easier solution; map the class onto the same table as for `AuthUser`:

```
package programming.grails

class Person {
    String name
    Organization organization

    static mapping = {
        table 'auth_user'
```

```
    }
}
```

This works, and will only select the mapped fields. You can't create new rows in the table (assuming `password` is not-null), but that's not the function of this class. But you might want to update instances, either changing the username or the `Organization`. That will work, because the generated SQL for the update will include the mapped columns, and the unmapped columns will retain their previous values.

Selecting with a POGO

If you don't need all the features of a second domain class (i.e., GORM methods, finders, etc.) then you can take advantage of a Hibernate feature with HQL queries. Instead of creating `Person` as a domain class, create it as a POGO in *src/groovy* and use the HQL `select new` syntax in a query:

```
long userId = ...
def person = AuthUser.executeQuery(
    'select new programming.grails.Person(a.name, a.organization) ' +
    'from AuthUser a where a.id=:id',
    [id: userId])[0]
```

Note that because `executeQuery` always returns a list, and we're only expecting a single instance, we use `[0]` to get the instance.

Because Hibernate isn't aware of the Groovy map constructor, you will need a traditional parameterized constructor for this POGO:

```
package programming.grails

class Person {
    String name
    Organization organization

    Person(String name, Organization organization) {
        this.name = name
        this.organization = organization
    }
}
```

You can relax the return type even further and skip the POGO, returning a map created in the HQL query:

```
long userId = ...
def data = AuthUser.executeQuery(
    'select new map(a.name as name, a.organization as organization) ' +
    'from AuthUser a where a.id=:id',
    [id: userId])[0]
```

and this will return a `Map` where the keys are the names specified in the HQL as aliases.

And of course, you can always just select the fields to be returned as an Object[] array (or List of arrays when you return multiple records) using standard report query syntax:

```
long userId = ...
def data = AuthUser.executeQuery(
        'select a.name, a.organization from AuthUser a ' +
        'where a.id=:id', [id: userId])[0]
```

get(), load(), and read()

GORM offers multiple ways to access a single domain instance by ID.

get()

Retrieving a single domain class instance corresponding to a row in a table is a common action, so it has its own dedicated method, get(). This is a static method defined on all domain classes. It returns the corresponding instance, or null if no record is found.

get() should be used instead of the equivalent findById(), because get() uses the cache (first and second level) by default, whereas dynamic finders like findById() are only cached in the query cache. As we saw above, this is quite volatile and will be cleared pessimistically by Hibernate when any other instance is saved, deleted, or updated. But an instance cached by a get() call is only invalidated if that instance is affected by an update.

One use for findById() is as part of an ownership checking query. If you have access to the currently authenticated user and have an ownership relationship, for example a CreditCard having a User field. Rather than submitting the user ID and the card ID to load the card instance, a safer approach would be to just submit the card ID and use the authenticated user as a redundant check. The query then becomes:

```
def cardId = params.id
def user = ... // implementation-specific way of getting the User domain instance
def card = CreditCard.findByIdAndUser(cardId, user)
```

By adding the second comparison to the SQL WHERE clause, we return the record only if both match. A hacker attempting to load someone else's data would be blocked.

But there are two alternative methods that also return single instances that are useful in certain circumstances.

load()

load() appears to work the same way as get() but, in fact, doesn't actually query the database, at least not initially. It creates a proxy instance for the record and stores the specified ID, and always returns an instance (because it can't be known if the record exists yet). It's not until the first call to a method (or a property access that calls its getter method) that the ID is used to actually retrieve the data. At this point, if no record is found, Hibernate will throw an `org.hibernate.ObjectNotFoundException`.

Using this in general would lead to a rather chaotic application, because you don't know until you try to access object data that the record doesn't exist, and it triggers an exception that you need to catch. So in general, `get()` is preferable. Consider this domain model:

```
class Author {
    String name
}
class Book {
    String title
    Author author
}
```

and this typical code to persist a new Book:

```
long authorId = params.authorId as Long
Book book = new Book(title: params.title, author: Author.get(authorId))
if (book.save()) {
    ...
}
else {
    ...
}
```

We load the entire `Author` instance into memory just so we can use it to set the foreign key in the book table. In this case, that's not very expensive, but for real domain classes with many fields and possibly eagerly loaded collections, it can be quite wasteful to retrieve the whole instance. Instead, we can use `load()`:

```
long authorId = params.authorId as Long
Book book = new Book(title: params.title, author: Author.load(authorId))
...
```

and, as long as the `Author` instance exists, which it should in this scenario because the ID was submitted with the request, which presumably came from a persistent instance, then the foreign key will resolve. If it doesn't, there will be a foreign key violation, and you can handle that error.

We have a similar situation when querying. Suppose we want to find all books by an author and only have the author ID. We could create a criteria or HQL query, but dynamic finders are a lot more convenient. However, this:

```
long authorId = ...
def author = Author.get(authorId)
def books = Book.findAllByAuthor(author)
```

incurs the same unnecessary cost as above; there's no need to load and discard the Author instance just to get the Book instances. If we instead use load(), then there will be just the one query:

```
long authorId = ...
def author = Author.load(authorId)
def books = Book.findAllByAuthor(author)
```

because the SQL only needs the author ID for the foreign key reference in its WHERE clause.

read()

The read() method is similar to the get() method in that it returns a domain class instance and not a proxy, or null if the corresponding record doesn't exist. Where it's different is that it sets the object to "read-only" mode (which isn't actually read-only).

When a persistent instance is loaded using get(), or by a query that doesn't result in a proxy, the data for the instance exists twice in memory: once for the instance itself, and again in a copy in an Object[] array in the session. This copy of the data is used for dirty detection. Hibernate uses this cached data to do a field-by-field check comparing the current state in the domain class instance with the original data that was loaded from the database to determine if any fields were modified. If you have configured a domain class to do dynamic updates, then it can use this information to update just the changed fields. Otherwise, any changed field triggers a full update.

Because you've indicated to Hibernate with a read() call that you don't intend to update the data, it doesn't bother with the copy of the data. This will reduce memory usage, which could be significant if you were loading a large number of instances that won't be modified.

The instance isn't really read-only, however. If you change one or more fields and save() the instance, it will update the record in the database. In fact, because there's no cached data to check, even if you don't change anything and call save(), it will update the record with the current values (ordinarily, dirty checking would render this a no-op). And you could also delete() the instance. So the instance is fully mutable, it's just not automatically updated for you during a flush.

Performance

Because Hibernate is a wrapper API around SQL, it does affect performance somewhat. In general, using hand-tuned SQL queries will often be faster than those generated by a tool. But Hibernate has several optimizations that help mitigate this and can actually be faster than using direct SQL.

Caching

One optimization is the caching described above. If you retrieve an instance using the get() method and call it again for the same ID in a session, Hibernate will only go to the database for the first call, because it will have stored the instance in the instance cache. And, if you have second level caching enabled for that domain class, it might not have to hit the database at all if there's a cached instance in the second level cache.

If you use the query cache, you will also save time by retrieving instances from the cache instead of rerunning the query and hitting the database again only to return the same instances as from a previous query with the same parameters.

Lazy Loading

By default, mapped collections (one-to-many) and many-to-one relationships are lazily loaded. They can easily be configured to eagerly load [e.g., see this blog post (*http://blog.springsource.org/2010/07/28/gorm-gotchas-part-3/*)], but because they're often secondary data that isn't needed every time you retrieve a containing instance, it's more common to leave the default lazy loading behavior enabled.

Keep in mind though that Grails collections can be "extra-lazy." resulting in N+1 queries. For example, given an Author class with a one-to-many relationship with a Book class using a hasMany property:

```
class Author {
    String name
    static hasMany = [books: Book]
}
```

and a Book class that doesn't specify a back-reference to the Author (making this a unidirectional relationship):

```
class Book {
    String title
}
```

you'll end up with a join table:

```
create table author_book (
    author_books_id bigint,
    book_id bigint
);
```

Accessing data from the books collection will initialize the collection by running a query similar to select * from author_book where author_books_id=? to retrieve the Book IDs. The collection will be populated with proxies, one for each Book ID. Then each access to data for a Book instance will trigger a query to load the data (similar to select * from book where id=?). If you loop through all of the instances, you'll end up with N + 1 queries; one for the IDs and one for each instance.

If you make the relationship bidirectional, either with an Author field in the Book class:

```
class Book {
    String title
    Author author
}
```

or with a "named" belongsTo (which creates a property named author in addition to configuring cascading):

```
class Book {
    String title
    static belongsTo = [author: Author]
}
```

then you'll get different behavior. The book table will have a foreign key into the au thor table and loading Book instances will be done in one query, similar to select * from book where author_id=?. The instances will not be proxies; all of the data will be loaded. The tradeoff is one big query that loads 100% of the data (the nonlazy prop-erties) versus N+1 queries that load data on demand.

Note that if you use the simpler belongsTo syntax, you will end up with a join table and proxies like the case where the relationship isn't bidirectional:

```
class Book {
    String title
    static belongsTo = Author
}
```

Transactional Write-Behind

Transactional write-behind is another feature that can help reduce the number of times you go to the database. Hibernate will queue save() calls for updated instances and delete() calls as long as possible, ideally until the flush() call that will be done before closing the session. This means that if you have a complex workflow where you retrieve an instance and modify it multiple times in various places in your code, you will often only end up with a single update in the database.

You can explicitly flush the session early, either by accessing the current session and calling flush() or by adding flush: true as a parameter to a save() or delete() call (e.g., book.save(flush: true)). In addition, Hibernate will flush the session early if necessary. This happens most often when you execute a query that might be affected by queued updates or deletes. It's rather pessimistic and flushes more often than it needs to, but it would be computationally complex to determine that query results wouldn't be affected, and you might have database triggers that would affect the results. So to be safe, Hibernate flushes for most queries. get() calls are an exception because they return a specific instance and there's no ambiguity.

Integration

Working with Java Enterprise Edition (JEE) techologies in Grails is very similar to using them in traditional Spring applications. For the most part, you can use them directly, writing classes in Java or reusing existing shared code and JAR files. Often it can be easier to take advantage of an existing Grails plugin that configures the necessary dependencies for you, and often adds convenience methods, services, or DSLs to hide some of the complexity and boilerplate.

Of course, like in Spring applications, you often have easier ways to implement features than using JEE techologies. GORM is a lot easier to use than JPA, Grails services behave much like EJB stateless session beans, and you can use services like EJB stateful session beans by setting their scope to "session" so each user gets a separate instance and the life cycle is automatically tied to HTTP session creation and destruction. Integrate whatever existing functionality you have, especially if it's tested and working, because it often doesn't help to rewrite for the sake of doing everything the "Grails way," but when adding new functionality, be sure to see if there's already a solution in Grails or in a plugin.

JMS

Messaging with the Java Message Service (JMS) is very straightforward in Grails. As with many technologies, "there's a plugin for that"—in this case, the jms plugin (*http://grails.org/plugin/jms*). It doesn't provide an implementation, just the core functionality, leaving the actual JMS implementation details to a provider. ActiveMQ (*https://activemq.apache.org/*) is a popular choice.

The jms plugin adds a lot of useful features and Grails integration, but let's start with a more manual integration (using Spring's support for JMS) for now, because it's easy to set up and will be more familiar if you've used JMS in a traditional Spring application.

The first step is to add the required dependencies in *BuildConfig.groovy* (make sure that `mavenCentral()` is uncommented in the `repositories` block):

```
dependencies {
    compile('org.apache.activemq:activemq-core:5.7.0') {
        transitive = false
    }

    runtime('org.apache.activemq:kahadb:5.7.0') {
        transitive = false
    }

    runtime('org.apache.geronimo.specs:geronimo-j2ee-management_1.1_spec:1.0.1') {
        transitive = false
    }

    compile('org.apache.geronimo.specs:geronimo-jms_1.1_spec:1.1.1') {
        transitive = false
    }
}
```

Then, we need to add some bean definitions in *grails-app/conf/spring/resources.groovy*. First, we'll need a `javax.jms.ConnectionFactory`:

```
import org.apache.activemq.ActiveMQConnectionFactory

...

jmsConnectionFactory(ActiveMQConnectionFactory) {
    brokerURL = 'vm://localhost'
}
```

This is configured to run in-memory, which is convenient for testing, or if you have a small application that only needs a single server. Connecting to an external JMS server or cluster is a simple matter of changing the `brokerURL` property—for example, `brokerURL = 'tcp://your_jms_server:61616'`.

We'll need at least one queue or topic as our message destinations:

```
import org.apache.activemq.command.ActiveMQQueue
import org.apache.activemq.command.ActiveMQTopic

...

myQueue(ActiveMQQueue) {
    physicalName = 'myQueue'
}

myTopic(ActiveMQTopic) {
    physicalName = 'myTopic'
}
```

Sending JMS messages is fairly complicated, in the same way that executing an SQL query using JDBC is—there is a lot of boilerplate plumbing code. Spring makes using JDBC significantly easier with its `org.springframework.jdbc.core.JdbcTemplate` helper class, and it does the same for Hibernate with the `org.springframework.orm.hibernate3.HibernateTemplate` class; when working with JMS, the `org.springframework.jms.core.JmsTemplate` helper class does a lot of the same repetitive work for you, so you can focus on sending and receiving messages. All of the template classes are stateless, so it's common to configure one as a singleton Spring bean:

```
import org.springframework.jms.core.JmsTemplate

...

jmsTemplate(JmsTemplate, ref('jmsConnectionFactory'))
```

Everything is ready to go, but let's create a couple of helper classes. The first will be a listener, so we can be sure that things are working (put this in the *src/groovy* folder):

```
package book.jms

class MyQueueMessageListener {

    void handleMessage(String message) {
        println "Received text message '$message'"
    }

    void handleMessage(Map message) {
        println "Received Map message '$message'"
    }

    void handleMessage(byte[] message) {
        println "Received byte[] message with length $message.length"
    }

    void handleMessage(Serializable message) {
        println "Received Serializable message '$message'"
    }
}
```

Note that the class doesn't implement any interfaces or extend a base class. This is the standard pattern for Grails artifacts, but this isn't a Grails class—it's a regular POGO (or a POJO if you prefer) that is being used by Spring. But we can use an adapter class, `org.springframework.jms.listener.adapter.MessageListenerAdapter`, which implements the `javax.jms.MessageListener` interface and uses reflection to find the method in your class to call based on the type of each message. So we'll register the listener class as a standalone bean in *resources.groovy* (although it could be an inner bean) and create an adapter bean that references it. We also need a third bean to access the queue (or topic) and call our message listener; we'll use Spring's `org.springframework.jms.listener.DefaultMessageListenerContainer` for this:

```
import book.jms.MyQueueMessageListener
import org.springframework.jms.listener.DefaultMessageListenerContainer
import org.springframework.jms.listener.adapter.MessageListenerAdapter

myQueueMessageListener(MyQueueMessageListener)

myQueueMessageListenerAdapter(MessageListenerAdapter,
                              ref('myQueueMessageListener'))

myQueueMessageListenerContainer(DefaultMessageListenerContainer) {
    connectionFactory = ref('jmsConnectionFactory')
    destination = ref('myQueue')
    messageListener = ref('myQueueMessageListenerAdapter')
}
```

It's pretty easy to use the JmsTemplate class directly, but let's create a utility class that sends various types of messages to a particular destination. In practice, you probably wouldn't have a general purpose class like this and would just send the message types that you need, but this demonstrates how to send each of the common message types:

```
package book.jms

import javax.jms.BytesMessage
import javax.jms.MapMessage
import javax.jms.Message
import javax.jms.Queue
import javax.jms.Session

import org.springframework.jms.core.JmsTemplate
import org.springframework.jms.core.MessageCreator

class MyQueueMessageSender {

    JmsTemplate jmsTemplate
    Queue queue

    void sendText(String text) {
        jmsTemplate.send(queue, new MessageCreator() {
            Message createMessage(Session session) {
                session.createTextMessage text
            }
        })
    }

    void sendMap(Map<String, Object> map) {
        jmsTemplate.send(queue, new MessageCreator() {
            Message createMessage(Session session) {
                MapMessage message = session.createMapMessage()
                map.each { String key, value ->
                    message.setObject key, value
                }
                message
```

```
        }
    })
}

void sendBytes(byte[] bytes) {
    jmsTemplate.send(queue, new MessageCreator() {
        Message createMessage(Session session) {
            BytesMessage message = session.createBytesMessage()
            message.writeBytes bytes
            message
        }
    })
}

void sendObject(Serializable object) {
    jmsTemplate.send(queue, new MessageCreator() {
        Message createMessage(Session session) {
            session.createObjectMessage object
        }
    })
}
}
```

Register it in *resources.groovy* with a reference to the JmsTemplate and the queue:

```
import book.jms.MyQueueMessageSender

...

myQueueMessageSender(MyQueueMessageSender) {
    jmsTemplate = ref('jmsTemplate')
    destination = ref('myQueue')
}
```

Run grails console and execute this to check that everything is working:

```
def sender = ctx.myQueueMessageSender

sender.sendMap([foo: 'bar', baz: 5])
sender.sendObject([1, 2, 5])
sender.sendText('Grails JMS')
sender.sendBytes('Grails JMS'.bytes)
```

and you should see the println statements in the console as each message is received.

XA Support with the Atomikos Plugin

The previous examples are a rather simplistic use of JMS; in practice, it's often the case
that messages are sent transactionally. One use case is to send a JMS message after
creating or modifying a domain class instance so some work can be done asynchro-
nously. If the JDBC transaction that the update is being done in rolls back, it's important
that the JMS message not be sent. Using a transactional JMS connection factory that is

configured to use XA transactions uses Two Phase Commit (2PC), which only commits the global transaction if the underlying JDBC and JMS transactions commit. This can also be used with just JDBC if you have multiple datasources and have transactions that update two or more databases at once.

The configuration of XA is more involved than the simpler cases, so it's best to use the `atomikos` plugin (*http://grails.org/plugin/atomikos*). It makes the process of converting each JDBC `DataSource` and JMS `ConnectionFactory` to use XA much simpler, but this depends on having the `jms` plugin (*http://grails.org/plugin/jms*) installed.

Add the `jms` and `atomikos` plugins to *BuildConfig.groovy*:

```
plugins {
   ...
   compile ':jms:1.2'
   compile ':atomikos:1.0'
}
```

and remove the `geronimo-j2ee-management_1.1_spec` and `geronimo-jms_1.1_spec` dependencies, because they're provided by the `jms` plugin:

```
dependencies {
   compile('org.apache.activemq:activemq-core:5.7.0') {
      transitive = false
   }

   runtime('org.apache.activemq:kahadb:5.7.0') {
      transitive = false
   }
}
```

The beans in *resources.groovy* need to change a bit; change `ActiveMQConnectionFacto ry` to `ActiveMQXAConnectionFactory`, and there's no need for a `jmsTemplate` bean, because one is created by the `jms` plugin. Also, we don't need a listener anymore, because we'll configure a service as a listener. So the complete *resources.groovy* file is just:

```
import org.apache.activemq.ActiveMQXAConnectionFactory
import org.apache.activemq.command.ActiveMQQueue

beans = {

   jmsConnectionFactory(ActiveMQXAConnectionFactory) {
      brokerURL = 'vm://localhost'
   }

   myQueue(ActiveMQQueue) {
      physicalName = 'myQueue'
   }
}
```

By default, the `atomikos` plugin converts all Spring `JmsTemplate` beans to use the XA JMS `ConnectionFactory` (although this is configurable). It will also convert regular `DataSource` beans to XA `DataSource` beans, but there is no standard API for configuring properties, and usually the driver class is different. So for any `DataSource` that should participate in XA transactions, add an `xaConfig` block in *DataSource.groovy*. Here, I'll show an example for the H2 database that is configured by default, but it's easy to do for MySQL or other databases:

```
environments {
    development {
        dataSource {
            dbCreate = 'create-drop'
            url = 'jdbc:h2:mem:devDb;MVCC=TRUE'
            xaConfig = [
                driverClassName: 'org.h2.jdbcx.JdbcDataSource',
                driverProperties: [
                    URL: 'jdbc:h2:db/devDb;MVCC=TRUE',
                    user: 'sa',
                    password: ''],
                minPoolSize: 1,
                maxPoolSize: 50
            ]
        }
    }
    ...
}
```

Create a domain class that we can use to test JDBC rollbacks:

```
package book.jms.xa

class Person {
    String name
}
```

and a Grails service to test JMS:

```
package book.jms.xa

class MessageTestService {

    static exposes = ['jms']
    static destination = 'myQueue'

    static transactional = false

    // NOT THREAD SAFE - just for testing
    def mostRecentMessage

    void onMessage(Map message) {
        mostRecentMessage = message
        println "new message: $message"
```

```
      }

      void onMessage(String message) {
         mostRecentMessage = message
         println "new message: $message"
      }
   }
```

Here we're taking advantage of the jms plugin's ability to easily make a service act as a JMS listener by setting the exposes and destination attributes. It has transactions disabled, because it's just a listener.

Finally, let's create a transactional service that tests the three combinations. In the fail AfterJms method, we save and flush a domain class instance and then send a message, and force a rollback with a runtime exception. In failAfterJdbc the order is reversed, and in succeedJmsAndJdbc, everything should work. If either the DataSource or the JMS ConnectionFactory isn't configured correctly, we'll see extra messages and/or extra database inserts:

```
   package book.jms.xa

   class XaTestService {

      def jmsService

      void failAfterJms() {

         def person = new Person(name: 'test JDBC').save(flush: true)
         assert person

         def message = [personId: person.id, personName: person.name]
         jmsService.send 'myQueue', message

         throw new RuntimeException('forcing an auto rollback in failAfterJms')
      }

      void failAfterJdbc() {
         jmsService.send 'myQueue', "you won't get this"

         def person = new Person(name: 'test JDBC').save(flush: true)

         throw new RuntimeException('forcing an auto rollback in failAfterJdbc')
      }

      void succeedJmsAndJdbc() {
         def person = new Person(name: 'test JDBC').save(flush: true)
         assert person

         def message = [personId: person.id, personName: person.name]
         jmsService.send 'myQueue', message
```

```
        }
    }
```

Test this by running `grails console` and executing this:

```
import book.jms.xa.Person

def xaTestService = ctx.xaTestService

int startPersonCount = Person.count()
xaTestService.succeedJmsAndJdbc()
assert startPersonCount + 1 == Person.count()

int startPersonCount2 = Person.count()
try {
    xaTestService.failAfterJms()
    println "ERROR, should have thrown an exception"
}
catch (e) {
    println "OK"
}
assert startPersonCount2 == Person.count()

int startPersonCount3 = Person.count()
try {
    xaTestService.failAfterJdbc()
    println "ERROR, should have thrown an exception"
}
catch (e) {
    println "OK"
}
assert startPersonCount3 == Person.count()
```

The output should look like this:

```
new message: [personId:1, personName:test JDBC]
OK
OK
```

indicating that when there is no forced rollback, a message is received and the database insert succeeds, and in both failure cases, there is no message and no database insert.

More information is available online for the `atomikos` plugin (*http://grails-plugins.github.com/grails-atomikos/*).

Mail

If you send a significant amount of email, you should probably look into a third-party service such as SendGrid (*http://sendgrid.com/*) or Postmark (*https://postmarkapp.com/*). But it is straightforward to send email from Grails using JavaMail (*http://www.oracle.com/technetwork/java/javamail/index.html*). The easiest way to do this is with the mail plugin (*http://grails.org/plugin/mail*), because it configures the dependencies for you and adds a DSL for sending emails.

Install the mail plugin by adding a plugin dependency in *BuildConfig.groovy*:

```
plugins {
    ...

    compile ":mail:1.0.1"
}
```

The mail plugin provides a service that has convenient methods for sending email. It wraps the Spring email support, which itself wraps the JavaMail APIs. The plugin adds a sendMail method to all controllers and services, but I prefer to call the method directly on the plugin's mailService bean.

Unless you're sending mail from a server on localhost and port 25, you'll need to add configuration options in *Config.groovy*; for example:

```
grails.mail.host = 'smtp.yourcompany.com'
grails.mail.port = 1025
```

If the server requires authentication, you can specify the username and password:

```
grails.mail.username = 'your_username'
grails.mail.password = 'your_password'
grails.mail.props = ['mail.smtp.auth': 'true']
```

and, if you are using SSL, you can configure that with properties in the grails.mail.props map:

```
grails.mail.props = [
    'mail.smtps.auth': true,
    'mail.smtps.socketFactory.class': 'javax.net.ssl.SSLSocketFactory',
    'mail.smtps.socketFactory.fallback': false]
```

Note that these properties start with mail.smtps. because SSL is being used.

Some servers (e.g., Gmail) require that you send a STARTTLS command; configure this by adding 'mail.smtp.starttls.enable': true to the grails.mail.props map. Be aware that this is inconsistent with the rest of the properties; I found in testing that I had to use the mail.smtp.starttls.enable property name instead of mail.smtps.starttls.enable.

If things aren't working, try enabling debug logging by adding 'mail.debug': true to the grails.mail.props map. There are various JavaMail properties (*http://java mail.kenai.com/nonav/javadocs/com/sun/mail/smtp/package-summary.html*) that are supported in the grails.mail.props map.

Sending Email

Having configured the server, you can now send email. The plugin provides a DSL to configure the messages; you call the sendMail method passing a closure containing DSL method calls for the various attributes of the message. Table 6-1 shows the available DSL methods.

Table 6-1. Mail sender DSL methods

Name	Arguments	Notes
to	Object[] or List	One or more recipient addresses
cc	Object[] or List	One or more "carbon copy" (CC) addresses
bcc	Object[] or List	One or more "blind carbon copy" (BCC) addresses
from	CharSequence	The sender's address
replyTo	CharSequence	Optional reply-to address (if different from the sender's address)
subject	CharSequence	The email subject
multipart	boolean or int	Either true or an int specifying the multipart mode (see the Spring documentation for details)
headers	Map	Header values to set on the underlying javax.mail.internet.MimeMessage
text	CharSequence or Map	Specifies either the string to use as the text body or a map configuring a GSP to use
html	CharSequence or Map	Specifies either the string to use as the HTML body or a map configuring a GSP to use
attach	Various	Specifies a File, InputStreamSource, or byte[] array as the content of an attachment
inline	Various	Specifies a File, InputStreamSource, or byte[] array as the content of an inline resource
locale	String or Locale	The Locale (or name) to use when rendering GSPs

If a message has attachments, be sure to call multipart true before any attach method calls. Note that email addresses can be of the form *user@host.domain* or Personal Name *<user@host.domain>*.

Sending a simple text email is easy:

```
def mailService

...

mailService.sendMail {
    to "someone@someplace.com"
    from "me@myserver.com"
    subject "The Subject"
    text 'The body of the email'
}
```

You can also send an HTML email; typically it makes sense to send both an HTML body and a text body to support various email clients and user preferences (be sure to call `multipart true`, because having two bodies requires a multipart message):

```
mailService.sendMail {
    multipart true
    to "someone@someplace.com"
    from "me@myserver.com"
    subject "The Subject"
    text 'The body of the email'
    html 'This is the <strong>HTML</strong> version of the email body'
}
```

It's often not practical to have large blocks of text or HTML in your code, so the plugin supports rendering GSPs to either text or HTML as the message body. To do this use a Map argument for the `text` or `html` method calls:

```
mailService.sendMail {
    multipart true
    to "someone@someplace.com"
    from "me@myserver.com"
    subject "Welcome to the site"
    text view: "/mail-templates/register-text"
    html view: "/mail-templates/register-html"
}
```

This will look for *grails-app/views/mail-templates/register-text.gsp* containing text and *grails-app/views/mail-templates/register-html.gsp* containing a mix of text and HTML tags. The GSPs can use variables just like those used by controllers; to specify the data to use when rendering the GSP use the `model` attribute:

```
def model = [foo: 'bar', answer: 42, ...]
mailService.sendMail {
    multipart true
    ...
    text view: "/mail-templates/register-text", model: model
    html view: "/mail-templates/register-html", model: model
}
```

You can also refer to a GSP from a plugin using the `plugin` argument:

```
def model = [foo: 'bar', answer: 42, ...]
mailService.sendMail {
    multipart true
    ...
    text view: "/mail-templates/register-text", model: model, plugin: 'myplugin'
    html view: "/mail-templates/register-html", model: model, plugin: 'myplugin'
}
```

Note that because there are separate methods for HTML and text, there's no need to specify the content type in the GSPs with a `<%@ page contentType="..." %>` directive.

If you use the message tag in your GSPs, be sure to call the locale method so the correct translation is used for the message codes.

Don't include section tags such as <html>, <head>, and <body>, but you can use other tags like <div> and <span>. Unlike regular GSPs used for rendering browser pages, you can't specify a layout, at least not directly. The GSP rendering used here is simpler than the full-blown implementation used by controllers, so you can't just add a <meta name='layout' content='main'> tag. You do have a few options though. One is to use inline styles on individual elements, such as <span style='...'>...</span>. This is cumbersome, but you cannot reference a stylesheet using a <link rel="stylesheet" href=...> tag, because the rendered HTML will be viewed in an email client, not a browser.

Fortunately, there is a way to use a template to keep your GSPs DRY; use the applyLayout tag in the GSPs:

```
<g:applyLayout name='email'>
<body>
...
</body>
</g:applyLayout>
```

This will look for the template *grails-app/views/layouts/email.gsp* and it might look something like this:

```
<style>
...
</style>

<g:layoutBody/>
```

You can't reference *.css* files, but you can inline the CSS for the template inside a style tag.

Attachments and inline references are also supported; for details on how to use these features and more general information about the plugin, refer to the plugin documentation (*http://gpc.github.com/grails-mail/docs/*). For information about the underlying Spring email support, refer to the Spring documentation (*http://static.springsource.org/spring/docs/3.1.x/spring-framework-reference/html/mail.html*).

Sending Email Asynchronously

The mail plugin has most of the features that you would expect, but one limitation is that all email sending is synchronous. The sendMessage call blocks until the message is sent by the email server, so if it is busy, it can affect user-initiated email sending such as a forgot-password workflow. The asynchronous-mail plugin (*http://grails.org/plugin/asynchronous-mail*) helps with this by storing the email information in your database using Grails domain classes, and providing Quartz jobs [the plugin depends on the quartz2 plugin (*http://grails.org/plugin/quartz2*)] that periodically retrieve the cached messages from the database and send them. This can significantly improve the user experience by returning quickly from controller requests and sending the email in a background process. It takes basically the same overall time to send the email but the site will appear to be much faster.

Using the plugin is very similar to using the mail plugin, except for the additional configuration and some additional DSL methods; see the plugin documentation (*http:// grails.org/plugin/asynchronous-mail*) for more information.

Sending Email from Log4j

Ordinarily we use Log4j to log messages to the console or logfiles, but there are several alternate appenders that ship with the JAR (and others contributed by the community), including ones that will log to a database, a JMS destination, and even the Windows event log. org.apache.log4j.net.SMTPAppender is useful for notifying you that something bad happened during off hours. But be careful, because if you misconfigure it or set the threshold too low, you can easily send yourself thousands of emails in a very short time (I'm speaking from experience here).

Like the rest of the logging configuration in Grails, you add this appender in the log4j block in *Config.groovy*:

```
log4j = {
    appenders {

        appender new org.apache.log4j.net.SMTPAppender(
            name:           'smtp',
            to:             'error_mailing_list@yourcompany.com',
            from:           'application_error@yourcompany.com',
            subject:        'Danger, Will Robinson',
            SMTPHost:       'smtp.yourcompany.com',
            SMTPPort:       1025,
            SMTPUsername:   'your_username',
            SMTPDebug:      false,
            SMTPPassword:   'your_password',
            layout: pattern(conversionPattern:
              '%d{[ dd.MM.yyyy HH:mm:ss.SSS]} [%t] %n%-5p %n%c %n%C %n %x %n %m%n'))
    }

    error 'org.codehaus.groovy.grails',
          'org.springframework',
          'org.hibernate',
          'net.sf.ehcache.hibernate'

    error 'smtp': ['com.yourcompany.yourapplication']
}
```

There's no need to set the `mail.smtp.auth` property if your server requires authentication, because the appender does it for you if you set the username and password.

If you're using Gmail, use `"smtp.gmail.com"` for the host, 587 for the port, and be aware that the from address will be ignored—the emails will show as having been sent from the authenticating account holder. Also, note that there is a limit of 500 emails per day, so only use Gmail if you expect a moderate volume of email. You will also need to send a STARTTLS command, but this isn't configurable in the appender, so set the appropriate system property at the beginning of the `log4j` block so that it's available to the appender when it's configured:

```
log4j = {
    System.setProperty 'mail.smtp.starttls.enable', 'true'

    appenders {
    ...
    }

    ...
}
```

You can enable SMTP debugging with `SMTPDebug: true` in the appender constructor call. You can also set the highest log level that is logged to email by adding:

```
appender new org.apache.log4j.net.SMTPAppender(
    ...
    threshold: org.apache.log4j.Level.ERROR
    ...
)
```

Use whatever threshold level makes sense for you. It's a good idea to do this for the `SMTPAppender` to limit the message volume. Note that the appender queues messages and only sends them when a "triggering event" occurs; this is defined by default as a message at the ERROR level or higher. So, if several messages are logged at lower levels (INFO, WARN, etc.) and one is logged at the ERROR level, one email is sent with all of the messages. You can configure the triggering behavior by implementing the `org.apache.log4j.spi.TriggeringEventEvaluator` interface (e.g., in *src/groovy* or *src/java*) and specifying the class name in the appender constructor call:

```
appender new org.apache.log4j.net.SMTPAppender(
    ...
    evaluatorClass: 'book.email.log4j.FatalTriggeringEventEvaluator'
    ...
)
```

In this example, I'm just changing the triggering level to FATAL (it would probably make sense to change the `threshold` attribute to `org.apache.log4j.Level.FATAL`), but you can use whatever logic you want:

```
package book.email.log4j

import org.apache.log4j.Level
import org.apache.log4j.spi.LoggingEvent
import org.apache.log4j.spi.TriggeringEventEvaluator

class FatalTriggeringEventEvaluator implements TriggeringEventEvaluator {
    boolean isTriggeringEvent(LoggingEvent event) {
        event.level.isGreaterOrEqual(Level.FATAL)
    }
}
```

Using imports can cause compilation problems depending on the dependency resolution order, so I've inlined the full `org.apache.log4j.Level` and `org.apache.log4j.net.SMTPAppender` class names.

In the configuration above, I've attached the appender to a single category (although you can add more to the list), but you can also add it to the root appender so all applicable messages across all loggers are sent:

```
root {
    error 'stdout', 'smtp'
    additivity = true
}
```

Note that if you don't have the `mail` plugin installed and aren't already sending email, you'll need to add this dependency in *BuildConfig.groovy*:

```
dependencies {
    compile 'javax.mail:mail:1.4.5'
}
```

and ensure that the `mavenCentral()` repository is uncommented.

You can read more about the configuration options for `SMTPAppender` in the Javadoc (*https://logging.apache.org/log4j/1.2/apidocs/org/apache/log4j/net/SMTPAppend er.html*).

Testing

There are a few libraries available that start an in-memory SMTP server that you can use to test your email workflows. The `greenmail` plugin (*http://grails.org/plugin/green mail*) integrates the GreenMail (*http://www.icegreen.com/greenmail/*) library and registers a `greenMail` Spring bean that you can use to verify that emails were sent correctly.

Similarly, the `dumbster` plugin (*http://grails.org/plugin/dumbster*) integrates the Dumbster (*http://quintanasoft.com/dumbster/*) library to also start an in-memory SMTP server.

SOAP Web Services

Creating SOAP-based web services can be a daunting task, given the number of APIs and acronyms involved. The `wslite` plugin (*http://grails.org/plugin/wslite*) is, as its name implies, a simple one to use. It doesn't have a lot of features but is lightweight. There is a more robust alternative though, based on the CXF framework (*https://cxf.apache.org/*). The `cxf` plugin (*http://grails.org/plugin/cxf*) configures the CXF dependencies and adds features to create your own web services, and the `cxf-client` plugin (*http://grails.org/plugin/cxf-client*) adds features to be a web service client. There is a third option, the `springws` plugin (*http://grails.org/plugin/springws*), but it is dated and not actively maintained.

I'll focus here on the CXF plugins because they provide a lot of features and are easy to use. It will be helpful to create a server and a client application to test things out.

The Server Application

First we'll create an application to be the server for our web services:

```
$ grails create-app server
```

Installing the `cxf` plugin is easy, just add it to *BuildConfig.groovy* (be sure to use the latest version):

```
plugins {
    ...
    compile ":cxf:1.1.0"
}
```

There are several different types of supported web services, but I'll describe just two here: the "simple" type and JAX-WS. The "simple" type is convenient, because no annotations are required, and by default, all public methods are automatically exposed as web service methods. JAX-WS services are preferred though, because they're more configurable and flexible.

In addition, you can put your service classes either in the *grails-app/services* folder or in *grails-app/endpoints*. There is no difference between the two other than the option of taking advantage of transaction support in services. If a web service writes to the database, it makes sense to make it a service, but otherwise, it's probably better to add it in the *endpoints* folder to maintain a separation of concerns. Another option would be to put all of the classes in the *endpoints* folder and dependency-inject transactional services that aren't exposed as web services. In any case, do what works for you.

The plugin comes with four scripts that generate web service classes for you. `create-endpoint` and `create-cxf-service` create identical JAX-WS classes, the only difference being that `create-endpoint` generates in the *endpoints* folder and `create-cxf-service` in the *services* folder. `create-endpoint-simple` and `create-cxf-service-`

`simple` create identical "simple" web services in the *endpoints* and *services* folders, respectively.

To get started, create a JAX-WS endpoint:

```
$ grails create-endpoint book.soap.hello
```

and edit the generated class so it looks like this:

```
package book.soap

import javax.jws.WebMethod
import org.grails.cxf.utils.EndpointType

class HelloEndpoint {

    static expose = EndpointType.JAX_WS

    @WebMethod
    String ping(String s) { s }

    @WebMethod
    String sayHello(String name) { "Hello, $name" }
}
```

Then create a "simple" service:

```
$ grails create-cxf-service-simple book.soap.math
```

and edit that generated class so it looks like this:

```
package book.soap

import org.grails.cxf.utils.EndpointType

class MathService {

    static expose = EndpointType.SIMPLE

    int add(int i1, int i2) { i1 + i2 }

    int multiply(int i1, int i2) { i1 * i2 }
}
```

There's a lot of customization that you can do at this point, but you have everything you need to get started. Start the server with `grails run-app`, and you can open *http:// localhost:8080/server/services* in a web browser to see a simple summary page that CXF generates for you. There will be links to the WSDL URLs there: in this case, *http:// localhost:8080/server/services/hello?wsdl* and *http://localhost:8080/server/services/ math?wsdl*.

The Client Application

Create an application to be the client for the web services:

```
$ grails create-app client
```

Install the `cxf-client` plugin by adding it to *BuildConfig.groovy*:

```
plugins {
    ...
    compile ":cxf-client:1.5.0"
}
```

The plugin has a `wsdl2java` script to read a WSDL file and create Java classes from it. The script has no command-line arguments; instead, everything is configured in *Config.groovy* under the `cxf.client` key:

```
cxf {
    client {
        helloService {
            wsdl = 'http://localhost:8080/server/services/hello?wsdl'
            namespace = 'book.soap.hello'
        }

        mathService {
            wsdl = 'http://localhost:8080/server/services/math?wsdl'
            namespace = 'book.soap.math'
        }

        stockquoteService {
            wsdl = 'http://www.webservicex.net/stockquote.asmx?WSDL'
        }
    }
}
```

At this step, the only required attribute is `wsdl`, which can be a path to a local file or a URL. The other attributes you can set are `namespace`, `client`, `bindingFile`, `output Dir`, and `wsdlArgs`. By default, the files will be generated in *src/java*. In addition to the two services from the server application, I've also configured a well-known stock quote service often used for testing. Run the script to generate the client code:

```
$ grails wsdl2java
```

Now that the code is available, we need to configure the runtime attributes. The two important ones are `clientInterface` and `serviceEndpointAddress`. `serviceEndpoin tAddress` is the URL of the web service; in all three cases, it's the same as the WSDL URL without the querystring, but this won't always be the case. The value for `clien tInterface` is an interface with the `@WebService` annotation. The names will vary, even for classes generated from our server application services, because one is a "simple" service and the other uses JAX-WS. And the stock quote service has three annotated interfaces; I found in testing that only `net.webservicex.StockQuoteSoap` worked.

Update *Config.groovy* with the new values:

```
cxf {
    client {
        helloService {
            wsdl = 'http://localhost:8080/server/services/hello?wsdl'
            namespace = 'book.soap.hello'

            clientInterface = book.soap.hello.HelloEndpoint
            serviceEndpointAddress = 'http://localhost:8080/server/services/hello'
        }

        mathService {
            wsdl = 'http://localhost:8080/server/services/math?wsdl'

            namespace = 'book.soap.math'
            clientInterface = book.soap.math.MathServicePortType
            serviceEndpointAddress = 'http://localhost:8080/server/services/math'
        }

        stockquoteService {
            wsdl = 'http://www.webservicex.net/stockquote.asmx?WSDL'

            clientInterface = net.webservicex.StockQuoteSoap
            serviceEndpointAddress = 'http://www.webservicex.net/stockquote.asmx'
        }
    }
}
```

The WSDL attributes aren't needed at runtime because the generated classes will be used. But it's okay to leave them in, and will be needed if you change your services and have to update the client.

The plugin will create a Spring bean for each configuration—in this case, `helloService`, `mathService`, and `stockquoteService` (use whatever you want for the names). The bean will be an `org.apache.cxf.jaxws.JaxWsClientProxy` that implements your `@WebService` interface. This largely abstracts away the SOAP and XML aspects of the services, because you simply need to dependency-inject the bean and call the exposed methods. You can try this out by running `grails console` and executing:

```
def helloService = ctx.helloService
println helloService.ping('testing, testing')
println helloService.sayHello('World')

def mathService = ctx.mathService
println mathService.add(123 as int, 234 as int)
println mathService.multiply(123 as int, 234 as int)

def stockquoteService = ctx.stockquoteService
String xml = stockquoteService.getQuote('VMW')
```

```
def parsed = new XmlSlurper().parseText(xml)
println "$parsed.Stock.Symbol \$$parsed.Stock.Last"
```

and the output should be similar to this:

```
testing, testing
Hello, World
357
28782
VMW $91.78
```

The stock quote service returns an XML string as its response, so I'm using an `XmlSlurp` `er` to extract the useful information:

```
<StockQuotes>
    <Stock>
        <Symbol>VMW</Symbol>
        <Last>91.78</Last>
        <Date>12/3/2012</Date>
        <Time>4:02pm</Time>
        <Change>+0.83</Change>
        <Open>90.32</Open>
        <High>92.34</High>
        <Low>90.22</Low>
        <Volume>1760741</Volume>
        <MktCap>39.260B</MktCap>
        <PreviousClose>90.95</PreviousClose>
        <PercentageChange>+0.91%</PercentageChange>
        <AnnRange>74.69 - 118.79</AnnRange>
        <Earns>1.71</Earns>
        <P-E>53.19</P-E>
        <Name>Vmware</Name>
    </Stock>
</StockQuotes>
```

TCPMon

The TCPMon (*https://ws.apache.org/commons/tcpmon/*) tool (Figure 6-1) is useful for inspecting the SOAP XML that is sent to and from your web services. It can help debug issues when your web service calls are failing, because in general, the process is a black box. The convenience of having excellent wrappers for complex technologies comes with the cost that, when things go wrong, it can be very difficult to figure out what happened. The `tcpmon` plugin (*http://grails.org/plugin/tcpmon*) makes the library available and adds a `tcpmon` script that launches the application.

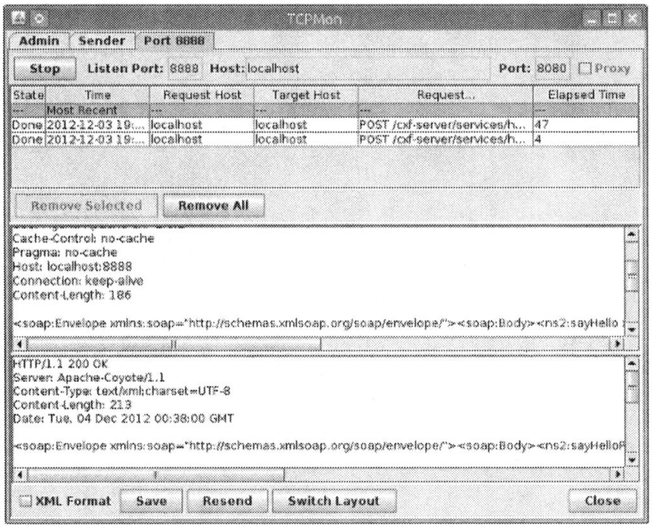

Figure 6-1. TCPMon

TCPMon acts as a proxy for your requests, so you configure what port it runs on and what server and port to intercept. While you're using it, change whatever client you're using to connect to the `tcpmon` instance instead of the real server, and it will capture your request, forward it to the server, and capture its response and forward that to your client. Afterward, you can inspect the XML, or manually submit requests with your own XML. Figure 6-1 shows TCPMon after some service calls.

By default, the `tcpmon` script connects to a server on `localhost` port 8080, and listens on port 8888. This is convenient if you have a local Grails application running as the server. Install the plugin by adding it to *BuildConfig.groovy*:

```
plugins {
    ...
    compile ':tcpmon:0.1'
}
```

and launch the script (in a separate console from your `run-app` console) with no arguments to use the defaults:

```
$ grails tcpmon
```

In the example applications above, you would change the endpoint addresses for the local services in *Config.groovy* to use port 8888 temporarily while you're working with TCPMon:

```
...

serviceEndpointAddress = 'http://localhost:8888/cxf-server/services/hello'
```

```
...
serviceEndpointAddress = 'http://localhost:8888/cxf-server/services/math'
...
```

It can proxy any server though; to proxy for the stock quote service, you would run the script with parameters to override the defaults:

```
$ grails tcpmon --target=80 --host=www.webservicex.net
```

and change the endpoint address to:

```
serviceEndpointAddress = 'http://localhost:8888/stockquote.asmx'
```

REST

There are many options for producing and consuming REST in Grails, including the support that is built into Grails (*http://bit.ly/ZsPUF4*) that provides RESTful URL mappings, automatic object graph conversion to XML with render ... as XML and to JSON with render ... as JSON, data binding, and content negotiation (*http://grails.org/doc/latest/guide/single.html#contentNegotiation*).

For more formal integration, use one of the various Grails REST plugins (*http://grails.org/plugins/search?q=rest*). The jaxrs plugin (*http://grails.org/plugin/jaxrs*) adds support for JSR 311 (JAX-RS), so I'll focus on that. To try it out, create a test application:

```
$ grails create-app resting
```

and install the plugin by adding a dependency in *BuildConfig.groovy*:

```
plugins {
    ...
    compile ':jaxrs:0.6'
}
```

Make sure that the mavenCentral() repository is uncommented and add http://maven.restlet.org as a custom repository:

```
repositories {
    inherits true
    grailsPlugins()
    grailsHome()
    grailsCentral()
    mavenLocal()
    mavenCentral()
    mavenRepo 'http://maven.restlet.org'
}
```

Create a simple "resource" by running the plugin's create-resource script:

```
$ grails create-resource book.rest.ping
```

and edit *grails-app/resources/book/rest/PingResource.groovy* so it looks like this:

```
package book.rest

import javax.ws.rs.GET
import javax.ws.rs.Path
import javax.ws.rs.Produces
import javax.ws.rs.QueryParam

@Path('/api/ping')
class PingResource {

    @GET
    @Produces('text/plain')
    String ping(@QueryParam('message') String message) { message }
}
```

This creates a simple action that accepts a GET request at /api/ping/ with a single parameter that it echoes back. Start the server with the run-app script, and test the resource by accessing *http://localhost:8080/resting/api/ping?message=testing,testing* in a browser, and it should echo the value of the message parameter.

You can see that the resource is available by generating the WADL file for your services by opening *http://localhost:8080/resting/application.wadl* in a browser. The relevant section of the generated XML will look something like this:

```
<resource path="/api/ping">
  <method id="ping" name="GET">
    <request>
      <param xmlns:xs="http://www.w3.org/2001/XMLSchema"
             name="message" style="query" type="xs:string"/>
    </request>
    <response>
      <representation mediaType="text/plain"/>
    </response>
  </method>
</resource>
```

WADL can be used by tools to generate client code and know how to call your services in the same way that WSDL makes information about SOAP services available.

The plugin has support for much more complicated resources and will generate REST-based scaffolding. Create a simple domain class:

```
$ grails create-domain-class book.rest.Person
```

and edit the file so it looks like this:

```
package book.rest

class Person {
    String firstName
```

```
    String lastName
}
```

Use the `generate-resources` script to create the scaffolding:

```
$ grails generate-resources book.rest.Person
```

This code creates the `book.rest.PersonCollectionResource` class in `grails-app/resources`:

```
package book.rest

...

@Path('/api/person')
@Consumes(['application/xml','application/json'])
@Produces(['application/xml','application/json'])
class PersonCollectionResource {

    def personResourceService

    @POST
    Response create(Person dto) {
        created personResourceService.create(dto)
    }

    @GET
    Response readAll() {
        ok personResourceService.readAll()
    }

    @Path('/{id}')
    PersonResource getResource(@PathParam('id') Long id) {
        new PersonResource(personResourceService: personResourceService, id:id)
    }
}
```

It has a method for GET requests that returns all `Person` instances, and a method for POST requests that creates a new `Person`. In addition, the script creates the `book.rest.PersonResource` class in `grails-app/resources`, which is mapped to `/api/person/{id}` URLs and through the `getResource` method in `PersonCollectionResource`:

```
package book.rest

...

@Consumes(['application/xml','application/json'])
@Produces(['application/xml','application/json'])
class PersonResource {

    def personResourceService
```

```
    def id

    @GET
    Response read() {
        ok personResourceService.read(id)
    }

    @PUT
    Response update(Person dto) {
        dto.id = id
        ok personResourceService.update(dto)
    }

    @DELETE
    void delete() {
        personResourceService.delete(id)
    }
}
```

All database persistence is handled by the generated service `book.rest.PersonResour`
`ceService`.

This provides a solid starting point for CRUD actions mapped to the various REST
verbs. Regenerate the WADL file to ensure that things are correctly wired. Testing these
methods is more involved than just issuing requests from a browser like in the earlier
simple example. There are browser addons to generate POST, PUT, and DELETE requests, but to actually use the REST API in an application, we'll need a proper client.
One great option is the Grails `rest-client-builder` plugin (*http://grails.org/plugin/*
rest-client-builder). It uses the Spring `org.springframework.web.client.RestTem`
`plate` with a convenient DSL.

Create a second application to be the test client and install the plugin by adding it to
BuildConfig.groovy:

```
plugins {
    ...

    compile ':rest-client-builder:1.0.3'
}
```

Run `grails console`, and to get things started, run this to do the same test as the earlier
browser-based test:

```
import grails.plugins.rest.client.RestBuilder

def rest = new RestBuilder()
def resp = rest.get(
'http://localhost:8080/resting/api/ping?message=testing,testing')
println resp.text
println resp.status
```

and the output should be:

```
testing,testing
200
```

We can also do more complex requests on the `Person` domain class. This will create a new instance using XML:

```
import grails.plugins.rest.client.RestBuilder

def rest = new RestBuilder()
def resp = rest.post('http://localhost:8080/resting/api/person') {
    accept 'application/xml'
    contentType 'application/xml'
    xml {
        person {
            firstName 'Foghorn'
            lastName 'Leghorn'
        }
    }
}

println resp.text
println resp.status
```

and the output should look like this:

```
<?xml version="1.0" encoding="UTF-8"?>
<person id="1">
<firstName>Foghorn</firstName>
<lastName>Leghorn</lastName>
</person>
201
```

I'm using the `text` property to view the result, but if you want to extract data from the response, use the `xml` property.

This will create an instance using JSON:

```
import grails.plugins.rest.client.RestBuilder

def rest = new RestBuilder()
def resp = rest.post('http://localhost:8080/resting/api/person') {
    accept 'application/json'
    contentType 'application/json'
    json {
        person {
            firstName = 'Hunter'
            lastName = 'Thompson'
        }
    }
}
```

```
println resp.text
println resp.status
```

and the output should look like this:

```
{"class":"book.rest.Person","id":2,"firstName":"Hunter","lastName":"Thompson"}
201
```

Like the XML example above, to work with the returned data, use the `resp.json` property.

We can retrieve all of the instances by making a GET call:

```
import grails.plugins.rest.client.RestBuilder

def rest = new RestBuilder()
def resp = rest.get('http://localhost:8888/rest/api/person')

println resp.text
println resp.status

resp.xml.person.each { person ->
    println "Person ${person.@id} '$person.firstName $person.lastName'"
}
```

and the output should look like this:

```
<?xml version="1.0" encoding="UTF-8"?>
<list>
<person id="1">
<firstName>Foghorn</firstName>
<lastName>Leghorn</lastName>
</person>
<person id="2">
<firstName>Hunter</firstName>
<lastName>Thompson</lastName>
</person>
</list>
200
Person 1 'Foghorn Leghorn'
Person 2 'Hunter Thompson'
```

We can edit an instance with a PUT using the ID of the instance to update:

```
import grails.plugins.rest.client.RestBuilder

def rest = new RestBuilder()
def resp = rest.put('http://localhost:8080/resting/api/person/1') {
    accept 'application/json'
    contentType 'application/json'
    json {
        person {
            firstName = 'Bugs'
            lastName = 'Bunny'
        }
```

```
    }
}

println resp.text
println resp.status
```

which should generate this output:

```
{"class":"book.rest.Person","id":1,"firstName":"Bugs","lastName":"Bunny"}
200
```

We can retrieve that instance again to verify the update:

```
import grails.plugins.rest.client.RestBuilder

def rest = new RestBuilder()
def resp = rest.get('http://localhost:8080/resting/api/person/1') {
    accept 'application/xml'
}

println resp.text
println resp.status
```

And, because we're asking for XML, the response will have the same data as before, except in XML format:

```
<?xml version="1.0" encoding="UTF-8"?>
<person id="1">
<firstName>Bugs</firstName>
<lastName>Bunny</lastName>
</person>
200
```

Finally, we can delete an instance using DELETE:

```
import grails.plugins.rest.client.RestBuilder

def rest = new RestBuilder()
def resp = rest.delete('http://localhost:8888/rest/api/person/1')
```

which doesn't generate a response body, so the output will be:

```
No Content
204
```

TCPMon

Just as when working with SOAP, things can easily go wrong when making REST requests, so the TCPMon tool can be useful to intercept requests and help diagnose issues.

Install the plugin as described in the SOAP section and launch it with the default settings:

```
$ grails tcpmon
```

or configure the host and ports as needed. Change the `RestBuilder` method calls to use port 8888 instead of 8080, and you will be able to view the requests and responses in the TCPMon GUI:

```
import grails.plugins.rest.client.RestBuilder

def rest = new RestBuilder()
def resp = rest.get('http://localhost:8888/resting/api/person/3') {
    accept 'application/json'
}
```

Figure 6-2 shows TCPMon displaying the request and the 404 response that results from requesting the nonexistent `Person` with ID 3.

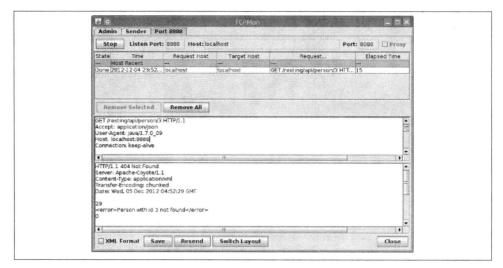

Figure 6-2. TCPMon

JMX

Java Management Extensions (JMX) isn't a JEE technology, but it is a convenient way to view and modify application configuration information, and it's already part of the JDK. Wiring things up isn't particularly complicated, but you should use the jmx plugin (*http://grails.org/plugin/jmx*) to do the work for you. It registers a few default MBeans but also has support for exposing your services as MBeans with a simple configuration.

By default, the plugin registers Hibernate's `org.hibernate.jmx.StatisticsService` MBean if the Hibernate libraries are available. This makes several usage statistics such as entity and collection load and update counts, cache hit, miss, and put counts, etc., available. Statistics gathering is disabled by default, but you can enable it with JMX, or programmatically at startup in *BootStrap.groovy*:

```
class BootStrap {

    def sessionFactory

    def init = { servletContext ->
        sessionFactory.statistics.statisticsEnabled = true
    }
}
```

The plugin also registers the Log4j `org.apache.log4j.jmx.HierarchyDynamicMBean` MBean to give you access to the Log4j configuration. You can view and update the root logger, and add MBeans for individual loggers to view and update their logging level. When a problem occurs, it can be convenient to temporarily change a logger's level to view debug information and restore it once the issue is resolved.

In addition, the plugin registers an MBean for each `DataSource` in your application. This allows you to view and modify connection pool information.

There are two ways to expose services as MBeans. The easier way is to add `static expose = ['jmx']` as a static property in the service. By default, all properties except `expose`, `jmxexpose`, `metaClass`, `scope`, and `transactional` are included, but you can use the `jmxexpose` property to customize the behavior. The other way is to annotate the class with `org.springframework.jmx.export.annotation.ManagedResource`. If you use this approach, the `jmxexpose` property is ignored, and you can annotate individual properties or getter methods with `org.springframework.jmx.export.annotation.ManagedAttribute`.

There are many JMX tools available, but the JDK comes with jconsole (*http://docs.oracle.com/javase/6/docs/technotes/guides/management/jconsole.html*), a Swing application that is easy to use. Figure 6-3 shows the beans for an application with the jmx plugin installed.

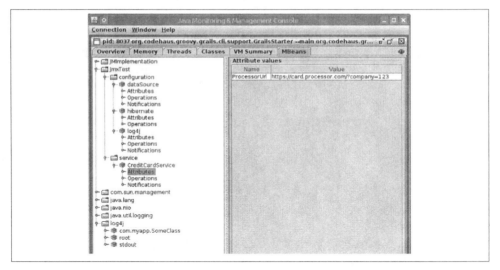

Figure 6-3. Viewing MBeans with JConsole

You can see the default MBeans `dataSource`, `hibernate`, and `log4j` nodes under the `configuration` node, and the `CreditCardService` MBean corresponding to this service:

```
package book.jmx

class CreditCardService {

    static expose = ['jmx']

    String processorUrl = 'https://card.processor.com/?company=123'

    ...
}
```

Exposing the `processorUrl` property makes it possible to change the URL at runtime without having to redeploy the application.

In addition, the top-level `log4j` node contains a `root` MBean corresponding to the root logger, a `console` MBean for the console appender, and an MBean for the `com.myapp.SomeClass` logger. Individual loggers MBeans are added with the `addLoggerMBean` operation of the `log4j` MBean. The plugin doesn't automatically configure individual loggers because a basic Grails application configures over 250 loggers.

Configuration

Grails uses a "convention over configuration" approach, but of course that doesn't mean that everything follows a convention. You should use the conventions where they make sense and override defaults as needed. And, beyond configuring core functionality, Grails has several configuration files under the *grails-app/conf* folder where you configure application settings, Spring bean definitions, library and plugin dependencies, and so on. Quite often, as an application grows, these configuration files can get large and unwieldy, so in this chapter, we discuss various approaches for partitioning and organizing various config files.

External config Files

The *Config.groovy* file that's generated by the `create-app` script contains this commented-out code at the top:

```
// locations to search for config files that get merged into the main config;
// config files can be ConfigSlurper scripts, Java properties files, or classes
// in the classpath in ConfigSlurper format

// grails.config.locations = [
//      "classpath:${appName}-config.properties",
//      "classpath:${appName}-config.groovy",
//      "file:${userHome}/.grails/${appName}-config.properties",
//      "file:${userHome}/.grails/${appName}-config.groovy"]

// if (System.properties["${appName}.config.location"]) {
//    grails.config.locations << "file:" +
//        System.properties["${appName}.config.location"]
// }
```

This provides a great way of defining one or more external config files that get merged into the main config that's defined in *Config.groovy*. You can define as many external files as you want in the `grails.config.locations` list. One convenient aspect of this feature is that the specified files don't have to exist; you'll just see a warning message in the console for each missing file (depending on your logging threshold). Each item must be a `String` or a `GString` with the location of a resource (typically file-based or classpath-based) or a class. Classes can be in your project or supplied by a plugin, or in a JAR file.

I usually remove the property file variants because Groovy files are more convenient, and change the file pattern to point to the project root directory:

```
grails.config.locations = [
    "classpath:${appName}-config.groovy",
    "file:./${appName}-config.groovy"]
```

This location list lets you define a per-developer local configuration override file in the root directory (`${appName}-config.groovy`) and another in the root of the classpath (`classpath:${appName}-config.groovy`). The local file lets you change database settings, the Log4j configuration, and any other setting defined in *Config.groovy* and gets around the classic problem where developers change configuration files locally and have to add them to their "never check these edited files into source control" list. This common practice is brittle and it's too easy to commit unintentional changes and also to miss important changes that should be committed. Using the external config file approach lets you edit *Config.groovy* for real changes and do whatever you want in your local override file(s). Be sure to add the local override filename to the exclusion list for your source control (i.e., `.gitignore`, `svn:ignore`).

The classpath location isn't particularly useful for local development; this is best used when deploying a WAR. One use case is to be able to create a generic WAR file that's deployable in any deployment environment. Any settings that are deployment-specific can be specified in a Groovy config file that's added to the classpath when deploying. A convenient location for Tomcat is its *lib* directory; all files there get automatically added to the classpath, and as long as each application's config file has a unique name, there won't be any overlap. Database passwords and other sensitive information that shouldn't be available to developers or in source control can also be specified here. The person responsible for deploying a WAR file can put the config file in a location that will put it in the classpath when starting up, and this keeps developers out of the production database. JNDI is another option, but it's less convenient because it requires server configuration. This approach just requires deploying a WAR file and a Groovy configuration file.

Note that this is just a suggested naming and location pattern, but you can add whatever you want to the filenames and paths; for example, making the files environment-specific:

```
grails.config.locations = [
    "classpath:${appName}-config-${Environment.current}.groovy"
]
```

The commented-out code also configures a way to specify an external file from the command line:

```
if (System.properties["${appName}.config.location"]) {
    grails.config.locations << "file:" +
        System.properties["${appName}.config.location"]
}
```

Add a -D flag when running the server startup script, or in a configuration file that the server reads (e.g., *setenv.sh* for Tomcat):

```
-DmyApp.config.location=/path/to/myconfig.groovy
```

Loading the Configuration

The process for loading the configuration is handled primarily by org.codehaus.groo vy.grails.compiler.GrailsProjectPackager and org.codehaus.groo vy.grails.commons.cfg.ConfigurationHelper. GrailsProjectPackager uses a Con figSlurper configured for the current Grails environment to load *Config.groovy* first and then merge in *DataSource.groovy*. Then it calls ConfigurationHelper.initCon fig() to finish the process.

ConfigurationHelper looks for the grails.config.defaults.locations setting, which has the same format as grails.config.locations. Properties specified in these files or classes are considered default values that can be overridden in *Config.groovy* or in any of the locations specified in grails.config.locations. So they're loaded first, then the previously loaded *Config.groovy* contents are overlaid over that (potentially overriding values), and this merged configuration becomes the current configuration. Then locations specified in grails.config.locations are loaded, and they will set new values and overwrite previously set values.

You can define environments blocks in the files to configure environment-specific values; anything not inside an environments block applies to all environments, but values within one are only set if the current environment matches.

So this defines the order of resolution as:

- Top-level attributes in each external "defaults" config file
- Environment-specific attributes in each external "defaults" config file
- Top-level attributes in *Config.groovy*
- Environment-specific attributes in *Config.groovy*
- Top-level attributes in each external config file
- Environment-specific attributes in each external config file

Partitioning Config Files

If you find that your *Config.groovy* is getting large, you can partition it into multiple files using the external config file approach. There's no best practice for how to split up the file, but in general, it's best to look for several related properties and put them in their own file. For example, if you have a lot of configuration for a security plugin, you might create a *Config-security.groovy* file:

```
grails.plugins.springsecurity.userLookup.userDomainClassName = 'com.foo.User'
grails.plugins.springsecurity.userLookup.authorityJoinClassName =
'com.foo.UserRole'
grails.plugins.springsecurity.authority.className = 'com.foo.Role'
grails.plugins.springsecurity.rememberMe.persistent = true
...
```

A complex logging configuration could go in *Config-logging.groovy*:

```
log4j = {
    error 'org.codehaus.groovy.grails',
          'org.springframework',
          'org.hibernate',
          'net.sf.ehcache.hibernate'
    ...
}
```

And you could put the Grails-specific configuration options in *Config-core.groovy*:

```
grails.project.groupId = appName
grails.mime.file.extensions = false
grails.mime.use.accept.header = false
...
```

and your application-specific configuration options in *Config-app.groovy*:

```
myapp.foo = 42
myapp.some.other.property = true
...
```

Remember that these config files also support environments, so you have that extra level of flexibility available too.

You can put these in *grails-app/conf* along with *Config.groovy* and the other configuration files, and then *Config.groovy* will just be a container for the grails.config.loca tions property, which now adds the partitioned files to the ${appName}- config.groovy files:

```
grails.config.locations = [
    "file:./grails-app/conf/Config-core.groovy",
    "file:./grails-app/conf/Config-security.groovy",
    "file:./grails-app/conf/Config-logging.groovy",
    "file:./grails-app/conf/Config-app.groovy",
    "classpath:${appName}-config.groovy",
    "file:./${appName}-config.groovy"]
```

The order here is important; you need the `${appName}-config.groovy` files to be listed last, because the files are parsed in the order specified, and these files must be last to properly override previously set values. The *Config-xxx.groovy* files should be independent, so they're unlikely to need a particular order.

Be careful though; this approach will work fine locally with `run-app` but will fail when you deploy the application as a WAR, because the `file:` locations won't be correct. So it's important that you sacrifice the convenience of keeping your configuration files together and convert the locations to use the classpath:

```
grails.config.locations = [
    "classpath:Config-core.groovy",
    "classpath:Config-security.groovy",
    "classpath:Config-logging.groovy",
    "classpath:Config-app.groovy",
    "classpath:${appName}-config.groovy",
    "file:./${appName}-config.groovy"]
```

Because Groovy files in the *conf* folder aren't copied to the classpath (only nonsource files are, and no files in the *conf/hibernate* and *conf/spring* folders are), you'll need to put these four files in *src/java* for them to be available in the classpath.

Splitting resources.groovy

If you have many Spring bean declarations in your *grails-app/conf/spring/resources.groovy* file, you should consider splitting it up into multiple files. There's no practical or performance benefit to this; it's purely an organizational improvement. You can take advantage of the `loadBeans` method and also conditional logic to partition your bean definitions in whatever way makes sense for your applications.

You can call `loadBeans` with a file path but this won't work in a deployed WAR. Loading files from the classpath works both in `run-app` and in a deployed WAR, so this approach is preferred. Non-Java files in the *src/java* directory get copied to the classpath, so this is a good place to put files like these. This *resources.groovy* example demonstrates loading three other files from the root of the classpath: */resources_security.groovy*, */resources_foo.groovy*, and */resources_bar.groovy*. It also conditionally loads *resources_test.groovy* only when running in the test environment, and defines a `dataSource` bean inline. Finally, it loads an optional list of dynamically specified external files as specified by the `customBeanLocations` config variable:

```
import grails.util.Environment

beans = {

    loadBeans('/resources_security.groovy')
    loadBeans('/resources_foo.groovy')
    loadBeans('/resources_bar.groovy')
```

```
    if (Environment.current == Environment.TEST) {
        loadBeans('/resources_test.groovy')
    }

    dataSource(MyCustomDataSource) {
        ...
    }

    if (application.config.customBeanLocations) {
        println '\nLoading bean definitions from' +
                application.config.customBeanLocations
        for (location in application.config.customBeanLocations) {
            loadBeans location
        }
    }
}
```

You can define `customBeanLocations` in any configuration file, but it makes most sense in an external config file. In particular, this could be useful in the development environment; you could add the property to your local `${appName}-config.groovy` file to support local Spring bean overrides:

```
customBeanLocations = ['file:grails-app/conf/spring/resources_dev.groovy']
```

and *resources_dev.groovy* could contain any number of new beans and bean overrides; for example:

```
beans {
    userDetailsService(MyMockUserDetailsService) {
        grailsApplication = ref('grailsApplication')
    }
}
```

It could also be set in the `classpath:${appName}-config.groovy` classpath file used for deployment to allow per-deployment Spring bean overrides:

```
customBeanLocations = ['classpath:resources_staging.groovy']
```

Modularizing Within resources.groovy

If your *resources.groovy* file becomes large, you can split it into multiple files as described above, but you can also reorganize it internally. You can break the large beans closure up into smaller closures and add helper methods like you would with any other code that is overly long. One issue you'll hit with this approach is that the bean builder DSL methods won't be available in your closures and methods, but there's a simple fix for this. For example, consider this simple file:

```
beans = {

    securityBean(SomeBeanClass) {
```

```
        prop1 = 'foo'
    }

    dataAccessBean(SomeOtherBeanClass) {
        prop2 = 'bar'
    }
}
```

We can split it into multiple methods easily:

```
beans = {
    createSecurityBeans()

    createDataAccessBeans()
}

private void createSecurityBeans() {
    securityBean(SomeBeanClass) {
        prop1 = 'foo'
    }
}

private void createDataAccessBeans() {
    dataAccessBean(SomeOtherBeanClass) {
        prop2 = 'bar'
    }
}
```

But this will fail with a `MissingMethodException` when calling the `securityBean` method. That's because the `beans` closure's `delegate` is set as the bean builder, and it interprets a `MissingMethodException` as a bean definition (assuming the signature is one of the expected patterns). But we can convert the methods to closures, and set their `delegate` as the bean builder:

```
beans = {
    createSecurityBeans.delegate = delegate
    createSecurityBeans()

    createDataAccessBeans.delegate = delegate
    createDataAccessBeans()
}

private createSecurityBeans = {
    securityBean(SomeBeanClass) {
        prop1 = 'foo'
    }
}

private createDataAccessBeans = {
    dataAccessBean(SomeOtherBeanClass) {
        prop2 = 'bar'
```

```
    }
}
```

Using this approach you can organize the file however you like, and even move the closures to helper classes:

```
import com.foo.SpringBeanConfigurationUtils

beans = {
   SpringBeanConfigurationUtils.createSecurityBeans.delegate = delegate
   SpringBeanConfigurationUtils.createSecurityBeans()

   SpringBeanConfigurationUtils.createDataAccessBeans.delegate = delegate
   SpringBeanConfigurationUtils.createDataAccessBeans()
}
```

with `SpringBeanConfigurationUtils` being a simple class in *src/groovy* with static closures:

```
class SpringBeanConfigurationUtils {

   static createSecurityBeans = {
      securityBean(SomeBeanClass) {
         prop1 = 'foo'
      }
   }

   static createDataAccessBeans = {
      dataAccessBean(SomeOtherBeanClass) {
         prop2 = 'bar'
      }
   }
}
```

This also has the significant benefit of making the bean building more easily tested, because you can conveniently call the helper classes in tests, but calling *resources.groovy* scripts requires more setup.

Environment-Specific Spring Beans

There's no support for an `environments` block in *resources.groovy* like there is in *Config.groovy*, *DataSource.groovy*, or *BootStrap.groovy*, but you can still fairly easily configure Spring beans differently for each environment. One way is to use a `switch` block; for example:

```
import grails.util.Environment

beans = {
   switch(Environment.current) {
      case Environment.PRODUCTION:
```

```
            userDetailsService(com.foo.RealUserDetailsService) {
                dataSource = ref('dataSource')
                someProperty = 24
            }

            break

        case Environment.DEVELOPMENT:

            userDetailsService(com.foo.MockUserDetailsService) {
                dataSource = ref('dataSource')
                someProperty = 42
            }

            break
        }
    }
}
```

This works, but it's not very flexible or DRY. Another option is to specify properties and even classes in the configuration (either *Config.groovy* or an external config file) and use them in *resources.groovy*. For example, you could define these properties in *Config.groovy*:

```
someBeanProperty = 42

environments {
    production {
        anotherBeanProperty = 'red'
    }
    development {
        anotherBeanProperty = 'blue'
    }
    staging {
        anotherBeanProperty = 'yellow'
    }
}
```

and use them in your bean definitions:

```
beans = {
    myBeanName(com.foo.Bar) {
        number = '${someBeanProperty}'
        color = '${anotherBeanProperty}'
    }
}
```

Here we're setting number to 42 in all environments, but color depends on the current environment. Note that even though we're setting number as a string, it works, because Spring's bean property resolution process uses converters that can convert between different formats.

Specifying a different bean class between environments is a little more work. The Grails bean builder doesn't support classes specified as a `String`, and there's no conversion from a `String` to a class, so these *Config.groovy* settings:

```
someBeanProperty = 42
someBeanClass = com.foo.RealImpl

environments {
    production {
        anotherBeanProperty = 'red'
        someBeanClass = com.foo.RealImpl
    }
    development {
        anotherBeanProperty = 'blue'
        someBeanClass = com.foo.MockImpl
    }
    staging {
        anotherBeanProperty = 'yellow'
        someBeanClass = com.foo.StagingImpl
    }
}
```

wouldn't work in this bean definition:

```
beans = {
    myBeanName('${someBeanClass}') {
        number = '${someBeanProperty}'
        color = '${anotherBeanProperty}'
    }
}
```

But there is a solution, it's just a little more verbose. The `GrailsApplication` is available as the `grailsApplication` binding variable, so we can access the config from there:

```
beans = {
    myBeanName(grailsApplication.config.someBeanClass) {
        number = '${someBeanProperty}'
        color = '${anotherBeanProperty}'
    }
}
```

You can also use this approach for more complicated property values or ones that Spring won't convert for you, and we could have used that approach the whole time:

```
def config = grailsApplication.config

beans = {
    myBeanName(config.someBeanClass) {
        number = config.someBeanProperty
        color = config.anotherBeanProperty
    }
}
```

Beans Closures in Config.groovy

One last option for environment-specific bean definitions uses an approach similar to the one above where we modularized within *resources.groovy* using closures. We can create bean-defining closures in *Config.groovy* in an `environments` block and invoke them in *resources.groovy*. For example:

```
environments {
    production {
        envBeans = {
            someBean(com.foo.BeanClass) {
                // prod-specific attributes
            }
        }
    }
    development {
        envBeans = {
            someBean(com.foo.MockBeanClass) {
                // dev-specific attributes
            }
        }
    }
    staging {
        envBeans = {
            someBean(com.foo.BeanClass) {
                // staging-specific attributes
            }
        }
    }
}
```

Then in *resources.groovy* we can configure the closure's `delegate` and invoke it:

```
beans = {
    def envBeans = grailsApplication.config.envBeans
    envBeans.delegate = delegate
    envBeans()
}
```

Options for BuildConfig.groovy

There's not a lot you can do to modularize *BuildConfig.groovy*. Because the settings that are specified there are used to build the application, you can't refer to other application classes, because they won't be available in the classpath yet. There's also no mechanism like `grails.config.locations` in *Config.groovy* to merge in external files. Fortunately it would be somewhat unusual for a *BuildConfig.groovy* file to become very large, so these limitations aren't a significant problem.

We do have some options though. The file is a Groovy script containing a DSL, so you can mix in logic in Groovy code along with repository, dependency, and plugin declarations. And you can certainly have environment-specific configuration, either with a switch block or using the executeForCurrentEnvironment in Environment; for example:

```
inherits("global") {
    Environment.executeForCurrentEnvironment {
        development {
            // development env exclusions
            excludes 'dep1', 'dep2', ...
        }
        production {
            // production env exclusions
            excludes 'dep3', 'dep4', ...
        }
    }
}

dependencies {
    Environment.executeForCurrentEnvironment {
        production {
            // environment-specific jar dependencies
            compile '...'
        }
    }
}

plugins {
    Environment.executeForCurrentEnvironment {
        production {
            // environment-specific plugin dependencies
            runtime '...'
        }
    }
}
```

Adding Additional Source Folders

By default, artifact source classes are kept in a subfolder of *grails-app*; nonartifact Groovy classes are in *src/groovy* and *src/java*. This should be sufficient in general, but if you have a lot of classes in *src/groovy* and *src/java*, you can create additional source folders, although there is some configuration required to get Grails to recognize and use them.

This first thing you need to do is to make the classes available to the project compiler. It's not enough to just compile the code though; you need to make sure the compiled classes end up in the *WEB-INF/classes* directory of your WAR files. And, if you have nonsource files, you should copy those to the classpath so they're available as resources. All of these tasks can be implemented using event handlers in *events/_Events.groovy* (create a new empty file if you don't already have one):

```
extraSrcDirs = ["$basedir/src/extra1", "$basedir/src/extra2", ...]

eventCompileStart = {
   for (String path in extraSrcDirs) {
      projectCompiler.srcDirectories << path
   }
   copyResources buildSettings.resourcesDir
}

eventCreateWarStart = { warName, stagingDir ->
   copyResources "$stagingDir/WEB-INF/classes"
}

private copyResources(destination) {
   ant.copy(todir: destination,
            failonerror: false,
            preservelastmodified: true) {
      for (String path in extraSrcDirs) {
         fileset(dir: path) {
            exclude(name: '*.groovy')
            exclude(name: '*.java')
         }
      }
   }
}
```

In this example, the `extraSrcDirs` property defines a list of one or more extra source paths to use; group your source however you want and in as many extra folders as you need. Keep in mind that although the classes will be compiled, there's no support for development-mode class reloading like there is for the standard folders, so changes to source in these folders will require a server restart.

Extra Folders Under grails-app

You can add additional source folders under the *grails-app* folder and get most of this functionality without configuration. Grails will automatically compile all Groovy and Java source for you; the only missing feature will be automatic copying of nonsource files to the classpath and your WAR files as resources. So one option would be to just keep source files under *grails-app* and resources in folders where they're handled correctly. And you can always add these extra *grails-app* subfolders to your `extra SrcDirs` list in *_Events.groovy*; this will result in the folders being registered twice, but this won't have any adverse effects.

Plugins

Plugins are a great way to add functionality to a Grails application. They're structurally nearly identical to an application, so they can add any of the artifacts that an application can (domain classes, services, etc.) and even create new artifact types. They can also contribute static resources (e.g., JavaScript or CSS files) and Gant scripts. And there are startup hooks that let plugins register Spring beans, add elements to the *web.xml* file, add dynamic `MetaClass` methods and properties, and listen for and respond to file modifications during development.

Plugins can also be used to modularize an application. Ordinarily, when thinking of plugins, you probably think about the hundreds of plugins that have been released to the central Grails plugin repository. These were created by community members and Grails team members to be reused by anyone who is interested, but you can create private plugins and even host your own plugin repository. If you find that you have common code that you want to share between applications, you can extract it out into a plugin and install it in all the applications that use it.

Creating a Plugin

Creating a new Grails plugin is very similar to creating a Grails application, but instead of running `grails create-app <appname>`, you run `grails create-plugin <plugin name>` (or use your IDE). The directory structure of an application and a plugin are very similar (Figure 8-1). This is intentional, because a plugin can contribute any of the standard artifacts that an application can have.

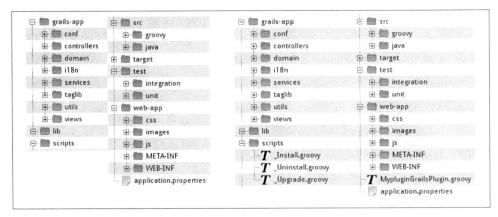

Figure 8-1. Application versus plugin directory structure

The most significant difference between a plugin project and an application project is that a plugin has a plugin descriptor, `<PluginName>GrailsPlugin.groovy`, in the root of the project. In addition, three scripts are created by default: `_Install.groovy`, `_Uninstall.groovy`, and `_Upgrade.groovy`.

Initial Steps

The initial plugin code is great to get you started, but having written dozens of plugins, I now have a routine when I first create a new plugin that includes cleaning up the generated code and deleting unnecessary files.

By default, Grails keeps installed plugins and other generated code for both plugin and application projects in the associated project folder in your *$HOME/.grails* folder. But I prefer to keep things in one place, so after creating the project (using `grails create-plugin <pluginname>`), I change these lines in *BuildConfig.groovy*:

```
grails.project.class.dir = "target/classes"
grails.project.test.class.dir = "target/test-classes"
grails.project.test.reports.dir = "target/test-reports"
```

to just:

```
grails.project.work.dir = 'target'
```

While I'm in *BuildConfig.groovy*, I remove this line:

```
//grails.project.war.file = "target/${appName}-${appVersion}.war"
```

because the WAR attribute isn't applicable to a plugin project. This has been removed from the template in more recent versions of Grails. I also delete the Tomcat plugin from the `plugins` section, because it's rarely needed when developing a plugin, only in the containing application—you will certainly want to create test applications that use your plugin and need a web server, but it's rare to run a plugin like an application with run-app.

I also update the release plugin to the latest version, and add a dependency on the plugin's rest-client-builder plugin so both the release and rest-client-builder plugins are properly excluded by the export = false attribute (depending on the version of Grails you're using, this may already be configured correctly):

```
build(':release:2.2.0', ':rest-client-builder:1.0.3') {
    export = false
}
```

Next, I remove most of the comments, so my final *BuildConfig.groovy* looks like this:

```
grails.project.work.dir = 'target'

grails.project.dependency.resolution = {

    inherits 'global'
    log 'warn'

    repositories {
        grailsCentral()
    }

    dependencies {
        // runtime 'mysql:mysql-connector-java:5.1.23'
    }

    plugins {
        build(':release:2.2.0', ':rest-client-builder:1.0.3') {
            export = false
        }
    }
}
```

I leave the commented-out dependency example in the dependencies block for a while to remind me of the syntax. If I end up with a plugin with no dependencies, I remove the block, and the same goes for the plugins block: if I don't have any plugin dependencies, I delete the block, because it's clutter and I can easily put it back if needed (old versions will be in source control).

I also clean up the *application.properties* file, removing the app.name attribute because it's rarely used in a plugin project:

```
app.grails.version=2.0.4
```

Then I import the project into GGTS (unless I used GGTS to create it of course). GGTS changes its compiled classes folder to the *target-eclipse* folder but, as I said, I like to have everything that's generated in the *target* folder, so I change that to *target/eclipseclasses* (under Project→Properties→Java Build Path→Source→Default output folder).

Most of the time, I will have no use for *grails-app/conf/UrlMappings.groovy*, *grails-app/views/error.gsp*, and the whole *web-app* directory, because they're really more for application projects than plugins, so I delete those. I also delete *scripts/_Uninstall.groovy* and *scripts/_Upgrade.groovy* because I rarely use either, and will also delete *scripts/_Install.groovy* if I don't use it.

Because I typically won't be using multiple environments when developing a plugin, I collapse *grails-app/conf/DataSource.groovy* into a flat file, using an in-memory database, because that will be useful for integration tests. While I'm there, I enable SQL logging with `logSql = true` in the `dataSource` block and SQL formatting and comments with `format_sql = true` and `use_sql_comments = true` in the `hibernate` block (I can easily comment them out if the logging gets in the way):

```
dataSource {
    pooled = true
    driverClassName = 'org.h2.Driver'
    username = 'sa'
    password = ''
    dbCreate = 'update'
    url = 'jdbc:h2:mem:testDb;MVCC=TRUE'
    logSql = true
}

hibernate {
    cache.use_second_level_cache = true
    cache.use_query_cache = true
    cache.region.factory_class = 'net.sf.ehcache.hibernate.EhCacheRegionFactory'
    format_sql = true
    use_sql_comments = true
}
```

So, to summarize, here are the cleanup steps (the order isn't particularly important) that I perform when creating a new plugin:

- Move all files into the *target* folder by setting `grails.project.class.dir='target'` in *BuildConfig.groovy* (or *settings.groovy*)
- Remove the `grails.project.war.file` property in *BuildConfig.groovy*
- Remove the dependency on the `tomcat` plugin, and update the `release` plugin dependency
- Delete *grails-app/conf/UrlMappings.groovy*, *grails-app/views/error.gsp*, the *web-app* directory, *scripts/_Uninstall.groovy*, *scripts/_Upgrade.groovy*, and *scripts/_Install.groovy* (if they're not needed)
- Flatten *grails-app/conf/DataSource* and configure SQL logging, formatting, and comments

The Plugin Descriptor

Every plugin has a plugin descriptor class in the root of the plugin project. The name of the class is the camel-case project name plus `GrailsPlugin.groovy`, such as `Hiber nateGrailsPlugin.groovy`, `SpringSecurityCoreGrailsPlugin.groovy`, etc. The descriptor has two sections: one for metadata about the plugin (its version, which versions of Grails it works with, etc.) and one with zero or more closures that are called during startup to let the plugin integrate itself into your application (`doWithWebDescriptor`, `doWithSpring`, etc.).

Metadata

When you initially create a plugin project, a starter descriptor class is created for you, and it has several comments describing what each setting and closure is for. Be sure to fill in all of the metadata attributes, because there's no check for unchanged default values, and you can easily publish a plugin to the central repository that looks like Figure 8-2 (yes, this is a real plugin!).

Plugin summary/headline
Tags : / | Latest : 0.1 | Last Updated: 23 May 2011 | Grails version : 1.2.2 > *

Documentation

Summary

Description

Brief description of the plugin.

Figure 8-2. An information-free plugin portal page

The top section for a "book" plugin will look like this:

```
class BookGrailsPlugin {
    // the plugin version
    def version = "0.1"
    // the version or versions of Grails the plugin is designed for
    def grailsVersion = "2.0 > *"
    // the other plugins this plugin depends on
    def dependsOn = [:]
    // resources that are excluded from plugin packaging
    def pluginExcludes = [
```

```
    "grails-app/views/error.gsp"
]
```

The initial version is 0.1. This value can be a number or a string, and can contain as many subparts as you want. A common pattern is to include major, minor, and point release values of the form major.minor.point, such as 1.2.5. I tend to take the approach of leaving the version below 1.0 (or 1.0.0) while things are changing frequently, but try to get to 1.0 as soon as possible to indicate that the plugin is stable and safe to use. There are a few popular Grails plugins that are quite stable but aren't yet at a version beyond 1.0, but this should be the exception.

The grailsVersion attribute defaults to the major.minor version of Grails that was used to create the plugin. So, for example, a plugin created with Grails 2.0.4 will default to 2.0 > *. You should make this value as low as possible to make the plugin available to as many users as you can. If you set it to a very recent version, users can't even test the plugin out without installing that version, if they're currently on an older version. If you do drop the minimum required version, be sure to test with at least one version of Grails in that minor version range. So if you drop it to 1.3 > *, test it in 1.3.8 and the most recent version of 2.0.x, 2.1.x, etc.

dependsOn is an older way of specifying plugin dependencies, but this is now deprecated and will cause problems if you have it specified and install your plugin in a 2.0+ application. Instead, add a dependency in the plugins section of your *BuildConfig.groovy* and remove the attribute from the descriptor. This means that your plugin won't work in Grails 1.2 or lower, but most users have upgraded to 1.3 and 2.x at this point, so that's not a major concern.

pluginExcludes is a convenient way of specifying individual files or name patterns for files that shouldn't be packaged in the plugin ZIP file. By default, these files and file patterns are included:

- *application.properties*
- *dependencies.groovy*
- **GrailsPlugin.groovy*
- *LICENSE*
- *LICENSE.txt*
- *plugin.xml*
- *docs/api/***
- *docs/gapi/***
- *grails-app/***
- *lib/***

- *scripts/***
- *src/***
- *web-app/***

and these default excludes are used:

- *grails-app/conf/BootStrap.groovy*
- *grails-app/conf/BuildConfig.groovy*
- *grails-app/conf/Config.groovy*
- *grails-app/conf/*DataSource.groovy*
- *grails-app/conf/UrlMappings.groovy*
- *grails-app/conf/spring/resources.groovy*
- *test/***
- *web-app/plugins/***
- *web-app/WEB-INF/***
- ***/.svn/***
- ***/CVS/***

You can use `pluginExcludes` to extend the exclusion list; this is typically for domain classes, services, and other artifacts to be used for local development and testing, but not included in the released ZIP files. As I said before, I rarely need an *error.gsp*, so if I delete it and have nothing else to exclude, I delete this property.

The next section of properties contain dummy values and should all be updated with the appropriate information:

```
        // TODO Fill in these fields
        def title = "Book Plugin" // Headline display name of the plugin
        def author = "Your name"
        def authorEmail = ""
        def description = '''\
Brief summary/description of the plugin.
'''

        // URL to the plugin's documentation
        def documentation = "http://grails.org/plugin/book"
```

The initial `title` attribute is probably sufficient, but be sure to add your name and email, and a brief synopsis of the plugin's features and uses in the `description` attribute. You should create proper documentation for your plugin (more on this later) so that will usually mean that you can have a rather short `description` string. By default, the string is a triple-quoted multiline string, so if you want, you can span multiple lines.

The `documentation` link will be correct if you put all of your documentation in the plugin portal page that is created for your plugin when your release it. If you write more extensive documentation somewhere [e.g., in your GitHub repository using their GitHub Pages feature (*http://pages.github.com/*)], then be sure to update the URL.

The final section of metadata attributes has to do with plugin publishing and POM generation:

```
    // Extra (optional) plugin metadata

    // License: one of 'APACHE', 'GPL2', 'GPL3'
//    def license = "APACHE"

    // Details of company behind the plugin (if there is one)
//    def organization = [name: "My Company", url: "http://www.my-company.com/"]

    // Any additional developers beyond the author specified above.
//    def developers = [ [name: "Joe Bloggs", email: "joe@bloggs.net"]]

    // Location of the plugin's issue tracker.
//    def issueManagement = [system: "JIRA", url:
//    "http://jira.grails.org/browse/GPMYPLUGIN"]

    // Online location of the plugin's browseable source code.
//    def scm = [url: "http://svn.codehaus.org/grails-plugins/"]
```

You can specify the name of the license, your company or organization, additional developers (don't add yourself to the `developers` list, because you're already in the list having set the `author` and `authorEmail` attributes above), the type and URL of your bug tracker, and the URL for your source control. These attributes are all optional, but it's a good idea to add the information, because it's used to populate the links in your plugin portal page and will make it easier for users to get access to the source of your plugin and report issues and feature requests.

There are also several attributes that can be set but that aren't included in the generated plugin descriptor:

Table 8-1. Plugin descriptor attributes

Attribute name	Description
loadBefore	A List of plugin names (camelCase, e.g., springSecurityCore) that this plugin should load before.
loadAfter	A List of plugin names (camelCase, e.g., springSecurityCore) that this plugin should load after.
scopes	The execution scope(s) that the plugin can execute in; valid options are test, war, run, functional_test, and all. Valid syntax includes a single String value, a List of one or more String values, or a Map with includes and/or excludes keys and values that are a single String or a List of String values that should be included or excluded.

Attribute name	Description
environments	Environment name(s) that the plugin can execute in; valid options are dev, test, prod, and any custom environments you have defined. Valid syntax is the same as for scopes.
watchedResources	One or more file locations or Ant-style location patterns to watch for changes in the development environment; changes will trigger an event and a call to your plugin's onChange handler. If you want to watch all artifacts of a particular type that are already watched by a plugin, use the observe attribute instead.
observe	A List of plugin names (camelCase, e.g., springSecurityCore) that this plugin should observe for changes in the development environment; if a resource in the observed plugin's watchedResources is changed, your plugin will be notified of the change so you can react to it.
evict	A List of plugin names (camelCase, e.g., springSecurityCore) that this plugin should evict; use this with caution, because there may be unexpected coupling between the application or another plugin and one that is evicted.
artefacts	A List of ArtefactHandler classes or instantiated instances that provide custom artifacts.
providedArtefacts	A List of artifact classes that are provided by the plugin that can be overriden by application classes with the same name and package; this is a rarely used attribute, but is used by CodecsGrails Plugin, ConvertersGrailsPlugin, and GroovyPagesGrailsPlugin.
packaging	How to package the plugin, either source (the default) or binary. Can be overridden from the package-plugin script command line.

Life Cycle Callbacks

In addition to metadata, the plugin descriptor contains closures that are called at various phases of the plugin life cycle at startup and during runtime. None are required, so I always delete any that aren't used; implement whichever ones you need for your plugin.

 The GrailsApplication instance is available in all of the life cycle closures as the application variable.

doWithWebDescriptor

```
def doWithWebDescriptor = { xml ->
  // TODO Implement additions to web.xml (optional)
}
```

You can use doWithWebDescriptor to modify the *web.xml* file that is generated when you build a WAR or start an embedded web server (e.g., when you execute the run-app script or when you run functional tests). Your closure will be passed the root org.w3c.dom.Element of the parsed XML template that is being used (either the one from the Grails distribution corresponding to the current servlet API version, or one you have customized after running grails install-templates) and you can use the *web.xml* DSL that is active in the scope of this closure.

There are two main features of the DSL that are most commonly used: getting a reference to all elements of a particular name, and adding one or more new elements. Typically, you'll want to position a new element in a particular location in the *web.xml* file. So, for example, you can get a reference to all of the `context-param` elements with this:

```
def contextParams = xml.'context-param'
```

This GPath expression will return a `org.w3c.dom.NodeList`, and it's most common to use the `length()` method (or the `size()` method added by Groovy) to position a new element after these elements. For example, you could add a new `filter` element after the last `context-param` element using the + operator with an element-defining closure:

```
contextParams[contextParams.size() - 1] + {
    'filter' {
        'filter-name'('springSecurityFilterChain')
        'filter-class'(DelegatingFilterProxy.name)
    }
}
```

This will generate this XML in your *web.xml* file:

```
<filter>
   <filter-name>springSecurityFilterChain</filter-name>
   <filter-class>
   org.springframework.web.filter.DelegatingFilterProxy
   </filter-class>
</filter>
```

See the Grails reference documentation (*http://bit.ly/115MZVS*) for more details and examples on the usage of this DSL. Also note that, if you need to position a `filter-mapping` element in a particular location (e.g., before or after another filter to ensure it is called in the correct order), you should use the `webxml` plugin (*http://grails.org/plugin/webxml*).

doWithSpring

```
def doWithSpring = {
   // TODO Implement runtime spring config (optional)
}
```

You use `doWithSpring` to register Spring beans in the `ApplicationContext`. This is implemented by the Spring beans DSL that you will be familiar with if you've worked with an application's *grails-app/conf/spring/resources.groovy* file. One convenient feature of the process that Grails uses to build the `ApplicationContext` is that the `Bean Builder` and `RuntimeSpringConfiguration` instances that are used when parsing the *resources.groovy* and the plugin descriptors store singleton bean definitions (the default scope) in a `Map` keyed by the bean names. So you can override any previously defined bean definition by just declaring a bean definition with the same name. You can order plugin loading using the `loadAfter` and `loadBefore` metadata attributes, so this lets plugin developers override beans registered by Grails or other plugins, and lets application developers override any bean in *resources.groovy*. You can even design your plugin to be customized in this way.

One prominent example of this is the `userDetailsService` bean in the Spring Security Core (*http://grails.org/plugin/spring-security-core*) plugin. By default, domain classes and GORM are used to store and retrieve user and role data for use in authentication and authorization, but the plugin was designed to not care where the data comes from, so you're free to create your own `userDetailsService` bean to customize where the data is stored however you like. The `spring-security-openid` plugin does this, overriding the core plugin definition (*http://bit.ly/YKomiP*) with its own (*http://bit.ly/135YJeW*) that adds an additional search by OpenID identifier. But, in general, this is an implementation detail, and users of the bean access it with dependency injection or as a bean reference in the bean builder DSL, in both cases by name.

See the Grails reference documentation (*http://bit.ly/115MZVS*) for more details and examples on the usage of the bean builder DSL.

doWithDynamicMethods

```
def doWithDynamicMethods = { ctx ->
  // TODO Implement registering dynamic methods to classes (optional)
}
```

You can use the `doWithDynamicMethods` callback to add custom methods or properties to one or more classes, working with `MetaClass` instances. The argument of the closure is the Spring `ApplicationContext` in case you need to reference any Spring beans in a metamethod.

It is common to add a method to all instances of a particular artifact type—for example, all controllers or all services. You can use the `GrailsApplication` to find all artifact instances using its `get<Artifact Type>Classes` dynamic method. This method returns `GrailsClass` instances, but you can access each wrapped `Class` with the `get Clazz()` method. So for example, you could add an `isPost` method to all controllers, which would be slightly more convenient than calling the `isPost()` method that's added to the `HttpServletRequest` `MetaClass`:

```
def doWithDynamicMethods = { ctx ->
  for (controllerClass in application.controllerClasses) {
    controllerClass.clazz.metaClass.isPost = { ->
      request.method.toUpperCase() == 'POST'
    }
  }
}
```

Note that this example uses the property-access form of `getControllerClasses()` (`controllerClasses`) for compactness.

doWithApplicationContext

```
def doWithApplicationContext = { ctx ->
   // TODO Implement post initialization spring config (optional)
}
```

If you have any configuration needs that make use of the initialized Spring `Applica tionContext`, you can do that work in `doWithApplicationContext`. One use for this is to slightly change a bean: altering a simple property value or changing a referenced bean to use a different instance. You can redefine the whole bean in `doWithSpring` but this tends to be verbose, because you often must copy the entire bean definition and often change only a few properties. If you want to retain the same bean class but just change one or more properties, you can usually do that more compactly in `doWithApplica tionContext`; for example:

```
def doWithApplicationContext = { ctx ->
   def myBean = ctx.myBean // or ctx.getBean('myBean')
   myBean.maxElements = 200
   myBean.errorHandler = new MockErrorHandler(true)
}
```

onChange

```
def onChange = { event ->
   // TODO Implement code that is executed when any artefact that this plugin is
   // watching is modified and reloaded. The event contains: event.source,
   // event.application, event.manager, event.ctx, and event.plugin.
}
```

If you have specified one or more files or file patterns to be monitored for changes with the `watchedResources` or `observe` attributes, you will be notified of the changes in the `onChange` callback. The event closure parameter is just a `Map`, and it contains the `source` (typically the newly compiled `Class` when watching source files, or the `File` if it's a regular file), the `GrailsApplication` instance under the `application` key, the `Grails PluginManager` instance under the `manager` key, the Spring `ApplicationContext` under the `ctx` key, and the plug-in instance that was watching for changes (your plugin for `watchedResources`, the observed plugin for `observe`) under the `plugin` key.

If you had updated a metaclass in `doWithDynamicMethods` at startup you need to redo that work again, because the newly compiled class will have a new `MetaClass`. You can keep things DRY by sharing code between the two callbacks; for example:

```
def doWithDynamicMethods = { ctx ->
   for (controllerClass in application.controllerClasses) {
      updateControllerMetaclass controllerClass.clazz
   }
}

def onChange = { event ->
   if (event.application.isControllerClass(event.source)) {
```

```
        updateControllerMetaclass event.source
    }
}

private void updateControllerMetaclass(Class c) {
    c.metaClass.isPost = { ->
        request.method.toUpperCase() == 'POST'
    }
}
```

If you are only watching for controller changes, then the `application.isController` `Class` check isn't necessary. But, if you are watching for changes of multiple artifact types, the `is<Artifact Type>Class` `GrailsApplication` dynamic method is convenient to determine what work must be done.

Note that if you need to monitor changes for a file pattern that is already watched by another, you can "observe" that plugin to be notified of changes it watches for. For example, you can simply add:

```
static observe = ['controllers']
```

to be notified of changes to any `grails-app/controllers` classes because the `controllers` plugin is already watching those files.

onConfigChange

```
def onConfigChange = { event ->
    // TODO Implement code that is executed when the project configuration changes.
    // The event is the same as for 'onChange'.
}
```

If you use Grails configuration data for some of your startup configuration, you should monitor changes of *Config.groovy* and handle the update in `onConfigChange`. For example, the core Grails `LoggingGrailsPlugin` watches for configuration changes, because logging is configured by a `log4j` closure in *Config.groovy*.

onShutdown

```
def onShutdown = { event ->
    // TODO Implement code that is executed when the application shuts down
}
```

If you need to do any work during a clean shutdown, you can add that code in `onShutdown`. This is analogous to the `destroy` closure in *grails-app/conf/BootStrap.groovy*. Keep in mind that this only fires during a clean shutdown; if the JVM is stopped with Ctrl-C or another abrupt approach, such as the Unix `kill` command, the code won't have a chance to run.

You can add many features that are only available to plugins to an application (e.g., listening for changed files in development mode, editing *web.xml*, and registering custom artifact handlers) with the `plugina` `tor` plugin (*http://grails.org/plugin/pluginator*).

Splitting Applications into Plugins

There are many ways to split out part of an application into one or more plugins to modularize development and make the code reusable, but there are a few patterns you can use and things to consider.

One issue you may have is that a plugin has only limited visibility into its containing application. If it had more, it would be an indication of a design flaw, because the application should use its plugins, not the other way around. Grails further complicates this by compiling plugins first and then the application code. This has significant benefits including letting you override entire plugin classes with application classes, but it means that your plugin compile will fail if it refers to application classes. This is a good thing, because it points out a coupling that shouldn't exist; if you need this sort of behavior, you should consider moving the shared code into another plugin that both the application and your plugin depend on.

Because a plugin is so similar to an application—it's practically identical except for the addition of the plugin descriptor—you can put any class or resource file that is in your application into a plugin. This means you can have a plugin that only contains static resources and possibly some helper classes, such as the `famfamfam` (*http://grails.org/ plugin/famfamfam*) or JQuery (*http://grails.org/plugin/jquery*) plugins. It could contain only domain classes, or no resources or artifacts at all, and just behavior in the plugin descriptor, such as adding `MetaClass` methods in `doWithDynamicMethods`. Any time you find that you have code, files, or functionality that could be shared between applications, or is shared in an overly manual way, consider extracting it into a plugin.

Inline Plugins

Having created a plugin, whether it contains new features or was split off from an application, you'll find it tedious to continuously repackage and reinstall it for each change you make. You can do this, and using a custom plugin repository would make it a lot easier, but you'll probably find that using:

```
grails.plugin.location."<plugin-name>" = "<path to plugin dir>"
```

is a lot more convenient. The path to the inline plugin can be relative, which helps keep things portable between developers on a team:

```
grails.plugin.location.foo = "../foo"
```

Don't do all of your testing with inline plugins, though, because there are a few bugs and behavior differences between inline plugins and plugins installed the standard way. One is that plugin exclusions aren't respected, so test classes and files that wouldn't be packaged into the plugin ZIP file will be available when using an inline plugin. So be sure to test your plugins in an application by installing from a plugin ZIP, or with a snapshot release.

Building and Releasing

It's a good idea to automate your build process to the extent possible. This can include configuring Jenkins or another continuous-integration server to build your project, or just one or more scripts that reduce the manual (and error-prone) steps. Whether you use a continuous-integration server or a script, it's a good idea to release from a clean copy of the code from source control instead of your local working directory so you don't accidentally include uncommitted code. I often create a shell script that does this for me; for example, here's my release.sh script for the cloud-foundry plugin:

```
#!/bin/bash

rm -rf target/release
mkdir target/release
cd target/release
git clone git@github.com:grails-plugins/grails-cloud-foundry.git
cd grails-cloud-foundry
grails clean
grails compile
grails publish-plugin --noScm
```

One risk with this approach is forgetting to push local changes before doing the release, but I prefer that risk to the one of accidentally including unfinished or untested local changes in a plugin release.

Automated Testing

Testing plugins isn't all that different from testing an application. There are usually many testable classes in a plugin project, so traditional unit and integration tests should be used to ensure that your code works correctly. I also like to do functional testing, because testing the plugin in isolation only gets you so far. Manually installing the plugin into a test application is tedious and error-prone, and hard to do with multiple versions of Grails, so I usually automate this as much as possible.

I don't have a fully fleshed-out process for automated test application creation, so I'll outline the general approach.

A mini DSL to describe versions

Originally I started doing this for the spring-security-core plugin and its extension plugins, because security testing is critical. I've tried to support as many versions of Grails as possible, because often, users don't have the freedom or time to upgrade, so that means I need to test in 1.2.x, 1.3.x, 2.0.x, and now 2.1.x.

The script that creates the test applications is in source control: *CreateS2TestApps.groovy* (*http://bit.ly/15gbUdJ*). It requires a local file called *testapps.config.groovy* and the format is very simple—each block defines the required property values for one version of a test application:

```
String version = '1.2.7.3'
String grailsHomeRoot = '/usr/local/javalib'
String dotGrailsCommon = '/home/burt/.grails'
String projectDirCommon = '/home/burt/workspace/testapps/spring-security-test'

v12 {
    grailsVersion = '1.2.3'
    pluginVersion = version
    dotGrails = dotGrailsCommon
    projectDir = projectDirCommon
    grailsHome = grailsHomeRoot + '/grails-' + grailsVersion
}

v13 {
    grailsVersion = '1.3.7'
    pluginVersion = version
    dotGrails = dotGrailsCommon
    projectDir = projectDirCommon
    grailsHome = grailsHomeRoot + '/grails-' + grailsVersion
}

v20 {
    grailsVersion = '2.0.4'
    pluginVersion = version
    dotGrails = dotGrailsCommon
    projectDir = projectDirCommon
    grailsHome = grailsHomeRoot + '/grails-' + grailsVersion
}

v21 {
    grailsVersion = '2.1.0'
    pluginVersion = version
    dotGrails = dotGrailsCommon
    projectDir = projectDirCommon
    grailsHome = grailsHomeRoot + '/grails-' + grailsVersion
}
```

Dropping support for an older version of Grails is a matter of deleting that block, and adding support for a new version just involves adding a new section for it. The DSL and the script could be smarter (e.g., finding the plugin ZIP file instead of requiring that the version be specified), but it works for me.

When I run the script (with `grails create-s2-testApps`), it parses the configuration file and runs the `grails create-app` script for each version (using the specified version of Grails, so it doesn't depend on the version that I use to develop the plugin), building that version's test application in the specified location. Then, it edits some of the auto-generated files and copies other test files. Once it finishes, I then just need to go to each test application directory and run the Ant build for the project to execute the functional tests for that version. I use an Ant *build.xml*, because the various combinations of settings (e.g., the three different approaches to configuring guarded URLs) aren't compatible, so the build script copies configuration-specific files for each run. In general, it would only be necessary to run `grails test-app` to run the functional tests, however. These are just regular Grails tests, so any failures will be in the generated JUnit reports.

One other significant benefit of creating these test applications with a script is that they're great for testing user-reported bugs and prototyping new features. They're fully initialized and ready to work with, so using them saves the time of creating an application by hand to investigate an issue or new feature.

Continuous integration

Continuous integration (CI) is a good idea for both applications and plugins. You should consider using CI for your plugins, especially because it is so easy to install Jenkins (*http://jenkins-ci.org/*) or another CI server. This way, each time you push to your source control repository, the CI server can start a build and notify you of any failures. And there are even free, cloud-based options. CloudBees has a free product called Build-Hive (*https://buildhive.cloudbees.com/*) that you can use for your Grails applications and plugins. See this blog post (*http://bit.ly/10XUQ67*) for information about using it.

Testing scripts

If your plugin (or application) includes Gant scripts, you should test along with all of the other plugin classes. This isn't very practical though, because to properly test them in an automated fashion (i.e., hooking into the `test-app` script), you need to start an instance of Grails and send commands to its command line, and verify its output, the files that are generated, or whatever observable changes are made. Fortunately, this process is much easier if you use `grails.test.AbstractCliTestCase` as the base class for your tests.

`AbstractCliTestCase` has helpful methods to use in your tests:

- `protected void execute(List<String> command)`
- `int waitForProcess()`

- `String getOutput()`
- `void verifyHeader()`
- `void enterInput(String input)`

You use the `execute` method to specify the command and arguments to use. This starts a new `Process` to launch a separate JVM, so you need to call `waitForProcess()` to wait for the process to finish. This returns the exit code, which typically will be 0 when it successfully executes, so you should verify this. The process output is captured for you and is available by calling the `getOutput()` method or as the associated `output` property. `verifyHeader()` asserts that the output contains the expected "Loading Grails ..." message, so that should probably also be one of the things you check.

So, if you have a script *GenerateThing.groovy*, you would run it in an application using something like:

```
$ grails generate-thing foo --max=20
```

A test for this would look something like:

```
import grails.test.AbstractCliTestCase

class GenerateThing extends AbstractCliTestCase {

    void testGenerateThing() {
        execute(['generate-thing', 'foo', '--max=20'])

        assertEquals 0, waitForProcess()

        verifyHeader()

        // do other checks and assertions
    }
}
```

Note that you don't include the `grails` command, because it is added for you. The process won't run indefinitely; there is a two-minute timeout check to guard against a process that hangs. You can change the value in a test method or the `setUp` method to make it a larger value if your scripts can take a long time to run:

```
timeout = 5 * 60 * 1000 // 5 minutes
```

or a smaller value if it is unlikely that a process will run long and you want it to fail faster if it does:

```
timeout = 10 * 1000 // 10 seconds
```

If your scripts expect user input, you can specify values with one or more calls to the `enterInput` method:

```
enterInput 'yes'
```

Add these after the `execute` and before the `waitForProcess` call.

The Database Migration plugin includes over 30 scripts, and all have tests. You can view these on GitHub (*https://github.com/grails-plugins/grails-database-migration/tree/master/test/cli/grails/plugin/databasemigration*). The tests extend the plugin's `Abstract ScriptTests` base class, which contains code that is shared between the tests. You might want to borrow the two `executeAndCheck` methods that combine the `execute`, `wait ForProcess`, and `verifyHeader` calls and also print the command output to the console if the test fails (this is also available in the generated test reports, but printing it when the test fails is more convenient). One takes a single string for the case where you just want to run the script with no arguments:

```
protected void executeAndCheck(String command) {
    executeAndCheck([command])
}
```

and the other takes a list that includes the command and any arguments, plus a `boolean` argument for whether the command is expected to fail:

```
protected void executeAndCheck(List<String> command,
                               boolean shouldSucceed = true) {
    command << '--stacktrace'
    execute command
    int exitCode = waitForProcess()
    if (shouldSucceed) {
        if (exitCode != 0) {
            println output
        }
        assertEquals 0, exitCode
    }
    else {
        if (exitCode == 0) {
            println output
        }
        assertFalse 0 == exitCode
    }
    verifyHeader()
}
```

This would simplify the previous example to:

```
class GenerateThing extends MyCliTestCase {

    void testGenerateThing() {
        executeAndCheck(['generate-thing', 'foo', '--max=20'])

        // do other checks and assertions
    }
}
```

assuming you create a `MyCliTestCase` extending `AbstractCliTestCase` and including these methods.

In Grails 2.3, an initial test class will be generated for you when you run the `create-script` command, and you will be able to customize the test template file. Until then you will need to manually create the tests.

Running the Tests

The CLI tests will be included along with any unit, integration, and functional tests you have if you run `grails test-app`. You can run the CLI tests separately by specifying the "other" phase:

```
grails test-app --other
```

Note that these tests are slow. Really, really slow. Each test method starts a new JVM to launch Grails and execute your script, so this adds up. It takes around 45 minutes on my development machine to run all of the Database Migration plugin tests. So you probably won't want to run them each time you run your unit and integration tests. You can skip them by specifying the unit and integration phases:

```
grails test-app --unit --integration
```

and run the whole set with `grails test-app` somewhat less often.

Custom Plugin Repositories

If you always release your plugins to the central Grails plugin repository, then publishing is simple; you just need to be sure the `release` plugin (*http://grails.org/plugin/release*) is installed and run the `publish-plugin` command. But, if you have private plugins that can't be shared, or have needed to create custom versions of public plugins, you can publish and install them from a local plugin repository server. There are two excellent servers that have free versions: JFrog Artifactory (*http://www.jfrog.org/*) and Sonatype Nexus (*http://www.sonatype.org/nexus/*). I've used Artifactory, so that's the one I'll describe here, but both are powerful, easy to install, and relatively simple to configure.

Once you have your Artifactory server installed and running (see the documentation at the JFrog site (*http://wiki.jfrog.org/confluence/display/RTF/Installing+Artifactory*) for the required steps), you need to make some small changes in the plugins that you will be publishing there, and in the applications and plugins that will install plugins from there. First, add a new `grails.project.dependency.distribution` section to your plugin's *BuildConfig.groovy* containing the configuration(s) that you will be using. It's a good idea to have both a "snapshots" configuration and a "release" configuration, so this would be configured as:

```
grails.project.dependency.distribution = {

    String serverRoot = 'http://pluginserver:8090/artifactory'

    remoteRepository(id: 'internalPluginSnapshots',
                     url: serverRoot + '/plugins-snapshot-local/') {
        authentication username: 'admin', password: 'password'
    }
    remoteRepository(id: 'internalPluginReleases',
                     url: serverRoot + '/plugins-release-local/') {
        authentication username: 'admin', password: 'password'
    }
}
```

Change the serverRoot as necessary for your setup, and change the repository id values to whatever name you want to use. Now you can use publish-plugin with the reposi tory argument to tell the script not to publish to the default repository, but yours instead:

```
grails publish-plugin --noScm --repository=internalPluginSnapshots --snapshot
```

or:

```
grails publish-plugin --noScm --repository=internalPluginReleases
```

depending on whether the plugin version setting is a -SNAPSHOT version or a regular release version. If you go to the server's web UI, your plugin should show up in the tree, as shown in Figure 8-3.

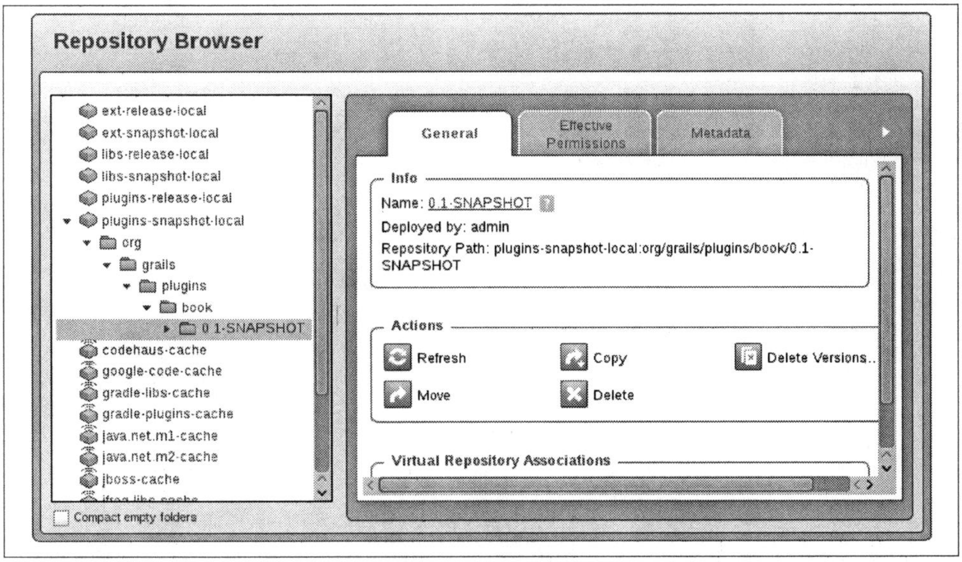

Figure 8-3. Successful publication of plugin to local repo

You probably don't want to leave the hardcoded usernames and passwords in source control, and fortunately, it's easy to store this information externally. Create a file in your *$HOME/.grails* folder named *settings.groovy* and add these lines (or add them to a preexisting file):

```
grails.project.repos.internalPluginReleases.username = 'admin'
grails.project.repos.internalPluginReleases.password = 'password'
grails.project.repos.internalPluginSnapshots.username = 'admin'
grails.project.repos.internalPluginSnapshots.password = 'password'
```

Now that the plugin is released, you can install it into an application or plugin by adding your local server as a custom repository in *BuildConfig.groovy*:

```
repositories {
    inherits true

    String serverRoot = 'http://pluginserver:8090/artifactory'
    mavenRepo serverRoot + '/plugins-snapshot-local/'
    mavenRepo serverRoot + '/plugins-release-local/'

    grailsPlugins()
    grailsHome()
    grailsCentral()
    mavenLocal()
    mavenCentral()
}
```

and adding it to *BuildConfig.groovy* in the plugins section:

```
plugins {
    runtime ":hibernate:$grailsVersion"
    runtime ':jquery:1.7.1'
    runtime ':resources:1.1.6'
    build ":tomcat:$grailsVersion"
    compile ":books:0.1-SNAPSHOT"
}
```

Once you have tested the plugin and released the non-snapshot version 0.1, be sure to update your plugin declaration:

```
plugins {
    runtime ":hibernate:$grailsVersion"
    runtime ':jquery:1.7.1'
    runtime ':resources:1.1.6'
    build ":tomcat:$grailsVersion"
    compile ":books:0.1"
}
```

Plugin Documentation

Your plugin won't be very usable if it has no documentation. Fortunately, the same documentation engine that is used to create the Grails reference documentation (*http://grails.org/doc/latest/*) is also available to applications and plugins. Using it is a matter of creating **.gdoc* files, which use an intuitive wiki-type syntax (based on Textile (*http://textile.sitemonks.com/*) syntax), and running `grails doc` to generate HTML files.

To get started, run:

```
$ grails doc --init
```

which will create the initial directory structure (under the *src/docs* directory) and some starter files. One of these is *toc.yml*, which defines the file layout in YAML format (*http://www.yaml.org/*).

Run `grails doc` to generate HTML output in the *target/docs* folder. You can change the output location by setting the `grails.project.docs.output.dir` property in *BuildConfig.groovy*; for example:

```
grails.project.docs.output.dir = 'docs/manual'
```

You can generate a single PDF version of the documentation in addition to the HTML docs by adding the `--pdf` flag:

```
$ grails doc --pdf
```

This will create the file *guide/single.pdf* in the root documentation directory.

There are several properties that you can set to customize the generated output. These start with `grails.doc.` and are set in *grails-app/conf/Config.groovy*. See the Grails documentation (*http://grails.org/doc/latest/guide/single.html#docengine*) for more information about these properties and the gdoc file syntax.

Custom Artifacts

Grails groups classes by type and uses the "artifact" concept to represent them. Typically, artifacts have their own folder in the *grails-app* folder, such as `controllers`, `domain`, and `services`. If your plugin adds functionality where a convention-based approach to defining application classes and adding behavior makes sense, you should consider adding a custom artifact type. A more traditional framework would more likely use interfaces and base classes, but this tends to be more restrictive and goes against the Grails "convention over configuration" approach.

The `GrailsApplication` instance has several methods to work with artifact classes:

`Class<?>[] getAllArtefacts()`
    Returns a class for each artifact instance

```
boolean isArtefact(Class theClazz)
```
Returns true if the class is a known artifact class

```
boolean isArtefactOfType(String artefactType, Class theClazz)
```
Returns true if the class is an artifact and of the specified type

```
boolean isArtefactOfType(String artefactType, String className)
```
Returns true if the class name is an artifact and of the specified type

```
GrailsClass getArtefact(String artefactType, String name)
```
Returns the GrailsClass instance of the specified type for the specified class name

```
ArtefactHandler getArtefactType(Class theClass)
```
Returns the artifact handler for the artifact class

```
GrailsClass[] getArtefacts(String artefactType)
```
Returns all GrailsClass instances for the artifact type

```
GrailsClass getArtefactForFeature(String artefactType, Object featureID)
```
Returns the GrailsClass of the specified type for the requested feature (e.g., the GrailsTagLibClass for a tag name or the GrailsControllerClass for a URI)

```
GrailsClass addArtefact(String artefactType, Class artefactClass)
```
Programmatically registers an artifact class

```
GrailsClass addArtefact(String artefactType, GrailsClass artefactGrail
sClass)
```
Programmatically registers an artifact class by name

```
void registerArtefactHandler(ArtefactHandler handler)
```
Programmatically registers an artifact handler

```
boolean hasArtefactHandler(String type)
```
Returns true if there is an artifact handler of the specified type

```
ArtefactHandler[] getArtefactHandlers()
```
Returns all known artifact handlers

```
ArtefactHandler getArtefactHandler(String type)
```
Returns the artifact handler for the specified name

```
GrailsClass getArtefactByLogicalPropertyName(String type, String logical
Name)
```
Returns the GrailsClass of the specified type for the requested logical property name [e.g., getArtefactByLogicalPropertyName('Service', 'person') or ge tArtefactByLogicalPropertyName('Controller', 'orderItem')]

```
void addArtefact(Class artefact)
```
Programmatically registers an artifact class

```
void addArtefact(String artefactType, Class artefactClass)
```
Programmatically registers an artifact class

```
void addArtefact(String artefactType, GrailsClass artefactGrailsClass)
```
Programmatically registers an artifact class

In addition, there are three dynamic methods that can be used to work with artifacts by type. The most commonly used is get<Artifact Type>Classes(); for example, get ControllerClasses() or getDomainClasses(). This can be used to loop through all known artifacts of a particular type. This method is more commonly used in its property form: application.controllerClasses or application.domainClasses. This calls the getArtefacts(String artefactType) method, using the artifact type from the method name as the artefactType argument value. In addition, there is an is<Arti fact Type>Class(Class) method, such as isServiceClass(Class), which calls the isArtefactOfType(String artefactType, Class theClazz) method. Finally, there is get<Artifact Type>Class(String), such as getTaglibClass(String), which calls getArtefact(String artefactType, String name).

Each artifact type must have an implementation of org.codehaus.groovy.grails.com mons.ArtefactHandler, an interface that extends org.codehaus.groovy.grails.com mons.GrailsClass to represent the artifact instances, and an implementation class for the interface. Typically, the artifact handler class extends org.codehaus.groo vy.grails.commons.ArtefactHandlerAdapter, which implements the interface and provides a sensible default implementation. The interface usually extends org.code haus.groovy.grails.commons.InjectableGrailsClass and the implementation class usually extends org.codehaus.groovy.grails.commons.AbstractInjectable GrailsClass.

As an example, consider a plugin that adds a MethodMixin class. It defines a destination class or interface, and closures to wire into the destination's metaclass. This can be done manually—for example, in *BootStrap.groovy*—but this could provide a convenient way of grouping the metaclass methods and also allow other plugins to provide mixin classes.

Once we're done, applications that use this plugin could define a ListMethodMixin class, which would automatically be discovered and would add methods to the List interface:

```
class ListMethodMixin {

    static destination = List

    static methods = [
        toStrings: { ->
            delegate.eachWithIndex { o, int i ->
```

```
                        delegate.set(i, o?.toString())
                    }
                },
                second: { -> delegate[1] }
            ]
        }
```

To support this, we'll need an interface to represent the GrailsClass and to provide access to the destination and methods values:

```
package com.mycompany;

import groovy.lang.Closure;
import java.util.Map;
import org.codehaus.groovy.grails.commons.InjectableGrailsClass;

public interface MethodMixinGrailsClass extends InjectableGrailsClass {

    String DESTINATION = "destination";
    String METHODS = "methods";

    /**
     * The class or interface to mix the methods into.
     *
     * @return the class or interface
     */
    Class<?> getDestination();

    /**
     * The closures to mix into the destination; the keys are method names and
     * the values are the closures to use for metamethods.
     * @return the methods
     */
    Map<String, Closure<?>> getMethods();
}
```

and an implementation of the interface:

```
package com.mycompany;

import groovy.lang.Closure;
import java.util.Map;
import org.codehaus.groovy.grails.commons.AbstractInjectableGrailsClass;

public class DefaultMethodMixinGrailsClass extends AbstractInjectableGrailsClass
        implements MethodMixinGrailsClass

    protected Class<?> destination;
    protected Map<String, Closure<?>> methods;

    @SuppressWarnings("unchecked")
    public DefaultMethodMixinGrailsClass(Class<?> wrappedClass) {
        super(wrappedClass, MethodMixinArtefactHandler.TYPE);
```

```
        destination = (Class<?>)getPropertyOrStaticPropertyOrFieldValue(
            DESTINATION, Class.class);
        methods = (Map<String, Closure<?>>) getPropertyOrStaticPropertyOrFieldValue(
            METHODS, Map.class);
    }

    public Class<?> getDestination() {
        return destination;
    }

    public Map<String, Closure<?>> getMethods() {
        return methods;
    }
}
```

And we'll also need an `ArtefactHandler` implementation:

```
package com.mycompany;

import org.codehaus.groovy.grails.commons.ArtefactHandlerAdapter;

public class MethodMixinArtefactHandler extends ArtefactHandlerAdapter {

    /** The artefact type. */
    public static final String TYPE = "MethodMixin";

    public MethodMixinArtefactHandler() {
        super(TYPE, MethodMixinGrailsClass.class,
            DefaultMethodMixinGrailsClass.class, TYPE);
    }
}
```

Register this in the plugin descriptor by adding the class to the `artefacts` list:

```
import com.mycompany.MethodMixinArtefactHandler

...

def artefacts = [MethodMixinArtefactHandler]
```

This will ensure that the artifact handler is discovered by Grails at startup. Because the `GrailsApplication` dynamic methods work for all registered artifact handlers, applications that use this plugin will be able to call `getMethodMixinClasses()` (or the property `methodMixinClasses`), `isMethodMixinClass(Class)`, and `getMethodMixinClass(String)`.

We will need code to apply the metaclass methods. This should be done at startup, and the `doWithDynamicMethods` callback is the best place for this:

```
import com.mycompany.MixinHelper

...
```

```
def doWithDynamicMethods = { ctx ->
    MixinHelper.mixinMethods application.methodMixinClasses
}
```

This depends on the `MixinHelper` utility class in *src/groovy*:

```
package com.mycompany

import org.codehaus.groovy.grails.commons.GrailsClass

class MixinHelper {

    static void mixinMethods(GrailsClass[] classes) {
        for (MethodMixinGrailsClass mm in classes) {
            mm.methods.each { String name, Closure impl ->
                mm.destination.metaClass."$name" = impl
            }
        }
    }
}
```

The code could have just been left in the plugin descriptor, but having it in a separate class makes it easier to access to test and to call from other parts of the plugin or application.

It's a good idea to support reloading so changes made in development are discovered and applied. Add a `watchedResources` property, which establishes the watch pattern for classes in the `methodMixins` folder and logic to update based on changes in the `onChange` callback:

```
def watchedResources = ['file:./grails-app/methodMixins/**/*MethodMixin.groovy']

...

def onChange = { event ->
    // put reloading logic here
}
```

It will be tricky to handle reloading for these artifacts, because methods could be removed. This is left as an exercise for the reader.

Applications that use this plugin will keep artifact classes in the *grails-app/methodMixins* folder, so it's a good idea to create that folder during plugin installation. Add the code to do that in *scripts/_Install.groovy*:

```
ant.mkdir dir: "$basedir/grails-app/methodMixins"
```

Having done all of this, we can now call the `toStrings` and `second` methods on any `List` in an application that includes the `ListMethodMixin` class:

```
def numbers = [1, 2, 5]
```

```
assert numbers.toStrings().every { it instanceof String }
assert numbers.second() == 2
```

Some Notes on Plugin Development Workflow

After creating a new plugin and doing the cleanup work I described above, at some point after some initial coding and testing, there will be a need to use the plugin in an application to verify that it works and to finish development. The inline plugin feature was added to Grails after I had written several plugins, so I tend to not use it. Instead, I change the plugin version from "0.1" to "0.1-SNAPSHOT," build the plugin with the `package-plugin` script, and install it into a test application using `grails install-plugin /path/to/the-new-plugin-0.1-SNAPSHOT.zip`. Adding the "SNAPSHOT" suffix is important because Grails doesn't cache snapshot plugins, so there's no risk of installing a stale cached version when creating a second test application.

Throughout this book, I've been advising against using `install-plugin` and using *BuildConfig.groovy* dependencies instead, but there is no convenient way (as of this writing) to register a dependency on a plugin ZIP. I could use a local plugin repository server, but that's overkill for my needs.

The big risk with this process is that it is more convenient to edit the application's version of the plugin code (under the *target* folder, because I use it as the work directory), but then it's far too easy to forget to update the original source, and it is a tediously manual process. But I found an excellent graphical diff tool that I use to keep the code in sync: Meld (*http://meldmerge.org/*). You can see a current diff for the HDIV plugin in Figure 8-4.

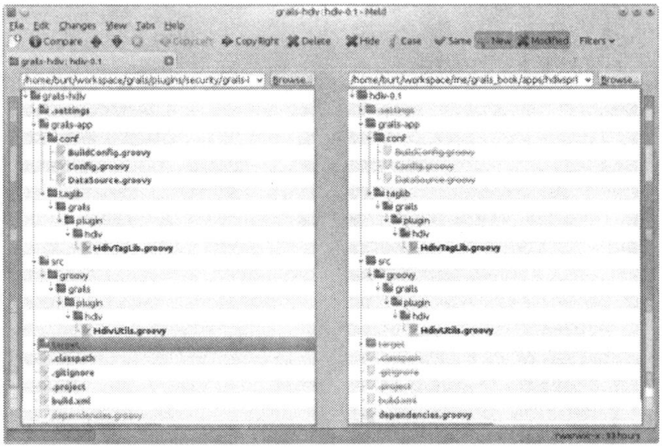

Figure 8-4. Using the Meld diff tool

Recall that the `package-plugin` script excludes several directories and files from the packaged ZIP file, so there will always be ignorable differences between the two directory trees. This will include the *.settings* directory (if you use GGTS), the *target* and *test* directories, along with *BuildConfig.groovy*, *Config.groovy*, and *DataSource.groovy*, and other miscellaneous files and directories. You can see that I have collapsed most of these nodes already. There are two real differences here: *HdivUtils.groovy* in *src/groovy* and *HdivTagLib* in *grails-app/taglib*.

It's easy to copy entire files from one tree to the other, or open a graphical diff and copy individual lines. It doesn't matter whether you edit the plugin project code or the code installed into the application; in either case, you can conveniently synchronize the files.

So, periodically, once I've made some changes and verified that the changes make sense, I update the plugin project code and commit the Git master repository. I keep Meld open, so after I have updated more files I use Ctrl-R to refresh the trees to synchronize the latest changes.

There is one exception to this workflow: *BuildConfig.groovy*. *BuildConfig.groovy* is included in the plugin ZIP, but it is copied as *dependencies.groovy*. This may change in the future where *dependencies.groovy* is only derived from *BuildConfig.groovy*, but currently it is simply copied. So, if I make any dependency changes in the installed plugin, I'll make them in *dependencies.groovy*, but I have to remember to manually make the same changes in the plugin project's *BuildConfig.groovy*.

Security

The purpose of this chapter is to scare you. You are most likely not doing enough to secure your application and your user data, and running a risk of an embarrassing security breach that could gain you a lot of unwanted attention. In Hollywood, they say that all publicity is good publicity, because whether it's good or bad, it gets people thinking about you. But for websites, this is far less true; users need to trust your site, and if you violate that trust, they will find an alternative. I often joke at conferences when I talk about security that you want to end up on Slashdot because you are awesome, not because you got hacked.

Please note that this is a very cursory discussion of an important topic, and you should make it a priority that at least someone on your team is knowledgeable about security best practices.

OWASP

The Open Web Application Security Project (OWASP (*https://www.owasp.org/index.php/Main_Page*)) is an organization that collects web application security information and publishes a list of its top 10 highest-priority security risks for web apps; this list is updated every three years, and the most recent is from 2010 (*https://www.owasp.org/index.php/Top_10_2010-Main*). Grails does help mitigate some of the risks by default, and using a security plugin helps with others, but it's important to be aware of the risks and to be security conscious.

A1: Injection

SQL injection is the most common type of injection attack, and Grails applications are largely immune to these, but not entirely. An SQL injection attack typically consists of tricking the application into running SQL queries or updates that either damage data or expose information. This can happen when you have a search form or other web page that accepts user input and you use the input as part of a dynamically generated SQL query without properly escaping the inputs.

Using regular JDBC, you can use a `java.sql.Statement` to run a `select` query; for example:

```
String sql = "select * from person where username ='" + params.username + "'"
ResultSet rs = statement.executeQuery(sql)
```

This works well if you have control over the inputs, but users can enter whatever they want in your form. If someone enters `foo`, then the `where` clause of your query will be `where username ='foo'`, but if a hacker enters `' or '1'='1`, then it will be `select * from person where username ='' or '1'='1`. Because `'1'='1'` is always true, the `or` results in the query returning unexpected records (in this case, all of them). Tricks like this can be used to bypass password checks during login or create a denial-of-service style attack where too much data is returned from the database repeatedly, or even to damage data or tables. If you use `execute` instead of `executeQuery`, you can mix `select` queries and updates and allow real damage:

```
boolean ok = statement.execute(sql)
```

If a hacker submits `'; drop table foo; --` or `'; truncate table foo; --`, you'll be scrambling to restore the database from the most recent backup.

The problem here is that we're trusting the users to do the right thing. The deeper problem is a failure to escape the user input properly before sending it to the database. You could look for patterns like the ones I've shown and implement a whitelist/blacklist filtering approach to using user-submitted data in your queries, but the best approach is to let the database driver do the work for you. Rather than using a `Statement`, use a `PreparedStatement` with parameter placeholders in the SQL:

```
String sql = "select * from person where username = ?"
PreparedStatement ps = connection.prepareStatement(sql)
ps.setString(1, params.username)
ResultSet rs = ps.executeQuery()
```

Now, if an unfriendly user submits a username with quote characters, they will be escaped properly (the approach is different for various databases, but the driver handles it for us) and the worst-case scenario now is an `SQLException`.

Fortunately for us, Hibernate uses a `PreparedStatement` for criteria queries, and all Grails queries are converted to criteria queries under the hood (the exception being single-element queries like `get()` or `read()`, which also use a `PreparedStatement`). You can see this by turning on SQL logging and enabling SQL comments in *Data-Source.groovy*:

```
dataSource {
    ...
    logSql = true
```

```
    }
    hibernate {
        ...
        format_sql = true
        use_sql_comments = true
    }
```

Given this simple domain class:

```
class Person {
    String username
}
```

You can use a few different approaches to find a user by username:

```
Person.findByUsername(params.username)

Person.where { username == params.username }.find()

Person.createCriteria().get {
    eq 'username', params.username
}
```

and each of these results in roughly the same SQL:

```
Hibernate:
    /* criteria query */ select
        this_.id as id0_0_,
        this_.version as version0_0_,
        this_.username as username0_0_
    from
        person this_
    where
        this_.username=?
```

You can see from the comment that Hibernate generated the SQL from a criteria query and, from the SQL, that a PreparedStatement is being used because the username parameter isn't the actual string being queried, but the ? placeholder.

So we're safe from SQL injection attacks in the general case, but we can also use HQL queries with the executeQuery and executeUpdate methods. Hibernate converts our HQL to SQL, so naive string concatenation of HQL can open up an SQL injection vulnerability:

```
Person.executeQuery("from Person where username='" + params.username + "'")
```

Hibernate has no way of knowing that a parameter should be escaped, because it just sees the final concatenated string. But, of course, HQL has the same support for placeholder replacement as SQL:

```
Person.executeQuery('from Person where username=?', [params.username])
```

and also has support for more readable named parameters:

```
Person.executeQuery('from Person where username=:username',
                    [username: params.username])
```

So, as long as you use the standard GORM methods to run your queries and are careful with HQL queries, you should be safe from SQL injection risks. Note that Groovy GStrings don't help here and, in fact, hide the problem to a certain extent. I could have written the SQL above as `"from Person where username='${params.username}'"` and the HQL as `"select * from person where username ='${params.user name}'"`; the lack of + characters in the code can make it more likely that this would get missed in a code review.

Command injection

Groovy makes it easy to execute arbitrary operating system commands by adding the `execute` method to the metaclass of the `String` and `String[]` classes. For example, it's simple to get a directory listing on a Unix or Linux system by running `'ls -l'.execute().text`. If your application uses this feature and creates the commands to be executed based on user input, you are at risk of a command injection attack. Unfortunately, there isn't a simple fix like there is for SQL; you will have to be vigilant and scan the user input based on a whitelist and/or a blacklist of allowed characters and expressions that are valid.

A2: Cross-Site Scripting (XSS)

A cross-site scripting (XSS) attack is one that takes advantage of unescaped input, much like the injection attacks in the previous section. In fact, you can think of XSS as script injection, because JavaScript is the most common input used.

Your site is vulnerable to XSS attacks if you fail to escape user-supplied input that you display on your site. This can include any type of input, such as a search form, comments, or editable content such as wikis. Most search engine sites display your original search query along with the results; this is fine if your search is "Grails books," but what if you "search" for "<script>alert(*Boo!*)</script>"? If your GSP naively redisplays this text without, at a minimum, HTML-encoding the bracket characters:

```
<div id='query'>You searched for '${originalQuery}'</div>
<div id='results'>
<g:each in='${results}' var='result'>
...
</g:each>
</div>
```

you will see a JavaScript pop-up when the results page loads because the rendered HTML will look like this:

```
<div id='query'>You searched for '<script>alert('Boo!')</script>'</div>
<div id='results'>
...
</div>
```

Remedies

Fortunately, Grails does have mechanisms to deal with this. When you initially create a Grails application, the generated *grails-app/conf/Config.groovy* file contains this configuration option:

```
grails.views.default.codec = "none" // none, html, base64
```

The default codec is the one that is used to escape content inside of ${} blocks, and the default is to do nothing. This is unfortunate but was chosen as the default because changing the behavior to automatically encode might break existing pages that explicitly encode, resulting in corrupted output from double-encoding. Luckily, it's simple to change to a sensible new value for your projects:

```
grails.views.default.codec = "html"
```

With this setting enabled, the HTML output would have been:

```
<div id='query'>You searched for '&lt;script&gt;alert('Boo!')&lt;/script&gt;'</div>
<div id='results'>
...
</div>
```

and you would have seen the original "query" in the browser as text instead of the JavaScript pop-up. Clearly, this should be one of the first things you do in a new Grails application.

The `fieldValue` tag is another standard way of displaying data, typically from a domain class or command object instance (the generated CRUD GSPs use this extensively). `fieldValue` does escape the field value by default, regardless of the `grails.views.default.codec` setting. For example, given this simple data class:

```
class Person {
    String name
}
```

and this simple controller:

```
class TestController {
    def index() {
        [person: new Person(name: '<script>alert("XSS!")</script>')]
    }
}
```

you can display the person's name attribute three ways:

```
${person.name}<br/>
```

```
${fieldValue(bean: person, field: 'name')}<br/>

<%=person.name%><br/>
```

The third one uses a `<% ... %>` block to write directly to the output stream; as you'll see, it's the most dangerous and should be avoided. With no default codec, the rendered HTML would be:

```
<script>alert("XSS!")</script><br/>

&lt;script&gt;alert(&quot;XSS!&quot;)&lt;/script&gt;<br/>

<script>alert("XSS!")</script><br/>
```

and you would see two JavaScript pop-ups. With the `"html"` codec you would only see one:

```
&lt;script&gt;alert(&quot;XSS!&quot;)&lt;/script&gt;<br/>

&lt;script&gt;alert(&quot;XSS!&quot;)&lt;/script&gt;<br/>

<script>alert("XSS!")</script><br/>
```

So, the lesson here is clear: use automatic escaping where practical and avoid directly writing to the output stream with `<% ... %>` blocks unless you are very confident that the content is safe.

As described so far, this isn't a particularly dangerous exploit. All the user has done is to manage to get search results to display a JavaScript pop-up. But much more extensive script code could have been used, along with HTML and CSS. Using input mechanisms that store the input and redisplay it for other users later (e.g., comments, wikis, etc.), you can inject script code that can bypass security checks, such as accessing authentication cookies to allow the attacker to impersonate someone else. You can also perform actions on the behalf of other users, such as executing a client-side GET or POST to transfer funds from one account to another.

Best practices

The first thing to do is make sure the default code is `"html"` to ensure that `${}` blocks are properly encoded. You may end up with double-encoded output if you had (or a plugin had) manually used the `encodeAsHTML()` method, such as `${someVariable.en codeAsHTML()}`, so those will have to be fixed. This would look bad, but encoding twice is better than not at all.

If you are using the Servlet 3.0 spec (this requires newer servers such as Tomcat 7) there is an option to set the `HttpOnly` flag for your cookies. This isn't in the cookie spec but is supported by all major browsers and disables JavaScript access to cookie values. You can call `setHttpOnly(true)` when creating your cookies to enable this. Tomcat 7 automatically sets this flag for your JSESSIONID cookie whether your application uses

Servlet 3.0 or not, and Spring Security uses reflection to call the method if it's available when creating remember-me cookies.

Also consider using SSL for your site and setting the `secure` flag so the cookies are only transmitted via SSL and are therefore always encrypted, even if the cookie value isn't; call `setSecure(true)` when creating the cookies. Spring Security creates secure cookies by default when you are using SSL.

Other options include using libraries that detect and block or encode risky input; these include AntiSamy, ESAPI, and HDIV, and are discussed later in the chapter.

There is a plugin that uses the ESAPI library to remove script tags and other malicious text from request parameters: the `xss-sanitizer` plugin (*http://grails.org/plugin/xss-sanitizer*). It registers a servlet filter to intercept all requests to make the necessary changes. The plugin is convenient in that it does the work of registering the filter and making the changes for you, but you could also use the ESAPI library directly.

See the OWASP XSS Prevention Cheat Sheet (*http://bit.ly/YXgY2O*) for much more information on this subject.

A3: Broken Authentication and Session Management

It is difficult to properly implement authentication. I find it very frustrating how often Grails tutorials describe a simple authentication mechanism using filters, because it encourages developers to implement security themselves and implies that it is easy to do. It is easy to create a Grails filter and implement a check for an active user before certain application URLs and redirect to a login page if one isn't found. But, it's too easy; there is far more to security than just this. As you continue development, you will find that more and more security-related features must be implemented (password hashing, session fixation protection, remember-me, forgotten password workflows, etc.) and each new feature that you implement yourself increases the likelihood that you will fail to properly implement the feature and create a vulnerability.

If you don't have extensive experience with security (and few of us do), then it's far too easy to expose information to hackers who are more clever than you (or have access to clever tools). Not enough people know that MD5 and SHA-1 are too easy to exploit and should be replaced with stronger alternatives (e.g., SHA-256, Bcrypt, etc.). Implementing a forgot-password approach too simplistically can allow hackers to change your password and authenticate as you. Using URL-rewriting and allowing users' session IDs to be added to URLs makes it easy for an attacker to capture authenticated users' session ID and perform actions as them. These are just a few examples; the number of things that can go wrong is significant.

Because HTTP is a stateless protocol, we must either resend authentication information in headers for each request or store the information in the HTTP session. This must be done securely. The best option is to disable URL rewriting and use cookies and SSL (ideally for all pages in your site). This ensures that the cookies are sent securely and cannot be seen by attackers. This is discussed in more detail in the upcoming section "A9: Insufficient Transport Layer Protection" on page 250.

Newer versions of Grails do not use URL rewriting; the `grails.views.enable.jses sionid` configuration setting defaults to `false`, and it determines whether or not to call the `encodeRedirectURL` response method when generating redirect URLs. If this is used, the session ID is appended to the querystring, so it's best to not enable this and only allow cookie-based authentication. In addition, if you manually create redirect URLs, use the `encodeURL` method but not the `encodeRedirectURL` method.

In addition, it is important to guard against session fixation. This is an attack where someone tricks a user into clicking a URL that contains the attacker's session ID. Then when the user authenticates, the attacker and the user share the same session and the attacker can perform actions as the user. The fix for this is simple; create a new session when authenticating, and copy all (or a safe subset) of the previous session variables into the new session. This is a feature of the Spring Security plugin; add this line in *Config.groovy* to enable it:

```
grails.plugins.springsecurity.useSessionFixationPrevention = true
```

As in several of the other sections, the best advice I can give is to use a proven framework and not "roll your own." Take advantage of the experience of others so you can spend time on the real features of your applications that provide business value.

A4: Insecure Direct Object References

An insecure direct object reference is one where you allow the user to choose the identifier for some data, potentially allowing the user to see another's data. For example, a user's personal information summary page might provide links to display purchases for each registered credit card:

```
<ul>
    <li><a href='/card/view/42'>Purchases for card xxxx-xxxx-xxxx-1234</a></li>
    <li><a href='/card/view/54312'>Purchases for card xxxx-xxxx-xxxx-1337</a></li>
    ...
</ul>
```

Once an attacker sees that this approach is used, it's a simple matter to loop through every value starting at 1 and request the page to view other users' transaction data. Any time you allow the identifier to be specified and don't protect access, you risk exposing information.

Remedies

For the credit card example above, the attack can only work if you access the credit card data only by ID; for example,

```
def card = CreditCard.get(params.id)
```

One way to defeat this is to take advantage of a relationship between the `CreditCard` domain class and the owning `User`; for example:

```
class CreditCard {
    String number
    CreditCardType type
    ...
    User owner
}
```

It should be easy to access the currently authenticated user's username or user ID, and you can use that to retrieve the card; for example:

```
def userId = ... // retrieve from authentication
def user = User.load(userId)
def card = CreditCard.findByIdAndOwner(params.id as Long, user)
```

or:

```
def username = ... // retrieve from authentication
def user = User.findByUsername(username)
def card = CreditCard.findByIdAndOwner(params.id as Long, user)
```

Using this approach, we still trust the provided card ID, but don't allow the user to specify the username or ID—it's already available from the authentication information. In this case, the generated SQL will fail to return a result if the card ID is valid but the user ID mismatches:

```
select ... from credit_card where id=? and user_id=?
```

Access control lists (ACLs) are a more rigorous but somewhat cumbersome approach that is also an excellent option for protecting access to data. This feature is available in the Spring Security ACL (*http://grails.org/plugin/spring-security-acl*) and Shiro (*http://grails.org/plugin/shiro*) plugins. This approach involves configuring access control information (typically stored in the database), specifying who can access what information and to what extent. You can grant different levels of access, such as read, edit, delete, create, etc. You could use this to register that only the user with ID 142352 can access the cards with IDs 42 and 54312. In the case of the Spring Security plugin, you would create a service method with an annotation that triggers the creation of a secure proxy that checks the data at runtime and throws an exception if a mismatch occurs:

```
@PreAuthorize("hasPermission(#id, 'com.yourapp.CreditCard', read)")
CreditCard getReport(long id) {
    CreditCard.get(id)
}
```

This has the benefit that the domain class method is not overly complicated—just a simple `get` call—but with the added complexity of having to populate and maintain the ACL data.

The HDIV library (described below) also has support for guarding against this type of attack. If you use it to postprocess your URLs, it can replace real identifiers with place-holder values and replace them at the server when the request is submitted. Using the example above, the generated HTML would be this instead:

```
<ul>
    <li><a href='/card/view/0'>Purchases for card xxxx-xxxx-xxxx-1234</a></li>
    <li><a href='/card/view/1'>Purchases for card xxxx-xxxx-xxxx-1337</a></li>
    ...
</ul>
```

and the real IDs would be stored on the server using the placeholder IDs as keys (0 → 42 and 1 → 54312). Now an attacker cannot simply choose the ID to view; only the placeholder value is valid. If an ID other than 0 or 1 is used, it will be detected as a tampering attempt. And this is all transparent to the server-side code, because a request wrapper is configured by a filter, so calls to request.getParameter() are intercepted to return the previously stored real IDs, not the actual submitted 0 or 1 values.

A5: Cross-Site Request Forgery

A cross-site request forgery (CSRF) attack is similar to an XSS attack. An attacker will often use XSS vulnerabilities to create pages that make requests on the behalf of other users and send personal information, cookies, or session IDs to the attacker's server, or perform some action on behalf of the user. One example of this is to insert an <img> tag into comment page. If the content isn't escaped, the tag will end up as valid markup in the HTML. Ordinarily, image URLs point to PNGs, JPGs, and GIFs, but the browser will execute a GET request for whatever URL is specified, so this is valid:

```
<img src='http://hacker.site.com?foo=bar'/>
```

The URL and querystring can be configured using JavaScript to include whatever in-formation is available (and this can be a lot). The request can initiate some action, or might just be used to add a record with captured information in the server log for retrieval later. The hacker could also create a local URL that would perform some action by the user. It is often simple for the hacker to create an account and log in, and then view the HTML source of the site's pages to see how requests are made, and craft URLs like this:

```
<img src='/account/transfer?destination=123&amount=1000'/>
```

Assuming that the hacker's account ID is 123, and the controller that handles the /account/transfer action uses the active authentication to determine the source user, this request could transfer $1,000 to the hacker's account.

Remedies

The first line of defense against CSRF attacks is to ensure that XSS attacks are not possible in your application, so refer to the discussion above for best practices there.

The best way to defeat CSRF attacks is to generate a token for each clickable URL (appended to the `href`) and form (using an `<input type='hidden'>` tag), and verify the token at the server. If a request is made (either a GET or a POST), and there is no token or it's not valid, the action is blocked. As long as the value is unique and generated for each request, even if an attacker accesses someone else's valid token, it won't be usable, because it is only valid for that user.

This would be cumbersome to implement yourself, because it would require changing all of your GSPs and controllers to add the tokens, and logic to properly generate and validate the tokens. Fortunately, there is a library that make this all fairly straightforward, HDIV (*http://www.hdiv.org/*). There is a Grails HDIV plugin (*http://grails.org/plugin/hdiv*) that helps to configure the library for you. Unfortunately, it depends on changes in Grails core that are only available as of version 2.3, so you will have to upgrade to take advantage of this. HDIV is discussed in more detail later.

In addition, actions that make changes should always use POST instead of GET; GET should only be used to retrieve information. Use the `allowedMethods` map in Grails controllers to define which actions require which methods. This isn't sufficient, because it's easy to craft client-side POST requests using JavaScript, but it raises the bar a bit.

See the OWASP CSRF Prevention Cheat Sheet (*http://bit.ly/11aBfAb*) for much more information on this subject.

A6: Security Misconfiguration

Misconfigured security is a much more extensive problem than many of the other risks, because it is impacted by potential issues with application, server, and operating system code. It's harder to automate any sort of fix; it's far from as simple as using a `Prepared Statement` for all database access or HTML-encoding rendered output.

Remedies

The general best practice to avoid security misconfiguration issues is to be proactive to ensure that all of the components of the system are hardened to the extent that is practical.

Never use a default password; if a software installation process doesn't require that you choose a password, change it ASAP. And use strong passwords, to the extent allowed by the verification rules, with a good mix of upper- and lowercase letters, numbers, spaces, and special characters.

You should disable unnecessary features; this reduces the "attack surface" and gives attackers fewer options to exploit. This includes uninstalling (or not installing in the first place) OS applications and features that won't be needed. Similarly, it's best to remove default or automatically created accounts for any software or servers that you use.

For example, MySQL configures a "test" user by default; the user can't do much of anything, but by removing the account, you again reduce the attack surface.

Be sure to routinely update software, especially when security fixes are available. This includes issues with development frameworks, server software, and OS patches. Don't be the last to know about available fixes; sign up for mailing lists and other information streams that will keep you aware of available updates.

A7: Insecure Cryptographic Storage

There are two general approaches to storing data in non-cleartext form: hashing and encrypting.

A hash function takes an input and generates a fixed-length output. Because large and small inputs generate an output of the same length, it's possible to generate the same hash value for two different inputs, but in practice they are of sufficient size that this is extremely unlikely. Hashing is "lossy"—that is, not all of the input information is recoverable from the output, and in fact, that is not the point of hashing; hashes are one-way conversions of the inputs into the outputs.

An encryption function similarly converts an input into an output, but in contrast to hash functions, encryption functions are designed to be decrypted. As such, they are more suitable for different data types than are hash functions.

Passwords are typically hashed. There is rarely a need to decrypt a password stored in a database, because during authentication, you merely need to hash the user's supplied password and compare it with the previously hashed value. If they agree (they may not be identical depending on the hash algorithm, but the implementation will have a way of determining that two hashes are equivalent), then it is very likely that the cleartext passwords were the same and you can authenticate the user. If they do not agree, then the inputs were definitely not the same and you deny access. Having decryptable passwords does allow us the convenience of sending the user the cleartext password when it is forgotten (and we have verified that the requesting user is the correct one), but this is a huge security risk. It is much safer to never store cleartext passwords and not be able to recover them, but instead deal with lost passwords by forcing the user (once validated) to create a new one.

There are many popular hashing algorithms, but you should be aware that some are no longer considered safe to use. One of these is MD5. When MD5 was originally created, it was very robust, but given advances in computation power, it is a simple matter to generate hashes of common (and not so common) passwords and store them in a database, and some of these are available online. Because these hashes are quick to compute and easy to store, MD5 is considered unsafe and should be avoided. SHA-1 has similar issues. You are better off using SHA-256 or SHA-512, or even better, Bcrypt. Bcrypt has the significant advantage of specifying a number of hash iterations. This slows down the computation of the hash, but because users only authenticate once per session (or less often if you use remember-me support), it's acceptable to incur this cost. But a hacker who is attempting a brute-force computational attack on your hashed passwords will be slowed down significantly if you use a large number of iterations.

One technique to make hashing more robust is using a "salt" for each password. This is a value that is included with the cleartext password when hashing, but is usually unique to the user. This way, two users with the same password will end up with different hash values, and this makes creating a lookup table of hash value much more computationally expensive.

On the other hand, other data that must be guarded in a datastore, but periodically must be available in its original form, is a candidate for encryption. Encryption is a complex subject, but there is support for it in the JDK with the Java Cryptography Extension (JCE). The Jasypt library (*http://www.jasypt.org/*) is an excellent tool to avoid having to deal with the implementation details of encrypting data, and there's even a Grails plugin for it: the `jasypt-encryption` plugin (*http://grails.org/plugin/jasypt-encryption*). Bouncy Castle (*http://www.bouncycastle.org/*) is another popular library with even more options than Jasypt, and the Jasypt plugin has support for using Bouncy Castle too, so you can use both if you want.

Best practices

It's important to secure the information that is used to generate your hashes and to encrypt and decrypt your data. Encryption algorithms typically use passwords and keys, so if a hacker is able to get access to these, then you might as well have stored the data in cleartext.

Do not store passwords in config files, or even in files on the filesystem. Instead, create a web page that you use to initialize the system where people trusted with passwords enter the passwords (using SSL!) when the application starts up. Ideally, you shouldn't trust any one person with all of the information to start the system. For example, to use JCE encryption, you will need to load a `java.security.KeyStore`, and this requires a password, and you use this to create a `javax.crypto.SecretKey`, which also requires a password. Use different passwords. If two people know the key store password and two other people know the key password (it's a good idea to have backup users in case someone isn't available), then no one person can decrypt the data or be coerced into giving someone else access.

Here are some general best practices:

- Use Bcrypt with a large number of iterations; alternatively, if you use a traditional hashing algorithm, use a strong one (e.g., SHA-256 or SHA-512, never MD5 or SHA-1), and use a salt value for each password.
- Don't store passwords on the filesystem, in code, or in source control.

- Rotate keys and change passwords frequently.

- Use crypto keys that are at least 128 bits.

- Don't write sensitive information to logfiles.

- Avoid native database encryption; use strong algorithms and encrypt the data yourself and store that.

- *Never* implement your own hash or crypto algorithm.

You can read the OWASP Guide to Cryptography (*https://www.owasp.org/index.php/Guide_to_Cryptography*) for more information.

A8: Failure to Restrict URL Access

When most people think about Grails application security, they think of the Spring Security and Shiro plugins. They are both excellent options for guarding access to various application URLs. They're not the only options, however; commercial options are also available, and application servers typically offer URL access protection features.

The Spring Security plugin offers three approaches to guarding URLs: annotations, database "requestmaps," and a simple mapping of URLs and their required roles. In addition, there is a "strict" mode option where URLs that do not have explicit access rules defined are blocked. This errs on the side of caution, assuming that it is better to have annoyed users and testers who cannot access URLs that they should have access to until the misconfiguration is fixed than it is to have users annoyed by discovering that information has been made available to unauthorized users because someone forgot to properly configure access to part of the site. Enabling this is simple, just a single line in *Config.groovy*:

```
grails.plugins.springsecurity.rejectIfNoRule = true
```

This vulnerability is relatively easy to test. You need to have a good sitemap to know what all of the available URLs are, but you should have this already for other uses. Given that information, it is typically just a mechanical process to write functional tests against a running server that request guarded URLs and assert that you are prompted to log in. Once you do authenticate, you can assert that all of the URLs that should be accessible to you (by virtue of granted roles, user type, etc.) are accessible, and that those that shouldn't be accessible are not.

A9: Insufficient Transport Layer Protection

It's relatively easy to intercept network traffic, so anything that shouldn't be viewable by an attacker should be guarded. One of the easiest ways to do this is to use SSL for your web traffic. This can lead to some unexpected behaviors though, especially related to the session ID cookie.

Authentication should be done using SSL, because you don't want to risk sending your users' passwords in the clear. It's simple enough to do this; using the Spring Security plugin, you can use the `forceHttps` property in *Config.groovy*:

```
grails.plugins.springsecurity.auth.forceHttps = true
```

and access to the login form will be redirected to the same URI but on the secure port (by default, 443). You can also use the "channel security" configuration to explicitly define that the login form URL (by default, `/login/auth`), and optionally other URLs, requires SSL. The problem here is that, if you only use SSL for authentication, the cookie has to be insecure in order to be usable on the other pages of the site. If you set the `secure` flag, the browser will only send the cookie over SSL, and accessing pages on the non-SSL port will not have access to it, and your users will appear to not be authenticated. But, if you omit this flag, the cookie can be intercepted, because it is sent as a request header with every request. So you trade encrypted passwords for the possibility that attackers can access your users' cookies and send them with their own requests, and access the site as an authenticated user.

Athough there is a small cost to using SSL due to the processing work encrypting the pages, you should consider using SSL for the entire site. Then, everything is transmitted securely and the data is significantly less likely to be accessed by attackers. This all hinges on proper SSL configuration, and ensuring that the certificates are renewed as needed and that they are purchased from reliable vendors. The certificate should use strong encryption, with a key size of at least 128 bits.

You can also encrypt traffic between servers such as between the web servers and database server. For example, in MySQL, you can configure the server to use an SSL certificate and create a user that requires SSL by appending `REQUIRE SSL` to the `GRANT` statement:

```
GRANT SELECT, INSERT, UPDATE, DELETE on database_name.* to username@servername
IDENTIFIED BY 'the password' REQUIRE SSL;
```

The web servers must also be configured to use SSL by configuring system properties for the location of the key store and trust store and their passwords. The JDBC URL must also be updated with the required SSL configuration options. This is typically overkill for most applications and will incur a performance cost for all database access, so only configure this if you need this level of security.

A10: Unvalidated Redirects and Forwards

Blindly redirecting or forwarding users to other URLs exposes them to being taken advantage of by attackers. For example, someone could use a cross-site scripting vulnerability in your site or fake an email containing a link that uses your site to redirect or forward to another site. This one could possibly install malware, or be styled like your site and trick users into revealing information, because they might think that they are still on your site.

If you do have a feature like this that accepts URLs as parameters, there are a couple of different approaches you can use to make the process safer. Don't create URLs like */some/url?nextPage=/user/home* because that could be changed to */some/url?nextPage=http://anyothersite.com/some/other/page*. In general, if you are building these URLs in GSP-generated pages, use `flash` scope to temporarily store the next URL and use a controller to retrieve the URL from `flash` scope and redirect or forward there. If the user can't see or set the values, you have the control. If you need to embed URLs in emails, use a placeholder code instead, such as */some/url?nextPage=a2*, and use the code to compute or look up the real URL.

And, of course, if you don't need to parameterize this process, don't. If the application always knows where the next page in the workflow is, there is no need to use hidden or obfuscated data.

Security Plugins

There are two primary plugins that secure Grails applications: `spring-security-core` (*http://grails.org/plugin/spring-security-core*) (and its secondary add-on plugins) and `shiro` (*http://grails.org/plugin/shiro*). Both are robust plugins with most or all of the authentication and authorization security features you will need and are backed by well-known security implementations. There are other plugins, and you have probably seen tutorials or blog posts promising how easy it is to "roll your own" security solution, typically with filters. I don't advise this approach; it's best to take advantage of the hard work and experience of others and use tested, proven frameworks and algorithm implementations.

I'll focus on the Spring Security plugins here because I'm most familiar with those, but don't take that as a quality judgement of Spring Security versus Shiro—Shiro is a great security framework and plugin, and if you find it more intuitive to use than Spring Security, then use it instead.

spring-security-core

The original security plugin based on Spring Security was the Acegi plugin (so named because at the time it was based on the Acegi security framework, before it was renamed to Spring Security). Over several releases, it became somewhat bloated with various features and support for several authentication providers (LDAP, OpenID, etc.) that weren't needed by every developer. One motivation in creating the `spring-security-core` plugin was to address this by creating a small "core" plugin with form-based authentication backed by database storage of users and roles, and optional add-on plugins that could be installed as needed to add extra functionality.

The `spring-security-core` plugin has many features available, including:

- Form-based authentication with a username and password
- HTTP Basic, Digest, and X509 browser certificate authentication
- URL-based access control (optionally stored in the database)
- Role-based access control
- Database storage of users and roles using Grails domain classes (although easily customizable to use any source)
- Password hashing, optionally salted
- Security-related GSP tags (`ifLoggedIn`, `ifAllGranted`, `ifAnyGranted`, etc.)
- A utility service
- Easy configuration of authentication and authorization event handlers
- Remember-me cookie support
- Support for Ajax authentication
- Configuration for URLs that require SSL
- Admin "run-as" support to temporarily act as another user
- Session fixation prevention

In addition, the plugin (like Spring Security itself) is highly customizable. All of the Spring beans that are needed are explicitly created by the plugin (rather than using schema-based autoconfiguration) so as to make it easy to override beans in the containing application. In addition, any default bean dependencies are explicitly created as their own beans—again, to make reconfiguring them easier. And all bean properties are set from the Grails configuration; there are sensible default values for most settings (except those that must be user-specified), and the settings are specified in *Config.groovy* to take advantage of configuration externalization, environment support, and using Groovy code to set the values. It's also easy to add additional authentication providers and filters, both in extension plugins and in your own application.

In addition, there are extension plugins that build on the core plugin to add additional features and authentication providers. These include:

Spring Security ACL
Adds support for object-level and method-level authorization using ACLs (access control lists)

Spring Security AppInfo
Provides a basic UI to view the security configuration

Spring Security CAS
Adds support for single sign-on using Jasig CAS

Spring Security OpenID
> Adds support for OpenID authentication

Spring Security Facebook
> Adds support for Facebook authentication

Spring Security Kerberos
> Adds support for single sign-on using Kerberos

Spring Security LDAP
> Adds support for LDAP and ActiveDirectory authentication

Spring Security Mock
> Adds support for fake/mock authentication during developement

Spring Security RADIUS
> Adds support for RADIUS authentication

Spring Security Shibboleth Native SP
> Adds support for `container provided` Shibboleth authentication

Spring Security Twitter
> Adds support for Twitter authentication

Spring Security UI
> Provides CRUD screens and other user management workflows

Getting started

It only takes a few minutes to get started and add security to your application. Like any plugin, you add a dependency in *BuildConfig.groovy* in the `plugins` section:

```
plugins {
    runtime ":hibernate:$grailsVersion"
    build ":tomcat:$grailsVersion"
    ...
    compile ':spring-security-core:1.2.7.3'
}
```

Run `grails compile` to trigger the dependency resolution and plugin installation. Then run the `s2-quickstart` script, which creates user and role domain classes as well as login and logout controllers and associated GSPs. Note that using domain classes and even a database at all is entirely optional. There is a chapter of the plugin's user guide that describes how to write your own `UserDetailsService` implementation that lets you decide where the user and role data is stored, if you need to use something other than a database, or a different database configuration than the default supplied by the plugin.

And that's all it takes to get started. Be sure to check out the plugin documentation for a more complete tutorial and more information about configuration options.

Access control

After running the `s2-quickstart` script, everything is ready to go but, of course, you need to define the access rules for the various pages in your application. By default, the plugin is configured to use annotations in your controllers:

```
import grails.plugins.springsecurity.Secured

class MyController {

    @Secured(['ROLE_USER'])
    def someAction() {
        ...
    }

    @Secured(['ROLE_ADMIN'])
    def someOtherAction() {
        ...
    }

    ...
}
```

This is my preference, because I like having the security information defined in the classes that are being guarded. But there are two other approaches that you can use; one is to specify a mapping of URLs and associated roles in the `interceptUrlMap` configuration property in *Config.groovy*, and the other uses a `Requestmap` domain class to store the mappings in the database. Here's an example of the `interceptUrlMap` property:

```
grails.plugins.springsecurity.interceptUrlMap = [
    '/secure/**':    ['ROLE_ADMIN'],
    '/finance/**':   ['ROLE_FINANCE', 'IS_AUTHENTICATED_FULLY'],
    '/js/**':        ['IS_AUTHENTICATED_ANONYMOUSLY'],
    '/css/**':       ['IS_AUTHENTICATED_ANONYMOUSLY'],
    '/images/**':    ['IS_AUTHENTICATED_ANONYMOUSLY'],
    '/*':            ['IS_AUTHENTICATED_ANONYMOUSLY'],
    '/login/**':     ['IS_AUTHENTICATED_ANONYMOUSLY'],
    '/logout/**':    ['IS_AUTHENTICATED_ANONYMOUSLY']
]
```

The advantage of the `interceptUrlMap` property is that everything is defined in one place, and because it's defined in *Config.groovy*, it can be programmatically generated or externalized. Storing the mappings in the database is flexible, because it supports updating the access rules while the application is running. Use whichever approach makes sense for your applications.

Other Plugins and Libraries

Spring Security and Shiro provide URL and object security but do little for other aspects of securing web applications—in particular, many of the items on the OWASP top 10 list. To protect your application against those types of attacks, there are a few good options that you can use in your applications.

AntiSamy

The AntiSamy library (*http://bit.ly/12eR0bF*) is helpful when you accept user input and display it again, such as allowing comments. You can avoid XSS attacks by using AntiSamy to remove malicious text (e.g., `<script>` and `<iframe>` tags) from user input. It uses an XML policy file with extensive rules for how to work with HTML, CSS, and JavaScript. The project includes policy files based on the rules used by Slashdot, eBay, and Myspace, so you can use those directly or use them as a starting point for your own policy file.

You can use the library directly, or install the Markup Sanitizer Plugin (*http://grails.org/ plugin/sanitizer*), which integrates AntiSamy. It adds a codec that provides an `encodeAs SanitizedMarkup` method, a service with utility methods, and a `markup` constraint for domain classes.

ESAPI

The OWASP Enterprise Security API (ESAPI (*http://bit.ly/10XJJKD*)) project is more extensive than AntiSamy, but has a different focus. It includes several features that overlap with Spring Security and Shiro, including authentication and authorization, but it has input validation and output encoding functionality that augment what Spring Security and Shiro offer.

The library has methods that are useful input validation and for escaping CSS, HTML, and JavaScript, such as `encodeForCSS`, `encodeForHTML`, `encodeForHTMLEntity`, and `encodeForJavascript`. It also has support for other formats, such as strings for SQL (`encodeForSQL`) and LDAP (`encodeForLDAP`) queries. Unlike AntiSamy, which removes tags, the ESAPI encoder replaces characters with format-specific safe strings.

You can use the library directly or install the `xss-sanitizer` plugin (*http://grails.org/ plugin/xss-sanitizer*). The plugin integrates ESAPI and adds a servlet filter that escapes all request parameters and headers.

HDIV

The HDIV (*http://www.hdiv.org/*) project adds protection against parameter tampering and XSS, SQL injection, and CSRF attacks. Using the library in Spring MVC (as of version 3.1) and Grails (as of version 2.3) is mostly transparent, because HDIV provides an implementation of the Spring `org.springframework.web.servlet.support.Re` `questDataValueProcessor` interface. This is used by the Spring and Grails form tags automatically. HDIV will also hook into the validation process, updating the `Errors` instance with information about SQL injection detection and other validation problems for fields.

HDIV can also help with "insecure direct object references" risks. It can replace object identifiers with generic values that are used as keys to retrieve the actual identifier values stored at the server. This reduces the risk that hackers can guess identifiers for objects that they don't have permission to view.

CSRF attack support is provided by hashing all form values (as long as you use Grails tags to generate the HTML) to generate a CSRF token. This is added to forms in a hidden tag and to links as an extra query string parameter. These tokens can then be validated at the server to detect tampering or other attacks.

To add HDIV to your project, install the `hdiv` plugin (*http://grails.org/plugin/hdiv*). It configures many sensible defaults for you and it is easy to customize the configuration in *Config.groovy*. Note that because HDIV support was only added to Grails for version 2.3, the plugin will not work with older versions of Grails.

General Best Practices

Don't trust users. You can't expect that users will do the right thing. Hackers will try to break in, and regular users might too. Don't assume that server requests will be the result of a click in or a form submission from your user interface—it's easy to create a GET or POST request programmatically. A corollary to this is that you cannot presume that client-side validations were used, so include them to make your site more usable and helpful, but always perform server-side checks.

Require strong passwords; don't trust that your users will make sensible decisions about security. If a user chooses a naive password and gets hacked, it is mostly the user's fault, but you are also at fault for not protecting users from themselves. Require a minimum length of at least eight characters, a mix of upper- and lowercase, special characters, etc. Here's an example of a user class that uses built-in constraints and a custom validator to ensure that the password cannot the same as the username, be null (the implicit default constraint), blank, shorter than 10 characters, longer than 128, and must include at least one number, one uppercase letter, and one special character (one of !, @, #, $, %, ^, or &):

```
class User {

    String username
    String password

    // other fields and methods
```

```
static constraints = {
    password blank: false, minSize: 10, maxSize: 128,
            validator: { password, user ->

        if (user.username && user.username == password) {
            return 'user.password.error.username'
        }

        if (!password.matches('^.*(?=.*\\d)(?=.*[a-zA-Z])(?=.*[!@#$%^&]).*$')) {
            return 'user.password.error.strength'
        }
    }

    // other validation checks
    }
}
```

Be careful when accepting user input. Be aware that users may be malicious, so don't trust their input when constructing queries, and be careful about concatenating strings when building HQL or SQL queries. If you will be redisplaying user input (either for them or for other users), ensure that the input is filtered or escaped to avoid XSS and CSRF exploits. Use automatic HTML encoding by ensuring that `grails.views.de fault.codec = "html"` is set in *Config.groovy*.

Validate and escape when processing submitted inputs, but also consider doing the same when redisplaying it, because otherwise you have to assume that all stored data was properly checked when submitted, and that it wasn't changed in a potentially unsafe way afterward. This will add a small processing cost, but given the risks, should be considered a worthwhile tradeoff.

Don't reinvent any wheels; use proven technologies and frameworks. Use Spring Security or Shiro, or a commercial security implementation. Use strong encryption when you need to be able to decrypt the data, and use robust hash algorithms for passwords and other data that won't be decrypted (e.g., Bcrypt or SHA-256/SHA-512, but never MD5 or SHA-1).

Consider not using the remember-me feature. Requiring passwords for each authentication makes it less likely that another person can use your site after someone has logged in and left the computer.

Use a CAPTCHA on your login pages to help ensure real people are attempting to authenticate. reCAPTCHA (*http://www.google.com/recaptcha*) is an excellent implementation, and there is a Grails plugin, the `recaptcha` plugin (*http://grails.org/plugin/recaptcha*).

Enforce password expiration policies. Store the date that each user changes their password, and use a Quartz job or some other scheduled process to look for users with passwords that have expired. Spring Security has a feature to help with this; the generated user domain class has a `passwordExpired` field that defaults to `false` but that you can set to `true`. Subsequent login attempts will fail, and you can use this to redirect users to a page where they must change their password; be sure to require the current password and to check that the new password is different from the expired one.

Use SSL for all of your site's pages. It will take slightly more processing power, but this isn't a problem with modern hardware.

Use a recent version of a web server that supports the Servlet 3.0 spec so you can set the `HttpOnly` flag to block script access to your session cookie.

Don't use HTTP Basic authentication, which sends the username and password very weakly encoded to the server for every request. If you must use Basic authentication, use SSL so at least the password is transmitted securely.

Think about security from the beginning of development. Just like testing and documentation, it's not always fun, but if you wait until the end of the project, it's unlikely that you will have the time to retrofit a sensible security implementation.

Don't use "security by obscurity" and hope that because it's not obvious that some parts of your application aren't locked down enough that hackers won't get access. Automated tools can find a surprising amount of information when given time.

Don't store production database passwords or other sensitive information in application code or configuration files like *DataSource.groovy* or *Config.groovy*, because the strings will end up in the *.class* files and can be read if an attacker gets access to your deployed WAR file. Use JNDI for your database connectivity, or use the `grails.config.loca tions` attribute in *Config.groovy* to externalize the production database values. You can either hardcode the file location, or if you're using Tomcat, you can take advantage of its *lib* directory being in the classpath and put an external configuration file there. Set the property to something like this:

```
grails.config.locations = [
    "classpath:${appName}-config.groovy",
    "file:./${appName}-config.groovy"]
if (System.properties["${appName}.config.location"]) {
    grails.config.locations << 'file:' +
            System.properties["${appName}.config.location"]
}
```

and put the database information in a file call *myappname-config.groovy* with the prefix `dataSource` for all of the properties you would have set in *DataSource.groovy*; for example:

```
dataSource.driverClassName = 'com.mysql.jdbc.Driver'
dataSource.dialect = org.hibernate.dialect.MySQL5InnoDBDialect
dataSource.username = 'the username'
```

```
dataSource.password = 'the password'
dataSource.url = 'jdbc:mysql://localhost/the_database_name'
```

To be even more secure, delete the external config file after the server has successfully started up because the information will be available in-memory.

Use `autocomplete='off'` in your authentication page's `<form>` element or at least for the username input. This will keep the browser from caching the form element information and make it less easy for others to authenticate as your users when using their computers. This can be disabled with browser plugins, so it isn't in any way a guarantee, but it will help.

Don't use the JavaScript `eval` function (or `setTimeout` or `setInterval`) with untrusted JSON inputs. Use `JSON.parse` or trusted toolkit APIs (e.g., jQuery) that use best practices.

Take advantage of the feature of servlet containers where files under the *WEB-INF* folder are not accessible by clients. Any datafile that should not be viewable in a browser should be under the *WEB-INF* and accessed using Spring's resource API.

Don't display stacktraces or other internal information on your error pages. In addition to being embarrassing, it gives hackers extra information that they might be able to use against you. Recent versions of Grails create an *error.gsp* similar to this one; if you are using an older version, use a similar environment check to display a simple error message in production and optionally the full stacktrace and error message in development:

```
<!DOCTYPE html>
<html>
   <head>
      <title><g:if env="development">Grails Runtime Exception</g:if>
            <g:else>Error</g:else></title>
      <meta name="layout" content="main">
      <g:if env="development">
         <link rel="stylesheet" type="text/css"
               href="${resource(dir: 'css', file: 'errors.css')}">
      </g:if>
   </head>
   <body>
      <g:if env="development">
         <g:renderException exception="${exception}" />
      </g:if>
      <g:else>
         <ul class="errors">
            <li>An error has occurred</li>
         </ul>
      </g:else>
   </body>
</html>
```

Use GSP comments, not HTML comments, to put notes in your GSPs. It's easy to view the source of your generated HTML and see the comments, so if you want to include comments that will not be rendered in the HTML, use either of these two comment syntaxes:

```
<%-- your comment here --%>
```

or:

```
%{-- your comment here --}%
```

Do regular code reviews or use pair programming to look for potential security vulnerabilities. It's too easy to accidentally make a mistake when you're rushing to get a feature completed, or even knowingly allow a vulnerability, assuming that you will have time to fix it before the code is deployed. A code review will keep you honest and get more eyes on potential issues, hopefully finding problems early while they're still inexpensive to fix.

Test your security. Do not use unit or even integration tests to test access control, because they use mocks, and your tests will only be checking the mocks, not the real security implementation. Use functional tests, and be as comprehensive as is practical, ideally checking all application URLs. Free and commercial automated testing tools are available that can scan your application for many known vulnerabilities and can automate the process of finding issues. This can be significantly more productive than human testing or code reviews (although these are still needed too).

Consider getting a security audit. Security companies are available and will attack your application to perform a penetration test using the same techniques as hackers, and will help you to find and fix vulnerabilities. It's impractical to expect developers to "think like hackers," in the same way that it is difficult to think like a naive user when trying to find usability issues. Except for rare cases, we're developers, not security experts.

You should also familiarize yourself with the new approach taken to parameter and data binding, described in this blog post (*http://blog.springsource.org/2012/03/28/secure-data-binding-with-grails/*). Changes were made in Grails 2.0.2 to the data binding process to change the binding order to ensure that dependency-injected Spring beans aren't changed, excluding static, transient, and dynamically typed properties by default, and adding whitelist and blacklist support in domain classes rather than having to clutter application code with inclusions and exclusions.

The Cloud

"The cloud" is a buzz topic right now, and for good reason. Cloud computing isn't the best approach for every deployment, but for many scenarios, using a cloud provider can save time and money, and make your applications less susceptible to traffic surges. It can also greatly simplify your deployment process and IT needs.

There is no one definition of cloud computing, and it is starting to become a misused term (some are now referring to any online service as a cloud service). In fact, there are three models of cloud computing: infrastructure as a service (IaaS), software as a Service (SaaS), and platform as a service (PaaS). They're all cloud services though—meaning, they're available over the Internet as metered ("pay as you go") services. SaaS examples include popular consumer services like Gmail, Hotmail, Facebook, and YouTube and also more specialized software services available in a metered fashion over the Internet. Amazon EC2, VMware vCloud, and Linode are popular IaaS options, and Amazon Elastic BeanStalk, Heroku, Cloud Foundry, and Cloudbees are popular PaaS options. Although Grails developers may integrate or create SaaS solutions, we will focus on IaaS and PaaS, because they are more integral to the development and deployment process. Also note that although Google App Engine is a viable option for traditional Java applications, Grails applications typically don't do well there; consider using Gaelyk (*https://gaelyk.appspot.com/*) instead to take advantage of a Groovy-based Grails-like environment.

The approach of hosting as a service rather than the more traditional product-based hosting typically means that the provider makes computing resources available to you over the Internet. So, instead of buying hardware that the provider hosts and monitors for you, they provide everything but your applications and data. This includes the "physical" servers (which are usually virtualized, to make it easier for them to provision new instances and decommission unused instances), as well as services such as relational databases, NoSQL datastores, storage, clustering, and others and features such as high availability, job scheduling, and even Hadoop and more.

Typically, cloud services are provided by a third party, but they can also be self-hosted, private cloud solutions that function like those provided externally, such as if you were to self-host an implementation of VMware's Cloud Foundry. The model is the same, and you have the same flexibility and elasiticity to add or remove capacity as needed, but you have the benefit of avoiding going out to the Internet, and security concerns are reduced. You can also implement hybrid solutions, mixing public and private cloud services (often at the expense of added integration complexity).

Cost Savings

Users will typically see savings in multiple ways when using cloud solutions. These include not having to purchase or maintain hardware; cloud providers can better take advantage of economies of scale because they buy significant amounts of hardware. They also often buy large servers with multiple processors and lots of RAM and use virtualization to create multiple virtual servers for each physical server. And you will also typically need a smaller IT staff when you outsource your hardware in this way, and can take advantage of the provider's often more experienced IT staff.

Typically, cloud providers implement a "utility computing" payment model where you pay for bandwidth, CPU time, disk storage, and other resources on a metered basis. You can use this to your advantage, because you only pay for what you use; if you anticipate an upcoming increase in site traffic (because of a sale, a holiday, students returning back to school in the fall, or another event), you can simply provision more servers. Once the traffic returns to regular levels, you return the temporary instances to the provider's pool.

What You Give Up

Although there are significant advantages to deploying to a cloud provider, there are also disadvantages. You lose a lot of freedom, because many choices are made for you. If you deploy to a traditional provider where you (or the provider) install or mirror an operating system, you get to install and/or configure some or all of the servlet container, database, a frontend static web server such as Apache or nginx, and other services and applications. You will be unlikely to have direct access to the filesystem, access to more than a few TCP/IP ports, or features such as IP multicast (which can make configuring distributed systems more convenient). You will even be limited in which version(s) of the Java JDK you can use (and, in the case of Google App Engine, many JDK classes and methods that you use often and take for granted). So there is a tradeoff when deploying to a cloud provider, and you need to consider what you gain and what you lose and determine if what the provider makes available is consistent with your deployment needs.

Cloud Foundry

Cloud Foundry (*http://cloudfoundry.com/*) is VMware's entry in the cloud space, and it's a strong one. VMware shook things up when they announced their open source cloud solution in April 2011. Offering a hosted solution (in beta at the time of this writing), as well as a downloadable "micro cloud" that runs in a virtual machine on your own laptop or server, and the option to view and enhance the code base (and even contribute new features back to VMware) make Cloud Foundry an interesting option. Although *cloudfoundry.com* is still a beta service and has no paid options or service agreements, there are commercial implementations of Cloud Foundry available that are independent of VMware, such as AppFog (*https://www.appfog.com/*).

The standard client that developers use to deploy applications is vmc (*http://start.cloud foundry.com/tools/vmc/installing-vmc.html*). It's a Ruby application, but it runs on Windows, Linux, and Mac OS, as long as you have Ruby and a few dependencies installed. Groovy/Grails Tool Suite (GGTS) (*http://grails.org/products/ggts*) also has excellent support for Cloud Foundry through its add-on; you can simply drag and drop your project onto the configured Cloud Foundry server node to deploy your application, and various wizards help you configure and attach services and configure your application runtime. But being Grails developers, your best bet is the `cloud-foundry` plugin (*http://grails.org/plugin/cloud-foundry*).

There are several services available to Cloud Foundry applications, including MySQL and PostgreSQL relational databases, MongoDB and Redis NoSQL stores, and RabbitMQ messaging, and all are supported with a corresponding Grails plugin and by the Cloud Foundry plugin.

Database Applications

To create a Grails application that uses a database (MySQL or PostgreSQL) and host it at Cloud Foundry, take the following steps:

1. Create an account (*https://my.cloudfoundry.com/signup*) if you haven't already.

2. Create the Grails application like you would for any hosting provider, but don't worry about the production datasource configuration yet.

3. Install the `cloud-foundry` plugin (*http://grails.org/plugin/cloud-foundry*) by adding it to *BuildConfig.groovy*.

4. Store your username and password in *$HOME/.grails/settings.groovy* or *Config.groovy*.

5. Configure a database service, either MySQL or PostgreSQL (or you can wait and have this automatically done for you when deploying).

6. Deploy the application, binding the database service that you already created, or creating and binding a new one as part of the deployment step.

That's not a lot of work, and once you've created an account and added your login credentials to *$HOME/.grails/settings.groovy*, it's even simpler for the second application (assuming you want to automatically create and bind a database service):

1. Create the Grails application.
2. Install the `cloud-foundry` plugin (*http://grails.org/plugin/cloud-foundry*).
3. Deploy the application, creating and binding a new database service.

You'll notice that there's no configuration mentioned other than specifying your login credentials. That's not an omission; it's how the deployment process works. The plugin includes a Spring bean postprocessor—`grails.plugin.cloudfoundry.AppCloudSer viceBeanPostprocessor`, although most of the functionality is in its `grails.plu gin.cloudsupport.AbstractCloudBeanPostprocessor` base class from the cloud-support plugin (*http://grails.org/plugin/cloud-support*)—that reconfigures the `Data Source` bean based on the runtime database service information that Cloud Foundry makes available during deployment. As long as you have a `dataSource` bean configured and the `VCAP_SERVICES` environment variable set, its JSON content is parsed and the database username, password, and URL values will be used to reconfigure the `data Source` bean for you. This is obviously convenient, because you don't have to run a command to find the cryptic connection values. But it also means there's next to zero coupling with the hosting provider. So you can easily change to a different cloud or more traditional hosting provider, or even deploy to multiple providers.

Creating an application

To make this more concrete, let's look at an example. I'll assume that you already have a Cloud Foundry account, and that you've added your username and password to *$HOME/.grails/settings.groovy* (the file isn't created for you, so create a new empty file if you haven't already done so) to avoid having your password in source control; for example:

```
grails.plugin.cloudfoundry.username = 'your_username'
grails.plugin.cloudfoundry.password = 'your_password'
```

Add a dependency on the `cloud-foundry` plugin to your application's *BuildConfig.groovy* in the `plugins` section:

```
plugins {
    runtime ":hibernate:$grailsVersion"
    runtime ':jquery:1.7.1'
    runtime ':resources:1.1.6'
    build ":tomcat:$grailsVersion"
```

```
    compile ':cloud-foundry:1.2.1'
}
```
and run `grails compile` to let the plugins resolve. If you want to use a MySQL database, add a dependency for its driver in the `dependencies` section:
```
dependencies {
    runtime 'mysql:mysql-connector-java:5.1.16'
}
```
otherwise, add a dependency for the PostgreSQL driver:
```
dependencies {
    runtime 'postgresql:postgresql:8.4-702.jdbc3'
}
```
Create a simple domain class so we can test the database persistence:
```
$ grails create-domain-class cloud.foundry.test.Person
```
and add some fields so it looks something like this:
```
package cloud.foundry.test

class Person {
    String firstName
    String lastName
}
```
Generate a static scaffolded UI:
```
$ grails generate-all cloud.foundry.test.Person
```
Enable the database console with the `grails.dbconsole.enabled` attribute in the `pro duction` section in *Config.groovy* so we can take a look at the database and run some queries once the application is deployed:
```
environments {
    ...
    production {
        ...
        grails.dbconsole.enabled = true
    }
}
```
Also add some logging code in *BootStrap.groovy* to display the database connection information so we can use it to connect with the database console UI:
```
import grails.converters.JSON

class BootStrap {

    def init = { servletContext ->
        String VCAP_SERVICES = System.getenv('VCAP_SERVICES')
```

```
            println "VCAP_SERVICES: ${System.getenv('VCAP_SERVICES')}\n"

            def json = JSON.parse(VCAP_SERVICES)
            def service = json.find { it.key.startsWith('mysql') }.value[0]
            def hostname = service.credentials.hostname
            def port = service.credentials.port
            def credentials = service.credentials
            def user = service.credentials.user
            def password = service.credentials.password
            println """
    MySQL url:     jdbc:mysql://$hostname:$port/$credentials
            user:     $user
            password: $password"""
        }
    }
```

And that's it—we'll leave the settings in *DataSource.groovy*, alone because the connection settings will be reconfigured for us when deploying. You can add some extra JDBC URL parameters to a placeholder URL to configure the database if you want; for example, to enable Unicode and UTF-8:

```
environments {
    ...
    production {
        dataSource {
            ...
            url = 'jdbc:mysql://localhost/db?useUnicode=true&characterEncoding=utf8'
        }
    }
}
```

> The cf-push (and cf-update) script can deploy an existing WAR file; for example, if you have a nonstandard build that requires more than running grails war, but by default will create a WAR for you. Because all Grails commands except war and test-app default to the development environment unless a different one is specified, it's very important that you always run grails prod cf-push and grails prod cf-update to ensure that you build a WAR optimized for a production deployment.

Run the cf-push command to deploy the application. You should see output similar to this if you don't already have a MySQL service configured and you let the script add and bind it for you (be sure to choose a unique application name):

```
$ grails prod cf-push
| Environment set to production.....
Building war file
| Done creating WAR target/cf-temp-1331686075902.war
>
```

```
Application Deployed URL: 'testing-testing-testing-1-2-3.cloudfoundry.com'? y
>
Would you like to create and bind a mysql service?[y,n] y
Service 'mysql-84fba3d' provisioned.
>
Would you like to create and bind a postgresql service?[y,n] n

Creating application testing-testing-testing-1-2-3 at
testing-testing-testing-1-2-3.cloudfoundry.com with 512MB and services [mysql-84fba3d]:
 OK
Uploading Application:
  Checking for available resources:
 OK
  Processing resources:
 OK
  Packing application:
 OK
  Uploading (452K):
 OK

Trying to start Application: 'testing-testing-testing-1-2-3'.
.....

Application 'testing-testing-testing-1-2-3' started at
http://testing-testing-testing-1-2-3.cloudfoundry.com
```

 Although the cf-push script builds an entire WAR file (typically at least 25 MB), you can see from the output that only 452 K was transferred to Cloud Foundry (this isn't a fixed value; the number will be different for each application). This is because the client is smart enough to calculate a hash of all of the files in your WAR file and compare them to previously uploaded files, and not upload anything that's already available at the server. This is particularly helpful for JAR files, because it's very likely that other users have already deployed applications with the Grails, Spring, Hibernate, and other library JARs that your application is using. So you only need to upload rarely used JARs and your actual application classes and files.

View the contents of the *stdout.log* file from the server with the cf-get-file script, and it should look something like this:

```
$ grails cf-get-file logs/stdout.log
| Environment set to development.....

VCAP_SERVICES: {"mysql-5.1":[{"name":"mysql-84fba3d","label":"mysql-5.1",
"plan":"free","tags":["mysql","mysql-5.1","relational"],
"credentials"{"name":"d2df723ab1f14440a9dcbd37af9c1a4d1",
"hostname":"172.30.48.22","host":"172.30.48.22","port":3306,
"user":"umASXSmfZneBu","username":"umASXSmfZneBu","password":"pMKFw9EqZNuOS"}}]}
```

```
MySQL url:    jdbc:mysql://172.30.48.22:3306/d2df723ab1f14440a9dcbd37af9c1a4d1
user:         umASXSmfZneBu
password:     pMKFw9EqZNuOS
```

If you navigate to the root URL of your application, it should display the start page with a link to the scaffolded controller you created, as shown in Figure 10-1.

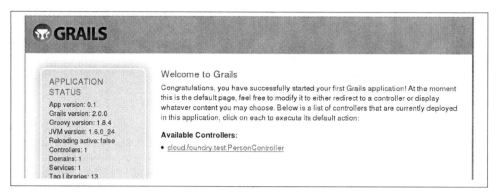

Figure 10-1. Home page of the test application

You can open up the database console by navigating to */dbconsole/*; choose Generic MySQL from the Saved Settings drop-down and enter the URL, username, and password that was in the server logfile to log in. Figure 10-2 shows the console after connecting.

Figure 10-2. Database console UI

There's not much to see yet, because the application just started, but you can open up the Person CRUD pages and add some data so you can run some queries. You can also run show create table person to see the DDL that was used to create the table; it should show that it's an InnoDB table (because the plugin configures the appropriate Hibernate Dialect for you) and that it uses UTF-8 charset (from the JDBC URL settings that you added to *DataSource.groovy*).

Scaling

Initially, your application will be deployed on a single Tomcat instance, but it's easy to scale up your deployment with the cf-update-instances script (*http://bit.ly/10XKAL8*) and view instance information with the cf-show-instances script (*http://bit.ly/117l19v*).

You can see the single instance running with the cf-show-instances script:

```
grails> cf-show-instances
| Environment set to development.....


+-------+---------+--------------------+
| Index | State   | Start Time         |
+-------+---------+--------------------+
| 0     | RUNNING | 03/14/2012 02:11AM |
+-------+---------+--------------------+
```

and increase it to four instances (the maximum, because the account is limited to 2 GB of memory across all instances, and each is 512 MB by default) with the cf-update-instances script:

```
grails> cf-update-instances 4

Scaled 'testing-testing-testing-1-2-3' up to 4 instances.
```

You can see that three new instances get allocated but aren't immediately available, because the Tomcat instances need some time to start up and deploy the WAR file:

```
grails> cf-show-instances


+-------+----------+--------------------+
| Index | State    | Start Time         |
+-------+----------+--------------------+
| 0     | RUNNING  | 03/14/2012 02:11AM |
+-------+----------+--------------------+
| 1     | STARTING | 03/14/2012 08:27PM |
+-------+----------+--------------------+
| 2     | STARTING | 03/14/2012 08:27PM |
+-------+----------+--------------------+
| 3     | STARTING | 03/14/2012 08:27PM |
+-------+----------+--------------------+
```

All four instances should be running soon afterward though:

```
grails> cf-show-instances

+-------+---------+--------------------+
| Index | State   | Start Time         |
+-------+---------+--------------------+
| 0     | RUNNING | 03/14/2012 02:11AM |
+-------+---------+--------------------+
| 1     | RUNNING | 03/14/2012 08:27PM |
+-------+---------+--------------------+
| 2     | RUNNING | 03/14/2012 08:27PM |
+-------+---------+--------------------+
| 3     | RUNNING | 03/14/2012 08:27PM |
+-------+---------+--------------------+
```

And you can scale back down at any time:

```
grails> cf-update-instances 1

Scaled 'testing-testing-testing-1-2-3' down to 1 instance.
```

HTTP sessions

Cloud Foundry uses sticky sessions between your instances, so functionality that depends on a consistent HTTP session will work well for the most part, because all requests will go to a single server. Sessions aren't replicated, however, so if the server that a user is on crashes, the HTTP session will be lost, and after getting redirected to another server, the session will have to be reinitialized. If authentication credentials are stored in the session, the user will no longer be authenticated and have to log in again.

Server crashes are rare, but you might consider using an alternative approach to session management. There are three plugins that you can use to change how sessions and session data are stored: `database-session` (*http://grails.org/plugin/database-session*) (which stores sessions in a relational database), `mongodb-session` (*http://grails.org/plugin/mongodb-session*) (which stores sessions in a MongoDB datastore), and `cookie-session` (*http://grails.org/plugin/cookie-session*) (which stores sessions in a cookie, limiting you to a total of 4 KB of session storage).

NoSQL, RabbitMQ, and Searchable

In addition to traditional relational databases, Cloud Foundry supports the MongoDB (*http://www.mongodb.org/*) and Redis (*http://redis.io/*) NoSQL stores and RabbitMQ (*http://www.rabbitmq.com/*) messaging. And, if your application uses one or more of the `mongodb` (*http://grails.org/plugin/mongodb*), `redis-gorm` (*http://grails.org/plugin/redis-gorm*), or `rabbitmq` (*http://grails.org/plugin/rabbitmq*) plugins and you have the corresponding Cloud Foundry services configured for your application, the bean postprocessor that updates the `dataSource` bean will do the same autoreconfiguration of the connection configuration for these services. The plugin also has support for ensuring that the Lucene index created by the `searchable` plugin (*http://grails.org/plugin/searchable*) gets created in a writeable directory.

Monitoring and the Cloud Foundry UI Plugin

The primary function of the Cloud Foundry plugin is to deploy and update your application, but it also has scripts that can give you a view into what's happening with your application.

Grails interactive mode makes monitoring your application from the command line a lot faster, because you only incur the JVM startup and Spring application context configuration once. Just execute `grails` to get started:

```
$ grails
| Enter a script name to run. Use TAB for completion:
grails>
```

Once the application is running, you can look at the *stdout.log* and *stderr.log* files with the `cf-logs` command (*http://bit.ly/XNnryC*):

```
grails> cf-logs
| Environment set to development.....
==== logs/stderr.log ====
Mar 14, 2012 1:06:23 AM org.apache.coyote.http11.Http11Protocol init
INFO: Initializing Coyote HTTP/1.1 on http-51810
Mar 14, 2012 1:06:23 AM org.apache.catalina.startup.Catalina load
INFO: Initialization processed in 379 ms
...

==== logs/stdout.log ====
VCAP_SERVICES: {"mysql-5.1":[{"name":"mysql-84fba3d","label":"mysql-5.1",
"plan":"free","tags":["mysql","mysql-5.1","relational"],
"credentials"{"name":"d2df723ab1f14440a9dcbd37af9c1a4d1",
"hostname":"172.30.48.22", "host":"172.30.48.22","port":3306,
"user":"umASXSmfZneBu","username":"umASXSmfZneBu",
"password":"pMKFw9EqZNuOS"}}]}


MySQL url:    jdbc:mysql://172.30.48.22:3306/d2df723ab1f14440a9dcbd37af9c1a4d1
      user:    umASXSmfZneBu
      password: pMKFw9EqZNuOS
```

Use the `cf-info` script (*http://bit.ly/16YtDEk*) to see your allocated memory, services, and application usage:

```
grails> cf-info

VMware's Cloud Application Platform
For support visit http://support.cloudfoundry.com
Target:   http://api.cloudfoundry.com (v0.999)
```

```
User:      beckwithb@vmware.com
Usage:     Memory   (512.0M of 2.0G total)
           Services (1 of 16 total)
           Apps     (1 of 20 total)
```

Use the `cf-stats` script (*http://grails-plugins.github.com/grails-cloud-foundry/docs/manual/ref/Scripts/cf-stats.html*) to see the runtime CPU, memory, and disk usage, and total uptime for your application:

```
grails> cf-stats

+-----------+-------------+----------------+--------------+---------------+
| Instance  | CPU (Cores) | Memory (limit) | Disk (limit) | Uptime        |
+-----------+-------------+----------------+--------------+---------------+
| 0         | 0.3% (4)    | 382.2M (512M)  | 41.0M (2G)   | 0d:1h:46m:42s |
+-----------+-------------+----------------+--------------+---------------+
```

You can also use the `cf-list-files` script (*http://grails-plugins.github.com/grails-cloud-foundry/docs/manual/ref/Scripts/cf-list-files.html*) to get a directory listing at the server:

```
grails> cf-list-files /tomcat/webapps/ROOT/js

application.js                     183B
```

and the `cf-get-file` script (*http://grails-plugins.github.com/grails-cloud-foundry/docs/manual/ref/Scripts/cf-get-file.html*) to view a file once you've found it with the `cf-list-files` script.

The cloud-foundry-ui Plugin

You can get a lot of information by using the command-line scripts, but they can be tedious and impractical to work with. There is an add-on plugin for the `cloud-foundry` plugin—the `cloud-foundry-ui` plugin (*http://grails.org/plugin/cloud-foundry-ui*)—that creates a simple but very useful monitoring frontend for your application. To use it, install it just like you did the `cloud-foundry` plugin; that is, add it to *BuildConfig.groovy*:

```
plugins {
    runtime ":hibernate:$grailsVersion"
    runtime ':jquery:1.7.1'
    runtime ':resources:1.1.6'
    build ":tomcat:$grailsVersion"

    compile ':cloud-foundry:1.2.1'

    compile ':cloud-foundry-ui:1.1.1'
}
```

There isn't much configuration required for this plugin, but you will need to add some controller mappings in *UrlMappings.groovy*. You have flexibility in the prefix of the URLs, but the other values must be the same as these:

```
class UrlMappings {

    static mappings = {
        "/$controller/$action?/$id?"{
            constraints {
                // apply constraints here
            }
        }

        "/admin/cfDashboard/$action?"(controller: 'cloudFoundryDashboard')

        "/admin/cfDashboard/application/$appName"(
                controller: 'cloudFoundryDashboard', action: 'application')

        "/admin/cfDashboard/service/$serviceName"(
                controller: 'cloudFoundryDashboard', action: 'service')

        "/admin/cfDashboard/files/$appName/$instanceIndex?"(
                controller: 'cloudFoundryDashboard', action: 'files')

        "/"(view:"/index")
        "500"(view:'/error')
    }
}
```

In this example, I've used the /admin prefix to differentiate the URLs from the main site, and to make it easier to guard the pages with security, because I can most likely use a wildcard pattern for /admin/**. Once you've installed the plugin and deployed the application with cf-push or updated an existing application with cf-update, you can navigate to the root URL that you defined in *UrlMappings.groovy*, such as *http://appname.cloudfoundry.com/admin/cfDashboard*.

If you set your Cloud Foundry username and password in *Config.groovy*, then you'll immediately see the UI screens. If you set the values in *$HOME/.grails/settings.groovy*, however, they're not available at runtime, so you'll be prompted with a login screen, as shown in Figure 10-3, to enter your credentials so the plugin can make API calls on your behalf.

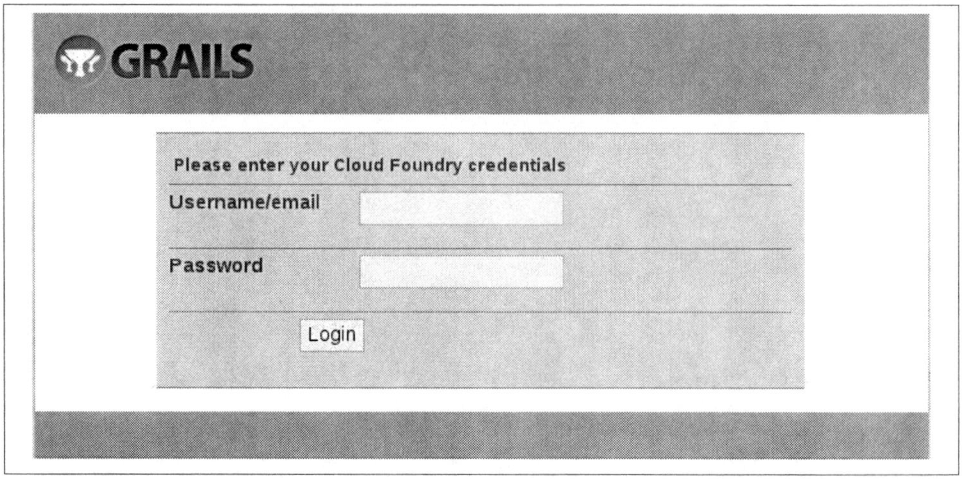

Figure 10-3. Login screen

Once you've logged in, click the toolbar button with your application name, and you'll see the statistics dashboard as shown in Figure 10-4.

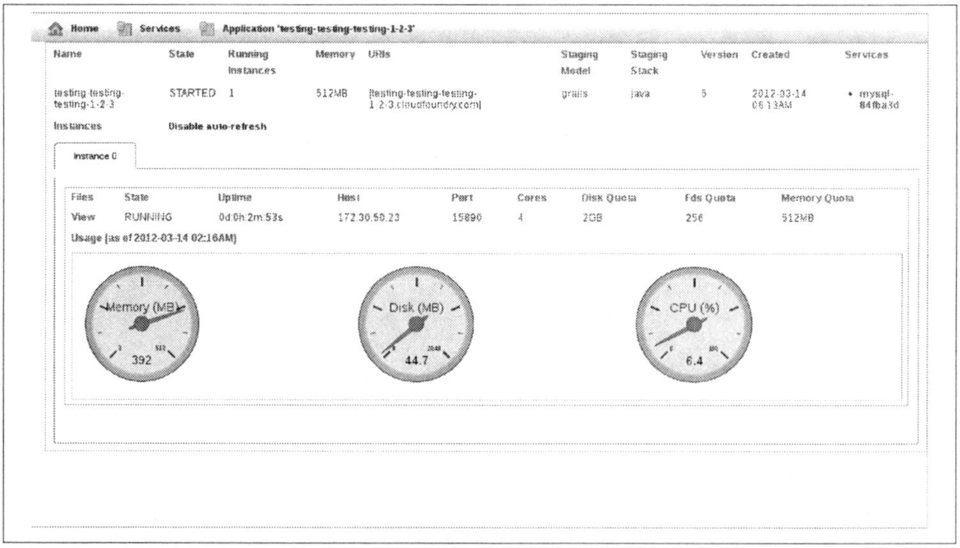

Figure 10-4. Statistics page

The gauges update themselves every five seconds unless you click the "Disable auto-refresh" link. If you click the View link on the left under Files, you'll see the file viewer pages like the example in Figure 10-5 that allow you to see the entire directory tree (as much as you're allowed to see, anyway) and view any file.

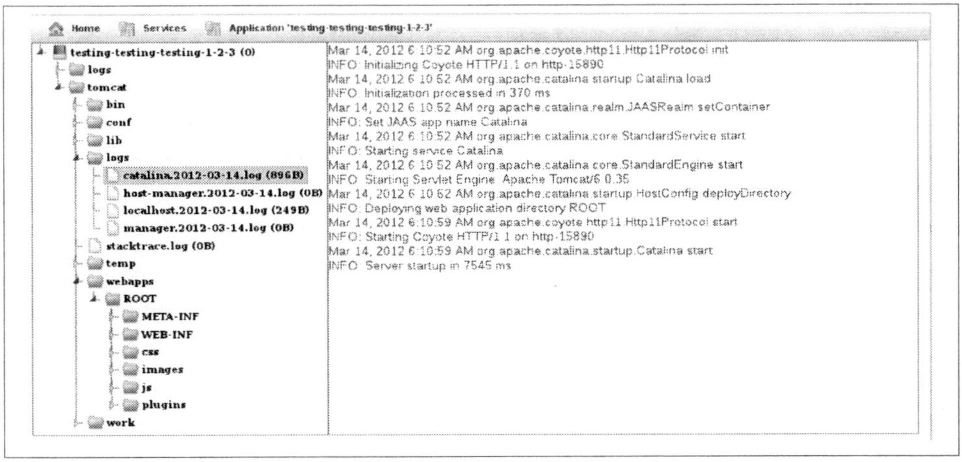

Figure 10-5. File viewer

You can also right-click on any file to download it to your local machine.

Heroku

Heroku (*http://www.heroku.com/*) is another great cloud hosting option for Grails applications. For a long time, Heroku was known for hosting Rails and other non-JVM platforms, but they have jumped into JVM hosting with both feet and provide a solid deployment option for Grails and Java applications. It's a more established solution than Cloud Foundry, so their add-on selection is much more extensive.

The workflow for creating Grails applications and deploying them to Heroku is quite similar to that for Cloud Foundry. As of this writing, there isn't a Java API client for Heroku's REST API yet, so you end up using a mix of the Grails plugin, the heroku command-line client, and Git tools to get everything going, but even so, it is still an easy process.

The Heroku deployment philosophy is quite different from that of Cloud Foundry; instead of building and deploying a standard WAR file, you create your project and commit it to a local Git repository, and configure a Git remote at the Heroku servers. Pushing to the Heroku remote triggers the deployment process, and the server-side components (a "build pack" in Heroku terminology) package up your application and deploy it.

The Heroku model is convenient, because you'll end up using less bandwidth to push the initial application and to update and redeploy changes. Cloud Foundry does use an intelligent hashing approach to avoid uploading files that are already available at the server so you don't actually upload an entire WAR in either case, but with Heroku, you only push application code. JAR files and plugin dependencies referenced in *BuildConfig.groovy* are resolved at the Heroku servers when building the WAR file. This convenience comes at a small cost, however; you cannot use unreleased or locally modified plugins. This isn't a general problem, because most of the time you will be using released plugins, but it makes testing new plugins somewhat harder. One workaround is to publish the in-progress plugins to your own plugin repository (as long as it's accessible to Heroku's servers), and you can also publish a snapshot release of an in-progress plugin in the central Grails plugin repository (if you're the plugin owner).

Heroku add-ons that work well with Grails applications include their PostgreSQL, Memcache, MongoHQ and MongoLab, RabbitMQ, and Redis To Go services. All are supported with a corresponding Grails plugin and by the Heroku plugin.

Database Applications

The general workflow for creating a Grails application that uses a PostgreSQL database and hosting it at Heroku is as follows:

1. Create an account (*https://api.heroku.com/signup*) if you haven't already.
2. Install the `heroku` client (*http://bit.ly/17eeP2R*) and a Git (*http://git-scm.com/*) client.
3. Create the Grails application like you would for any hosting provider, but don't worry about the production datasource configuration yet.
4. Install the `heroku` plugin (*http://grails.org/plugin/heroku*) by adding it to *BuildConfig.groovy*.
5. Commit your application code to a local Git repository.
6. Register the application with the `heroku create` command (this also creates a Git remote so you can push to deploy).
7. Deploy the application with `git push`.

You don't have to register a database add-on, because all Grails applications get a small, free PostgreSQL instance.

Like with the Cloud Foundry plugin, there's hardly any configuration needed, because the `heroku` plugin uses a similar approach where a Spring bean postprocessor (`grails.plugin.heroku.HerokuBeanPostprocessor`) reconfigures the `DataSource` bean based on the runtime database service information that Heroku makes available during deployment. Instead of one large JSON string in a single environment variable like Cloud Foundry, each add-on registers its own environment variable(s), such as `DATABASE_URL` for the PostgreSQL add-on; `MONGOHQ_URL` for the MongoHQ add-on; `MEMCACHE_SERVERS`, `MEMCACHE_USERNAME`, and `MEMCACHE_PASSWORD` for Memcache; and so on. You could run `heroku config` and use the connection information there to hardcode values in *DataSource.groovy*, but it's best to use the plugin and stay as decoupled as possible to leave your options open.

Creating an application

Let's look at an example of deploying to Heroku. I'll assume that you already have a Heroku account and that you've installed the `heroku` and `git` clients and have authenticated at Heroku.

Add a dependency on the `heroku` plugin to your application's *BuildConfig.groovy* in the `plugins` section:

```
plugins {
    runtime ":hibernate:$grailsVersion"
    runtime ':jquery:1.7.1'
    runtime ':resources:1.1.6'
    build ":tomcat:$grailsVersion"

    compile ':heroku:1.0.1'
}
```

and run `grails compile` to let the plugins resolve. Add a dependency for the PostgreSQL driver:

```
dependencies {
    runtime 'postgresql:postgresql:8.4-702.jdbc3'
}
```

Create a simple domain class so we can test the database persistence:

```
$ grails create-domain-class heroku.test.Person
```

and add some fields so it looks something like this:

```
package heroku.test

class Person {
    String firstName
    String lastName
}
```

Generate a static scaffolded UI:

```
$ grails generate-all heroku.test.Person
```

Enable the database console with the `grails.dbconsole.enabled` attribute in the `production` section in *Config.groovy* so we can take a look at the database and run some queries once the application is deployed:

```
environments {
    ...
    production {
        ...
```

```
        grails.dbconsole.enabled = true
    }
}
```

Also add some logging code in *BootStrap.groovy* to display the database connection information so we can use it to connect with the database console UI:

```
import grails.plugin.heroku.PostgresqlServiceInfo

class BootStrap {

    def init = { servletContext ->
        String DATABASE_URL = System.getenv('DATABASE_URL')
        if (DATABASE_URL) {
            try {
                PostgresqlServiceInfo info = new PostgresqlServiceInfo()
                println "\nPostgreSQL service ($DATABASE_URL): url='$info.url', " +
                        "user='$info.username', password='$info.password'\n"
            }
            catch (e) {
                println "Error occurred parsing DATABASE_URL: $e.message"
            }
        }
    }
}
```

Leave the settings in *DataSource.groovy* alone, because the connection settings will be reconfigured for us when deploying.

Now we just need to initialize the Git repo and configure the Heroku project. Run `git init`:

```
$ git init
Initialized empty Git repository in /home/burt/workspace/heroku_grails/.git/
```

Run `grails integrate-with --git` to create a *.gitignore* file, and add the files and commit them:

```
$ grails integrate-with --git
| Created Git project files..
$ git add .
$ git commit -m "initial commit"
[master (root-commit) 78181a3] initial commit
 69 files changed, 4487 insertions(+), 0 deletions(-)
 create mode 100644 .classpath
 create mode 100644 .gitignore
 create mode 100644 .project
 create mode 100644 application.properties
 ...
```

Create the application using `heroku create`:

```
$ heroku create --stack cedar
```

This command creates the application at Heroku's server (but doesn't deploy anything yet). You can verify this by going to *https://api.heroku.com/myapps* where it will be listed along with any other application you may have created. The command also registers a Git remote to Heroku, which you can see by running `git remote -v`.

And we're now ready to deploy. It's as simple as pushing the commited application files to the Heroku remote added by `heroku create`, so run `git push heroku master` and watch the output. You'll see that your application JAR and plugin dependencies are resolved at the server, and a WAR file will be created and deployed to a Jetty server instance. If there's an error during deployment, the Git push will fail and you can fix the issue, commit the changes, and push again to try deploying with the fixes applied.

If the deployment is sucessful, you can run `heroku logs` to see the server log output, and run `heroku logs -t` to "tail" the log and continuously display updated lines of output. The PostgreSQL connection information in the logs should look something like this:

```
PostgreSQL service (
postgres://syrmypn:Dp_RHcV@ec2-23-21-182-175.compute-1.amazonaws.com/syrmypn):
url='jdbc:postgresql://ec2-23-21-182-175.compute-1.amazonaws.com:5432/syrmypn',
user='syrmypn', password='Dp_RHcV'
```

If you navigate to the root URL of your application, it should display the start page with a link to the scaffolded controller you created. Figure 10-6 shows an example.

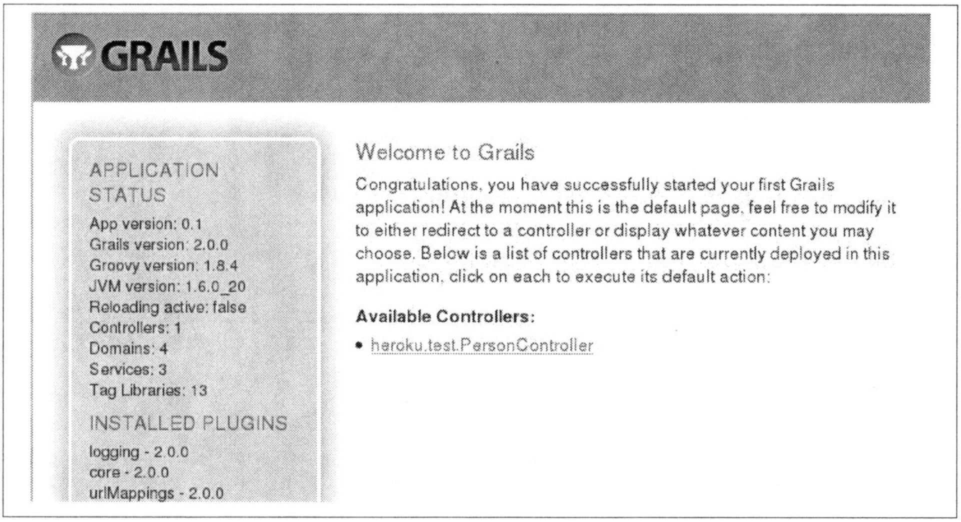

Figure 10-6. Home page of the test application

You can open up the database console by navigating to */dbconsole/*; choose Generic PostgreSQL from the Saved Settings drop-down and enter the URL, username, and password that was in the server logfile to log in. Figure 10-7 shows the console after connecting.

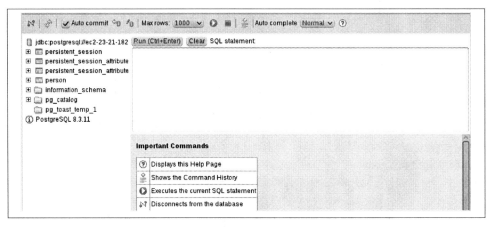

Figure 10-7. Database console UI

There's not much to see yet because the application just started, but you can open up the Person CRUD pages and add some data so you can run some queries.

Scaling

Initially, your application will be deployed on a single Jetty instance, but it's easy to scale up your deployment with the heroku scale command:

```
$ heroku scale web=4
Scaling web processes... done, now running 4
```

and if you rerun heroku logs -t after increasing the server count, you'll see the three new instances logging startup messages (each message contains the web instance it was generated by).

Unlike the equivalent Cloud Foundry command, this isn't limited by your account's quotas, because you pay for additional resources.

Each account gets 750 "dyno hours" free per month, and a single application deployed on one instance running full time for a month will use 744 hours; so, as long as you use the free versions of the various add-on services, you won't have to pay anything for your hosting. But once you add one or more web processes, you'll go beyond the 750 hour limit and have to pay for the rest.

Use the heroku ps command to get some state and uptime information about the various instances:

```
$ heroku ps
Process  State        Command
-------  ----------   ---------------------------------------
web.1    up for 38m   java $JAVA_OPTS -jar server/jetty-..
web.2    up for 4m    java $JAVA_OPTS -jar server/jetty-..
web.3    up for 4m    java $JAVA_OPTS -jar server/jetty-..
web.4    up for 4m    java $JAVA_OPTS -jar server/jetty-..
[source,java]
```

HTTP sessions

Heroku does not offer session affinity, sticky sessions, or session clustering options. This means that functionality that depends on a consistent HTTP session will not work on Heroku. This includes basic HTTP session storage, but also Grails `flash` scope, because that is implemented by storing the flash-scope data in the session until the next request. It also means that plugins like `spring-security-core` that store authentication details in your session will not work; you can authenticate, but because your requests will be randomly assigned to different servers, you'll appear logged in only on one instance but not the others. Whereas alternative approaches to session management are an option for Cloud Foundry, they're more necessary for Heroku.

The `heroku` plugin depends on the `database-session` plugin, so by default, your users will continue to split requests across multiple servers, but the session data will be stored in the PostgreSQL database and shared across all servers. If you prefer to use the MongoDB version of the plugin, add an exclusion for the `database-session` plugin in *BuildConfig.groovy* and add a dependency for the `mongodb-session` plugin (*http://grails.org/plugin/mongodb-session*):

```
plugins {
    runtime ":hibernate:$grailsVersion"
    runtime ':jquery:1.7.1'
    runtime ':resources:1.1.6'
    build ":tomcat:$grailsVersion"

    compile(':heroku:1.0.1') {
        excludes 'database-session'
    }

    compile ':mongodb-session:0.1'
}
```

Or if you prefer to use cookie-based storage (and you're confident that user sessions won't go beyond the 4 K limit), use the `cookie-session` plugin (*http://grails.org/plugin/cookie-session*) instead:

```
plugins {
    runtime ":hibernate:$grailsVersion"
    runtime ':jquery:1.7.1'
    runtime ':resources:1.1.6'
```

```
    build ":tomcat:$grailsVersion"

    compile(':heroku:1.0.1') {
        excludes 'database-session'
    }

    compile ':cookie-session:0.1.2'
}
```

Build Packs

The process for deploying applications in the various platforms that Heroku supports varies widely, so they have abstracted the process with the concept of a buildpack (*https://devcenter.heroku.com/articles/buildpacks*). For Grails applications, this involves downloading a Grails/Jetty bundle that is created separately for each version of Grails, running the Grails war script for your application source code in their copy of the Git repo, and generating a Procfile that defines how to start the Jetty server for your WAR file.

These buildpacks are open source and hosted at GitHub (*https://github.com/heroku/heroku-buildpack-grails*). This means that you can suggest changes to the standard Grails buildpack by submitting a pull request, or even create your own buildpack to customize the build process. Using a custom buildpack is very simple; all you need to do is reference the URL to the source. See the Heroku documentation (*https://devcenter.heroku.com/articles/buildpacks#using-a-custom-buildpack*) for more details.

Other Providers

Heroku and Cloud Foundry are far from the only cloud options for deploying Grails applications. There are many providers that can host JVM-based applications, with varying levels of direct or indirect support for Grails. Some of these include:

- Amazon Elastic BeanStalk (*https://aws.amazon.com/elasticbeanstalk/*) is a provider from Amazon that uses AWS services; there is a plugin (*http://grails.org/plugin/aws*) that simplifies the process of working with the available services. There is also a detailed blog post on deploying a Grails application (*http://www.bobbywarner.com/2011/10/14/grails-on-aws/*) to Elastic BeanStalk.
- CloudBees (*http://www.cloudbees.com/*) is another solid option, and there is also a Grails plugin (*http://grails.org/plugin/cloud-bees*).
- Jelastic (*http://jelastic.com/*)
- dotCloud (*https://www.dotcloud.com/*)
- openShift (*https://openshift.redhat.com/app/*)

Other Uses for Cloud Services

You use cloud providers for more than just deployment—continuous integration (CI) of applications and plugins. Travis CI (*https://travis-ci.org/*) is a free CI provider with support for Grails; see this blog post (*http://bit.ly/138I0nf*) for some pointers on getting started. CloudBees has a free cloud-based CI product called BuildHive (*https://build hive.cloudbees.com/*) that can support Grails. See this blog post (*http://bit.ly/ 10XUQ67*) for information about using it, and this slide deck (*http://slidesha.re/ 12fw0lg*) for an overview of the Grails CloudBees plugin and using BuildHive for CI.

CHAPTER 11
AOP

Aspect-oriented programming (AOP) is a powerful technique to simplify software by identifying "cross-cutting concerns," or functionality that cannot be cleanly modularized into a single component, class, or module, and applying that logic centrally rather than scattering copies across the code base. In a Grails application, this might involve recognizing that security checks (or logging, timing, or any other shared logic) are required in services, controllers, and Quartz jobs, for example; although the purpose of each of these artifacts is quite different, they share a common need that "cuts across" the different types. There are several simplistic approaches that could be used, but they involve code duplication, artificial class hierarchies, or other brittle approaches that make the code harder to maintain. But using AOP would more likely be a much cleaner and more maintainable approach, because there isn't a proper object-oriented approach that can solve the problem.

AOP is a large topic, but for the sake of this discussion, let's focus on `before`, `after`, `around`, and `after-throwing` interception, which is useful to separate *what* gets executed from *when* it gets executed. `before` interception is where code runs before one or more specified methods, and potentially blocks access to the method by throwing an exception (e.g., in a security check where it's determined that you're not allowed) or does some work before the method runs (e.g., starting or joining a transaction). `after` interception cannot block access to the method, because it will already have been invoked, but it is an opportunity to do some work afterward (e.g., committing a transaction). `around` interception can be thought of as a combination of `before` and `after` interception, where you can do work before and/or after the method is invoked, invoke the method with different arguments, or choose to not invoke the method at all and instead perform another action. Finally, `after-throwing` interception happens when an exception is detected, allowing work after having entered an error state.

Spring has excellent support for AOP using proxies and dedicates an entire chapter in its documentation (*http://bit.ly/XNo0Z8*) to the subject. In addition, we'll see that Grails has a few AOP-like techniques that can be used in a more limited fashion (including Grails filters and servlet filters), and even Groovy can provide an AOP-like approach by using metaclass method and property interception and mix-ins.

To be fair though, there are some risks and costs in using techniques like this. Grails adds a lot of "magic" to your code—this is the essence of the "convention over configuration" approach where, if you name classes correctly, put them in the correct folder, and possibly add some configuration information, a lot of cool stuff is added to your classes—and AOP can add more. But, when this magic code that you can't see (at least not directly or conveniently) fails, it can be difficult sometimes to even know where to start looking for a fix. And done incorrectly, using AOP can actually trade complexity for complexity; different isn't necessarily better. And tooling can be limited, because although there is excellent IDE support for AOP and Groovy, there isn't anything out there as of this writing that works with both at the same time in a project.

Grails Filters

Let's start with a simple example of a Grails filter. Filters are backed by Spring `Handler Interceptor` instances, so they're limited to intercepting controller actions, whereas HTTP filters can intercept any request. You can create them by hand, but it's more convenient to use the `create-filters` script; for example:

```
$ grails create-filters aop.Book
```

which creates this starter filters class:

```
package aop

class BookFilters {

   def filters = {
      all(controller:'*', action:'*') {
         before = {

         }
         after = { Map model ->

         }
         afterView = { Exception e ->

         }
      }
   }
}
```

See the Grails documentation (*http://grails.org/doc/latest/guide/single.html#filters*) for detailed information on filters.

All four interception types are supported here. The `before` closure fires before any matching controller requests (you can limit which controllers and/or actions are intercepted with the `controller` and `action` arguments) and you can return `true` or `false` from the closure. `true` means that you want to allow the controller action to execute, and `false` will stop the workflow and not call the controller action. Returning nothing is the same as returning `true`. So you can do both `before` and `around` interception depending on the state at the time of the request, the current request URL or query parameters, or other criteria. You can perform some action and let the controller action fire (`before` interception) or handle the request yourself, rendering a response directly or forwarding or redirecting to another URL (`around` interception). `around` interception isn't directly supported, but can be implemented as a combination of `before` and `after` interception.

The `after` and `afterView` closures support `after` interception, because in both cases, the controller action will have been invoked. In the `after` closure, you have access to the model map that will be used in the view (typically a GSP) and can alter its contents, and also perform other post-action tasks. The `afterView` closure is similar, but it is called after the view is rendered, so you don't have an opportunity to alter the model map but you can perform other post-action tasks. It also allows `after-throwing` interception because you can detect that an exception has occurred by testing that the e variable is null or not, and do work for the exception case there.

For example, you could manage redirecting from an older URL scheme to a new one (e.g., after a site rework) with a filter like this (note that the `redirects` filter name is arbitrary):

```
redirects(controller:'*', action:'*') {
    before = {
        if (request.forwardURI =~ '/old/action') {
            redirect controller: 'new', action: 'action',
                    params: params, permanent: true
            return false
        }
        if (request.forwardURI =~ '/other/action') {
            redirect controller: 'newer', action: 'action',
                    params: params, permanent: true
            return false
        }
        if (request.forwardURI =~ '/thing/show') {
            response.sendError 404
            return false
        }
        ...
```

```
    }
}
```

Here, we check the incoming requested URL, and redirect to a new controller action if it matches /old/action or /other/action. If the URL matches /thing/show, we send a 404 error code, and we could also add some logging or some other logic. The logic here involves only before interceptors, so the optional after and afterView closures have been deleted.

And, in this example, we use the after block to add the currently logged-in user's username to the model map:

```
username(controller:'*', action:'*') {
    after = { Map model ->
        if (model != null && springSecurityService.loggedIn) {
            model.username = springSecurityService.principal.username
        }
    }
}
```

Note that the null check of the model is important because it will be null for redirects.

 Grails also supports simpler interceptors with the beforeIntercep tor and afterInterceptor closures in controllers; these are the same as Grails filters but can only apply to the controller they're defined in, and there is no afterViewInterceptor. This means that there's no way to handle exceptions, or do work after the view has been rendered, but before, around, and after interception would be the same as for filters.

HTTP Filters

HTTP filters are classes that implement the javax.servlet.Filter interface. This is a simple interface with only three methods: init and destroy are used to do initialization work at startup and cleanup work at shutdown, respectively, and doFilter is called for each request that the filter is configured to support:

```
void doFilter(ServletRequest request, ServletResponse response, FilterChain chain)
```

Filters are registered in *web.xml* with a filter element; for example:

```
<filter>
    <filter-name>charEncodingFilter</filter-name>
    <filter-class>org.springframework.web.filter.DelegatingFilterProxy</filter-class>
</filter>
```

Filters are also registered with a filter-mapping element to configure the URL pattern that the filter applies to; for example:

```
<filter-mapping>
   <filter-name>charEncodingFilter</filter-name>
   <url-pattern>/*</url-pattern>
</filter-mapping>
```

To edit *web.xml*, run the `install-templates` script (if you haven't already):

```
grails install-templates
```

and edit `src/templates/war/web.xml`.

You can write the class in Groovy or Java, but because they will typically apply to all requests (including static resources), the small overhead that Groovy adds can add up, so Java is usually a better choice.

The registered filters are called in order, which is determined by the position of the `filter-mapping` elements in *web.xml*, and they form a filter chain. The chain is forward-only, and each filter calls the next filter in the chain by calling `doFilter()` on the `FilterChain` instance. You can do work before and/or after calling `doFilter()`, and can stop filter processing by not calling `doFilter()`, and this is how the different interception approaches can be implemented.

You can do `before` interception by doing work before calling `doFilter()`. You can do `after` interception by doing work after calling `doFilter()`. `around` interception is possible by writing to the response `Writer` or `OutputStream` directly or redirecting or forwarding to another URL, and not calling `doFilter()`. And you can implement `after-throwing` interception by wrapping the `doFilter()` call in a `try/catch` block:

```
public void doFilter(ServletRequest req, ServletResponse res, FilterChain chain)
      throws IOException, ServletException {

   // do "before" and/or "around" work here

   try {
      chain.doFilter(req, res);

      // do "after" work here
   }
   catch (Exception e) {
      // do "after-throwing" work here
   }
}
```

Groovy AOP

You can use metaclass techniques in Groovy to intercept method calls and property access. These techniques are limited by the fact that they only work when calling the methods from Groovy, although they can work when calling Groovy or Java classes.

Things could be much simpler if you edit your code to add in hooks directly, such as adding `methodMissing` or `propertyMissing` methods. You could also directly implement the `GroovyInterceptable` marker interface that is used as a flag to Groovy to route all calls through the `invokeMethod` method. Java classes can also participate by extending `GroovyObjectSupport` and implementing `GroovyInterceptable`. These changes are impractical in general and impossible for classes that are already compiled, and it would be problematic to alter your own code this way (e.g., if the code were also used in non-Groovy projects). In these cases, because we cannot use standard object-oriented approaches, we'll look at approaches that use runtime metaprogramming to weave in extra functionality instead.

Consider this simple utility class with very useful `add` and `multiply` methods:

```
class MathUtils {
    int add(int i1, int i2) {
        i1 + i2
    }

    int multiply(int i1, int i2) {
        i1 * i2
    }
}
```

Because it's a Groovy class, we can register a metaclass override for the `invokeMethod` method that does any combination of `before`, `after`, `around`, and `after-throwing` interception for all method calls:

```
def mc = MathUtils.metaClass
mc.invokeMethod = { String name, args ->

    // do "before" and/or "around" work here

    try {
        def value = mc.getMetaMethod(name, args).invoke(delegate, args)

        // do "after" work here

        return value // or another value
    }
    catch (e) {
        // do "after-throwing" work here
    }
}
```

This approach intercepts every method, but you can look at the method name and arguments to determine if a particular method is one that should be handled specially or if you should just let the standard logic apply. There is a small overhead added by intercepting all method calls, however, so you can intercept individual method calls too:

```
def realAdd = MathUtils.metaClass.pickMethod('add', int, int)
MathUtils.metaClass.add = { int i1, int i2 ->

    // do "before" and/or "around" work here

    try {
        def sum = realAdd.invoke(delegate, i1, i2)

        // do "after" work here

        return sum // or another value
    }
    catch (e) {
        // do "after-throwing" work here
    }
}
```

Here we get a reference to the real add method and register a metaclass override, calling the real method (or not, depending on your business rules).

We can do the same for getting (and setting) properties. Given this simple data class:

```
class Person {
    String firstName
    String lastName
}
```

we can intercept all property access:

```
def mc = Person.metaClass
mc.getProperty = { String name ->

    // do "before" and/or "around" work here
    try {
        def value = mc.getMetaProperty(name).getProperty(delegate)

        // do "after" work here
        return value // or another value
    }
    catch (e) {
        // do "after-throwing" work here
    }
}
```

or individual properties:

```
def mc = Person.metaClass
def firstNameProperty = mc.getMetaProperty('firstName')

mc.getFirstName = { ->

    // do "before" and/or "around" work here
    try {
        def value = firstNameProperty.getProperty(delegate)
```

```
        // do "after" work here
        return value // or another value
    }
    catch (e) {
        // do "after-throwing" work here
    }
}
```

Registering Metaclass Interceptors

In Grails, there are two standard locations to register metaclass changes. In a plugin, you can use the doWithDynamicMethods closure, and in an application, typically this is done in *BootStrap.groovy*. The examples so far have described intercepting all or some methods in individual classes, but Grails provides convenient access to all classes of a particular artifact type (e.g., controllers, services, and domain classes) via the GrailsAp plication.

```
class BootStrap {

    def grailsApplication

    def init = { servletContext ->

        for (sc in grailsApplication.serviceClasses) {
            def mc = sc.clazz.metaClass
            mc.invokeMethod = { String name, args ->

                long startTime = System.currentTimeMillis()
                try {
                    return mc.getMetaMethod(name, args).invoke(delegate, args)
                }
                finally {
                    delegate.log.trace "Service method $name with args $args " +
                                       "took ${System.currentTimeMillis() - startTime}ms"
                }
            }
        }
    }
}
```

In the previous examples, be sure to check that the `getMetaMethod` and `getMetaProperty` calls return nonnull values. `invokeMethod` and `get Property` interceptors can be used to handle nonexistent methods and properties (e.g., to create DSLs and builders), but here we are interested in working with existing functionality. If the requested method doesn't exist, throw a `MissingMethodException` such as `throw new Missing MethodException(name, delegate.getClass(), args)` and throw a `MissingPropertyException` for invalid properties such as `throw new MissingPropertyException(name, delegate.getClass())`.

Error Code URL Mappings

Grails provides a simple but useful approach to handling particular exceptions during controller action processing, and this is a form of `after-throwing` interception. The default *UrlMappings.groovy* class that is generated by the `run-app` script includes a catch-all handler for all exceptions that display errors with *error.gsp*:

```
"500"(view:'/error')
```

But you can define more fine-grained mappings too. The default example directly renders a GSP, but it is more convenient to use a controller action, because you can do arbitrary work before rendering an error page, and URL mappings allow either a view, or a controller and action (although the action can be omitted to use the default action). Here is an example that uses an `ErrorsController` to handle three exception types— `java.lang.IllegalArgumentException`, `java.lang.NullPointerException`, and `MyException` (a custom application-defined exception)—with an action for each type, and retains the catch-all mapping for exceptions not specifically listed:

```
"500"(controller: "errors", action: "illegalArgument",
    exception: IllegalArgumentException)
"500"(controller: "errors", action: "nullPointer",
    exception: NullPointerException)
"500"(controller: "errors", action: "customException",
    exception: MyException)
"500"(view: "/errors/serverError")
```

Spring AOP

The Spring Framework is well known for its bean container, but its AOP functionality makes a significant amount of power available to the Spring (and Grails) developer. Spring AOP makes it easy to complement your object-oriented code with aspect-oriented code without having to use a special compiler. In addition, you can write your advice code in Java or Groovy instead of having to write your code in aspects (as you would when using AspectJ). Spring AOP is implemented by creating proxies at runtime that intercept method calls to the target instance, so you are limited to only using method interception. Also, only Spring beans are candidates for interception, so this includes Grails services, beans registered by Grails and installed plug-ins, and beans you have registered in your application in *resources.groovy*. See the Spring documentation (*http://bit.ly/XNo0Z8*) for more detailed information.

Spring AOP is configured either in the application context configuration files (using XML syntax or the Grails bean builder) or using AspectJ annotations; I'll describe the annotation approach here, because I find it to be the more convenient approach. These include `Aspect`, `Pointcut`, `Before`, `After`, and `Around` (in the `org.aspectj.lang.annotation` package). Only a subset of the AspectJ annotation functionality is supported (e.g., you can intercept `execution` but not `call`), which is itself a subset of the functionality supported by defining aspects in **.aj* Aspect files, but in practice, it is a large subset and is very powerful.

One example of Spring AOP that you have likely used in Grails is in transactional services. By default, services are transactional unless this is disabled with `static transactional = false`, and it's possible to have more fine-grained control over transaction demarcation with the `@Transactional` annotation. The services become transactional by being wrapped in a proxy that enforces the transaction configuration for the class, and for individual methods if configured. This is implemented by dynamically subclassing your class with CGLIB and retaining a reference to an instance of your service, then intercepting method calls and calling your methods as needed. The general transaction logic flow is something like this:

- If a transaction is disallowed (e.g., with `Propagation.NEVER`), throw an exception.
- If a new one is required (e.g., with `Propagation.REQUIRES_NEW`), suspend the current transaction (if active) and start a new one.
- If the propagation is `Propagation.SUPPORTS` and one is active, "join" it.
- If the propagation is `Propagation.REQUIRED` and one is active, "join" it, or create one otherwise.
- Call your application code.
- If an exception occurs, check if it's a runtime exception or error and automatically roll back the transaction (although autorollback exception classes can be customized).
- If the work succeeds and the transaction was new, commit it (otherwise, let the initiator of the active transaction commit it).

Essentially, this boils down to multiple `before` checks and `after` checks. The Spring Security `@Secured` annotation is similar, although the logic is all `before`. You can set default behavior and settings at the class level, and override at the method level. The checks involved at runtime are basically these:

- Determine if there is an active authentication.
- Check potentially complex rules (a combination of roles, IP addresses, SpEL expressions, etc.) to determine which to enforce.
- Disallow access by throwing an exception if there is no authentication and one is required, or you are authenticated but are not authorized to perform this action.
- Call your application code.

In both cases, there are many items to check and work to do based on various scenarios, and these are both simplified descriptions of the real logic involved. You certainly would not want this tangled with your application code, so letting Grails configure default transaction rules or adding a few annotations helps reduce the clutter dramatically.

Enabling Spring AOP

The Spring documentation describes two ways to enable AOP support in an `Applica tionContext`; one is to include a namespaced tag `<aop:aspectj-autoproxy/>` element and the other is to register a bean for the `AnnotationAwareAspectJAutoProxyCrea tor` class, such as `<bean class="org.springframework.aop.aspectj.annotation.An notationAwareAspectJAutoProxyCreator" />`. The two approaches are essentially equivalent; the namespaced tag is handled by the `org.springframework.aop.con fig.AspectJAutoProxyBeanDefinitionParser` configuration class, which registers an `AnnotationAwareAspectJAutoProxyCreator` bean with the bean name `org.spring framework.aop.config.internalAutoProxyCreator`.

Luckily, none of this is necessary in Grails, because the work is done for you by `CoreGrailsPlugin` in `doWithSpring`. This is also where the `context` namespace is registered (`xmlns grailsContext:"http://grails.org/schema/context"`) and the `<context:annotation-config>` element is registered (using the BeanBuilder equivalent `context.'annotation-config'()`), which configures Spring to autodiscover and register beans based on the existence of annotations such as `@Component`, `@Service`, `@Controller`, and `@Repository` (in the `org.springframework.stereotype` package). For more information on the Grails bean builder DSL syntax, see the documentation (*http://grails.org/doc/latest/guide/spring.html#theBeanBuilderDSLExplained*).

There is a configuration step required to get Spring to discover your annotated classes; the `grails.spring.bean.packages` configuration option in *Config.groovy* specifies a list of one or more package names to search the classpath for (because scanning the entire classpath would be unnecessarily expensive); for example:

```
grails.spring.bean.packages = ['com.mycompany.myapp.beans']
```

This search is also configured in `CoreGrailsPlugin` with `grailsContext.'component-scan'('base-package':packagesToScan.join(','))`.

It uses the Grails ClosureClassIgnoringComponentScanBeanDefinitionParser to do essentially the same search as a traditional <context:component-scan> element. The Grails class extends the Spring ComponentScanBeanDefinitionParser class to add Groovy-awareness to the scanning process. Note that you don't have to use autodiscovery; you can manually register the beans in *resources.groovy* if you prefer.

Defining AspectJ-Annotated Aspects

Spring AOP aspects must be Spring beans, and although most Grails artifacts are registered as Spring beans, none are good candidates for being aspects, or even base classes for them. So your aspect classes must be registered in the application context, either in *resources.groovy* or by adding an annotation such as @Component and adding their packages to the grails.spring.bean.packages list.

 A discussion of the syntax for values in AspectJ annotations is beyond the scope of this book. See the Spring AOP documentation (*http://bit.ly/XNo0Z8*) and AspectJ documentation (*http://www.eclipse.org/aspectj/docs.php*) for useful information and examples.

Let's look at some examples to get a sense for what is possible here.

When using annotations, you create empty methods with the @Pointcut annotation whose value contains the pointcut definition as a string. This isn't required; you can define them inline in the advice annotations (e.g., @Before, @Around), but it makes more sense to split them logically and combine them in the advice annotations. That way, you can easily reuse them, for example, in an abstract base class:

```
package book;

import org.apache.log4j.Logger;
import org.aspectj.lang.annotation.Pointcut;

public abstract class AbstractAspect {

    protected Logger log = Logger.getLogger(getClass());

    @Pointcut("execution(public * *..*Service.*(..))")
    public void publicServiceMethod() {}

    @Pointcut("execution(public groovy.lang.MetaClass getMetaClass()) ||" +
            "execution(public void setMetaClass(groovy.lang.MetaClass)) ||" +
            "execution(public Object getProperty(String)) ||" +
            "execution(public void setProperty(String, Object)) ||" +
            "execution(public Object invokeMethod(String, Object))")
    public void groovyObjectMethods() {}
```

```
    @Pointcut("execution(public * *$*(..))")
    public void groovyDollarSignMethods() {}
}
```

Here we have a `publicServiceMethod` pointcut that will match public methods in classes in any package and with any signature, in classes with names that end in `Ser``vice`. This can find beans that aren't Grails services, but there isn't a practical way to find all services. Another approach would be to use the `bean()` pointcut, looking for any bean whose name ends in `Service`:

```
@Pointcut("bean(*Service) && execution(public * *(..))")
public void publicServiceMethod() {}
```

But, again, this can find beans with names that coincidentally end in `Service` but aren't Grails services, such as the `userDetailsService` bean that the Spring Security Core plugin registers. If this happens, you can further customize the pointcut, for example, by limiting it to being in a package pattern:

```
@Pointcut("execution(public * com.yourco.yourapp..*Service.*(..))")
```

or excluding beans that aren't really matches:

```
@Pointcut("bean(*Service) && !bean(userDetailsService) && " +
          "execution(public * *(..))")
```

The other two pointcuts are there to identify methods added by the Groovy compiler: `getMetaClass` and `setMetaClass`, `getProperty` and `setProperty`, and `invokeMethod`, and methods with $ characters in them, such as `__$swapInit`, `super$1$toString`, and `super$1$wait`. We typically use them to exclude the identified methods (via `!groovyOb``jectMethods()`).

Here's an aspect that subclasses `AbstractAspect` to reuse its pointcuts, and adds around advice for "real" public service methods to log the execution time of method calls:

```
package book;

import org.aspectj.lang.ProceedingJoinPoint;
import org.aspectj.lang.annotation.Around;
import org.aspectj.lang.annotation.Aspect;
import org.springframework.stereotype.Component;
import org.springframework.util.StopWatch;

@Aspect
@Component
public class ServiceMethodTimingAspect extends AbstractAspect {

@Around("publicServiceMethod() && !groovyObjectMethods() && " +
        "!groovyDollarSignMethods()")
    public Object traceServiceMethodCall(ProceedingJoinPoint jp) throws Throwable {
        String name = jp.getSignature().getDeclaringTypeName() + '.' +
                      jp.getSignature().getName();
```

```
    StopWatch stopWatch = new StopWatch(name);
    stopWatch.start(name);
    try {
        return jp.proceed();
    }
    finally {
        stopWatch.stop();
        log.trace(stopWatch.shortSummary());
    }
    }
}
```

and another (written in Groovy because Spring doesn't care) to log at the beginning and at the end of method calls:

```
package book

import org.aspectj.lang.ProceedingJoinPoint
import org.aspectj.lang.annotation.Around
import org.aspectj.lang.annotation.Aspect
import org.springframework.stereotype.Component

@Aspect
@Component
class ServiceMethodCallAspect extends AbstractAspect {

@Around("publicServiceMethod() && !groovyObjectMethods() && " +
        "!groovyDollarSignMethods()")
    def traceServiceMethodCall(ProceedingJoinPoint jp) throws Throwable {
        String invocationDescription =
            "method '$jp.signature.name' of class [$jp.signature.declaringTypeName]"
        log.trace "Entering $invocationDescription"
        try {
            def result = jp.proceed()
            log.trace "Exiting $invocationDescription"
            return result
        }
        catch (Throwable e) {
            log.trace "Exception thrown in $invocationDescription", e
            throw e
        }
    }
}
```

To try this out, add these aspect classes to your application (in *src/java* and *src/groovy*) and add a simple service to *grails-app/services*; for example:

```
package book

class BookService {

    String foo() {
        return 'bar'
```

```
        }
    }
```

The aspects log at the "trace" level, so be sure to enable that in the `log4j` block in *Config.groovy* (or change them to `println` statements):

```
log4j = {
    ...
    trace 'book'
}
```

When you call `bookService.foo()` (e.g., in a Grails console), you should see output like this:

```
Entering method 'foo' of class [book.BookService]

Exiting method 'foo' of class [book.BookService]

2013-02-18 04:55:32,626 [Thread-14] TRACE book.ServiceMethodTimingAspect
StopWatch 'book.BookService.foo': running time (millis) = 33 Result: bar
```

Compile-Time Weaving

Spring AOP is very powerful, but its features are somewhat limitated in that only Spring beans can be advised, and only a subset of the AspectJ functionality is supported. It is possible to use AspectJ in a more traditional way in Grails applications, where the aspect interception calls are actually added to the bytecode of advised classes. This opens up many more possibilities, because now any class that is part of your application (or even a plug-in, because most plugins are distributed in source form) can be compiled with AspectJ weaving activated. This is problematic for Groovy-based projects though, because AspectJ's `ajc` compiler isn't aware of or very compatible with Groovy's `groovyc` compiler. But, you're in luck, because AspectJ can weave into compiled classes. So it's possible to use `javac` and `groovyc` to compile your Grails classes just as you are now, and hook into the compilation process and call `ajc` after that.

This is straightforward to do manually, but there is a plugin that makes it much easier: the `aspectj` plugin (*http://grails.org/plugin/aspectj*). It registers event listeners to hook into the compilation process (for both local development using `run-app` and when building WAR files to deploy on a server) and weave aspects into advised classes. It also enables the full functionality supported by AspectJ annotations (e.g., advising `call` and not just `execution` pointcuts) and even aspects written as **.aj* files, which allow the full power of AspectJ.

An example illustrates the power that this approach affords. Database updates should be done in a transaction, even when there is only a single change, because the workflow may be different in the future, and it's better to refactor the code early. And, although you may think you're only updating a single instance, that might not be the case, given how much GORM does for you under the hood. For example, deleting or updating an instance that has a mapped collection can affect both the top-level instance and collection items, and an exception after a partial update can result in inconsistent database state. Unfortunately, the controllers generated by the `generate-controller` and `generate-all` scripts create, update, and delete domain class instances from the controller (as of this writing). These should be refactored to let the database work be done in a transactional service method, calling the dependency-injected service from the controller, and the same goes for updates from Quartz jobs and other nontransactional artifacts.

So to help detect updates made outside of a transaction, we can advise calls to GORM methods in domain classes that are executed outside the context of a running transaction. These include the variants of `save` and `delete`, as well as `lock` (which makes no sense outside of a transaction) and the lesser-known `mutex` method. Those are instance methods, but we also want to check calls to static methods, including `lock`, `executeUpdate`, `saveAll`, `deleteAll`, and `findOrSaveWhere`. While we're here, let's also look for calls to `withTransaction` that happen during a transaction; this isn't a problem, it's just redundant.

This aspect class defines the various pointcuts for all of these methods, and before advice for the instance methods and static methods (two are required in order to make the domain class instance available when checking instance methods):

```
package book;

import java.util.ArrayList;
import java.util.Arrays;
import java.util.List;

import org.aspectj.lang.JoinPoint;
import org.aspectj.lang.annotation.Aspect;
import org.aspectj.lang.annotation.Before;
import org.aspectj.lang.annotation.Pointcut;
import org.springframework.transaction.support.TransactionSynchronizationManager;

@Aspect
public class TransactionCheckAspect {

    @Pointcut("@within(grails.persistence.Entity)")
    public void isDomainClass() {}

    @Pointcut("execution(public Object save()) ||" +
            "execution(public Object save(java.util.Map)) ||" +
            "execution(public Object save(boolean))")
    public void saveMethod() {}

    @Pointcut("execution(public void delete()) ||" +
            "execution(public void delete(java.util.Map))")
```

```
    public void deleteMethod() {}

    @Pointcut("execution(public Object lock())")
    public void lockMethod() {}

    @Pointcut("execution(public Object mutex(groovy.lang.Closure))")
    public void mutexMethod() {}

    @Pointcut("execution(public static Object lock(java.io.Serializable))")
    public void staticLockMethod() {}

    @Pointcut("execution(public static Integer executeUpdate(..))")
    public void executeUpdateMethod() {}

    @Pointcut("execution(public static java.util.List saveAll(..))")
    public void saveAllMethod() {}

    @Pointcut("execution(public static void deleteAll(..))")
    public void deleteAllMethod() {}

    @Pointcut("execution(public static Object findOrSaveWhere(java.util.Map))")
    public void findOrSaveWhereMethod() {}

    @Pointcut("execution(public static Object withTransaction(" +
                "groovy.lang.Closure)) || " +
            "execution(public static Object withTransaction(" +
                "org.springframework.transaction.TransactionDefinition, " +
                "groovy.lang.Closure))")
    public void withTransactionMethod() {}


    @Before("isDomainClass() && (" +
                "saveMethod() || deleteMethod() ||" +
                "lockMethod() || mutexMethod()) " +
                " && this(instance)")
    public void ensureTransactionActive(JoinPoint jp, Object instance)
        throws Throwable {

        warn(jp, instance);
    }

    @Before("isDomainClass() && (" +
            "staticLockMethod() || executeUpdateMethod() || " +
            "saveAllMethod() || deleteAllMethod() || " +
            "findOrSaveWhereMethod() || withTransactionMethod())")
    public void ensureTransactionActiveStatic(JoinPoint jp) throws Throwable {
        warn(jp, null);
    }

    private void warn(JoinPoint jp, Object instance) {
        boolean txActive =
            TransactionSynchronizationManager.isSynchronizationActive();
```

```
        if ("withTransaction".equals(jp.getSignature().getName())) {
            if (txActive) {
                System.out.println("WARNING: withTransaction called inside of an " +
                                "active transaction:\n" + describeState(null));
            }
        }
        else {
            if (!txActive) {
                System.out.println("WARNING: Method '" + jp.getSignature() +
                                "' called outside of an active transaction:\n" +
                describeState(instance));
            }
        }
    }
}
```

This aspect is an example of an "architectural enforcement" aspect. It's slightly different from the security or transaction aspects, because it exists only to ensure the integrity of the system as a whole and not modularize any behavior.

We also need a pointcut that limits the method calls to those on domain classes; we don't want to log spurious warnings for any call to save, delete, etc., in any class. We can do this by leveraging AspectJ's ability to look for methods and classes with particular annotations, and the fact that Grails adds the grails.persistence.Entity annotation to domain classes when it adds GORM methods with its AST transforms:

```
@Pointcut("@within(grails.persistence.Entity)")
public void isDomainClass() {}
```

The two before methods, ensureTransactionActive and ensureTransactionActive Static, delegate to the warn method to check if there is an active transaction (with the help of TransactionSynchronizationManager.isSynchronizationActive()) and log a warning if needed. The implementation of describeState is omitted for brevity but can be whatever implementation makes sense for your use cases.

This aspect class uses Spring annotations, but isn't annotated with @Component because this is a compile-time aspect and you don't want Spring to autodetect it. That would be okay in this case, but if you were to use call, cflow, or other pointcut expressions that Spring doesn't support, you will get an exception at startup. Here's the same aspect written as a regular Aspect *.aj aspect:

```
package book;

import grails.persistence.Entity;
import groovy.lang.Closure;

import java.io.Serializable;
import java.util.ArrayList;
import java.util.Arrays;
```

```
import java.util.List;
import java.util.Map;

import org.aspectj.lang.JoinPoint;
import org.springframework.transaction.TransactionDefinition;
import org.springframework.transaction.support.TransactionSynchronizationManager;

public aspect TransactionCheckAspect {

    pointcut isDomainClass() :
        within(Entity);

    pointcut saveMethod() :
        execution(public Object save()) ||
        execution(public Object save(Map)) ||
        execution(public Object save(boolean));

    pointcut deleteMethod() :
        execution(public void delete()) ||
        execution(public void delete(Map));

    pointcut lockMethod() :
        execution(public Object lock());

    pointcut mutexMethod() :
        execution(public Object mutex(Closure));

    pointcut staticLockMethod() :
        execution(public static Object lock(Serializable));

    pointcut executeUpdateMethod() :
        execution(public static Integer executeUpdate(..));

    pointcut saveAllMethod() :
        execution(public static List saveAll(..));

    pointcut deleteAllMethod() :
        execution(public static void deleteAll(..));

    pointcut findOrSaveWhereMethod() :
        execution(public static Object findOrSaveWhere(Map));

    pointcut withTransactionMethod() :
        execution(public static Object withTransaction(Closure)) ||
        execution(public static Object withTransaction(
            TransactionDefinition, Closure));

    before(Object instance) :
            isDomainClass() &&
            (saveMethod() || deleteMethod() || lockMethod() || mutexMethod()) &&
            args(instance) {
        warn(thisJoinPoint, instance);
```

```
        }

    before() :
        staticLockMethod() || executeUpdateMethod() || saveAllMethod() ||
        deleteAllMethod() || findOrSaveWhereMethod() || withTransactionMethod() {
      warn(thisJoinPoint, null);
    }

    private void warn(JoinPoint jp, Object instance) {
      boolean txActive =
      TransactionSynchronizationManager.isSynchronizationActive();

      if ("withTransaction".equals(jp.getSignature().getName())) {
        if (txActive) {
          System.out.println("WARNING: withTransaction called inside of an " +
                            "active transaction:\n" + describeState(null));
        }
      }
      else {
        if (!txActive) {
          System.out.println("WARNING: Method '" + jp.getSignature() +
                            "' called outside of an active transaction:\n" +
                            describeState(instance));
        }
      }
    }
  }
}
```

It's interesting to note that the pointcuts are much shorter because we can move full class names from the annotation's defining strings to imports. Otherwise, the aspect is essentially equivalent beyond the syntax differences.

An implementation of the `describeState` method could capture the current call stack to give you information about where the method calls are coming from:

```
private static final List<String> IGNORED_PACKAGES = Arrays.asList(
    "com.springsource.loaded.", "groovy.lang.", "java.lang.", "sun.",
    "org.codehaus.groovy.reflection.", "org.codehaus.groovy.runtime.");

private String describeState() {
  List<StackTraceElement> elements = new ArrayList<StackTraceElement>();
  for (StackTraceElement element : Thread.currentThread().getStackTrace()) {
    if (element.getLineNumber() < 1) {
      continue;
    }
    if (element.getClassName().equals(getClass().getName())) {
      continue;
    }

    boolean ignore = false;
    for (String ignoredPackage : IGNORED_PACKAGES) {
      if (element.getClassName().startsWith(ignoredPackage)) {
```

```
        ignore = true;
        break;
      }
    }
    if (!ignore) {
      elements.add(element);
    }
  }

  StringBuilder sb = new StringBuilder();
  int i = 0;
  for (StackTraceElement element : elements) {
    if (i++ > 4) {
      break;
    }
    sb.append("\tat ").append(element).append('\n');
  }
  sb.append("\t...").append('\n');
  return sb.toString();
}
```

This will agressively prune the stack elements of rows that provide no useful information (e.g., the extra method calls added by Groovy) and print the first five frames. To try this out, create a Book domain class using grails create-domain-class aop.Book and generate a standard Grails scaffolded controller (either dynamic using grails create-scaffold-controller aop.Book or static with grails generate-all aop.Book). Start the application with grails run-app and create a new Book. You should see output like this:

```
WARNING: Method 'Object aop.Book.save(Map)' called without an active transaction:
    at aop.Book.save(Book.groovy:1)
    at aop.BookController.save(script13611782333350451886625.groovy:24)
    at org.codehaus.groovy.grails.web.servlet.mvc.MixedGrailsControllerHelper.
        invoke(MixedGrailsControllerHelper.java:69)
    at org.codehaus.groovy.grails.web.servlet.mvc.
        AbstractGrailsControllerHelper.handleAction(
        AbstractGrailsControllerHelper.java:330)
    at org.codehaus.groovy.grails.web.servlet.mvc.
        AbstractGrailsControllerHelper.executeAction(
        AbstractGrailsControllerHelper.java:211)
    ...
```

The AspectJ framework is large and powerful but has a rather steep learning curve. *Aspectj in Action* by Ramnivas Laddad (Manning, 2009) is an excellent resource if you find that your AOP needs are complex enough that you need AspectJ, or if you need its other features such as compile-time weaving.

Upgrading Applications and Plugins

New Grails versions are released fairly often, and they always contain bug fixes and new features that you probably want to have available in your applications and plugins. You might not be able to upgrade for every release, but you shouldn't get too far out of date. We try our best to limit breaking changes and other changes that will make upgrading harder, but sometimes progress has its costs.

Grails does have an upgrade script (*http://bit.ly/138GUbf*), but it doesn't do all of the work needed to upgrade between versions, and will likely be removed or at least renamed in a future version of Grails, because the name is a bit misleading. It is useful in some respects, but there will always be manual steps involved in upgrading to a newer version of Grails.

So what does the upgrade script do? There are a few fixes for very old (pre-1.0) applications:

- Delete *basedir/plugins/core* (core taglibs are now part of Grails, not files in the application)
- Move *basedir/grails-tests* test classes to *test/integration*
- Delete *basedir/tmp*
- Move *basedir/spring* and *basedir/hibernate* under *basedir/grails-app/conf*

and there are fixes for all versions:

- Copy current static resources (images, CSS, JS) to *basedir/web-app*
- Replace *basedir/web-app/WEB-INF/sitemesh.xml* and *basedir/web-app/WEB-INF/applicationContext.xml* with the latest versions
- Copy current **.tld* files to *basedir/web-app/WEB-INF/tld*

- Create missing *grails-app/conf* files (*Config.groovy*, *BuildConfig.groovy*, *Data-Source.groovy*, and *UrlMappings.groovy*)
- Update *Config.groovy* with new settings:
  - `grails.views.default.codec="none" // none, html, base64`
  - `grails.views.gsp.encoding="UTF-8"`
- Upgrade *DataSource.groovy* to use H2 instead of HSQLDB (only if the `update-data-source` flag is specified)
- Update *application.properties*
- Run the *scripts/_Upgrade.groovy* script for each plugin
- Ensure *basedir/grails-app/i18n/messages.properties* exists
- Install or upgrade the "core" plugins (Hibernate and Tomcat)

If you're upgrading a very old version of Grails, things will have changed so significantly that you'll have a lot more work to do than this script's changes. So, for moderately recent versions of Grails (say 1.2 or higher), these steps can be split into three groups:

- Necessary ones:
  - Updating *sitemesh.xml* and *applicationContext.xml*
  - Updating **.tld* files
  - Update *Config.groovy* with new settings
  - Upgrade *DataSource.groovy* to use H2
  - Update *application.properties*
- Unnecessary ones:
  - Create missing *grails-app/conf* files
  - Run *scripts/_Upgrade.groovy* scripts
  - Ensure *basedir/grails-app/i18n/messages.properties* exists
- Problematic ones:
  - Copy current static resources
  - Install or upgrade the "core" plugins (Hibernate and Tomcat)

The unnecessary steps aren't needed (in general), because the conf files and *messages.properties* will exist, and plugins rarely have upgrade scripts. The problematic ones should be avoided because your UI designers will probably have deleted many of the stock static resource files and customized the look and feel of your application; and, if you've uninstalled the Hibernate plugin (e.g., to use a NoSQL datastore instead) or the Tomcat plugin (to use Jetty instead), they will be reinstalled.

Using the dynamic `grailsVersion` instead of hardcoding the version (e.g., `runtime ":hibernate:$grailsVersion"`) will ensure you're always using the versions of the Hibernate and Tomcat plugins that correspond to the current Grails version anyway.

One potential pain point when upgrading is due to having installed and edited templates. You can install the templates that are used to create artifacts, GSPs, and *web.xml* by running the `install-templates` script. This copies the standard files into your application in the *src/templates* folder, and Grails will use those instead of its own when running scripts that generate files. Although this is convenient, it can be problematic during an upgrade because you will retain the old templates instead of the updated ones. This is primarily a UI issue, but differences in the *web.xml* template can cause your application to fail. So be sure to merge your template changes into the new templates in the destination version.

Another issue with the script is with preexisting files such as *BuildConfig.groovy*. For example, if you are upgrading from 1.2.3 to 2.1.1, the default 1.2.3 file (minus comments) is:

```
grails.project.class.dir = "target/classes"
grails.project.test.class.dir = "target/test-classes"
grails.project.test.reports.dir   = "target/test-reports"

grails.project.dependency.resolution = {

    inherits( "global" ) {}
    log "warn"
    repositories {
        grailsPlugins()
        grailsHome()
    }
    dependencies {}
}
```

whereas the default 2.1.1 file is:

```
grails.servlet.version = "2.5"
grails.project.class.dir = "target/classes"
grails.project.test.class.dir = "target/test-classes"
grails.project.test.reports.dir = "target/test-reports"
grails.project.target.level = 1.6
grails.project.source.level = 1.6

grails.project.dependency.resolution = {
    inherits("global") {}
    log "error"
    checksums true

    repositories {
        inherits true
```

```
        grailsPlugins()
        grailsHome()
        grailsCentral()

        mavenLocal()
        mavenCentral()
    }
    dependencies {}

    plugins {
        runtime ":hibernate:$grailsVersion"
        runtime ":jquery:1.8.0"
        runtime ":resources:1.1.6"
        build ":tomcat:$grailsVersion"
        runtime ":database-migration:1.1"
        compile ':cache:1.0.0'
    }
}
```

There isn't logic to add the missing configuration, so you'll need to do that yourself.

Why Doesn't the Upgrade Script Do More?

We could automate more of the process. This would involve carefully looking at application differences for every version delta and adding code to handle each. Then upgrading from 2.0.0 to 2.0.4 would involve making the necessary changes from 2.0.0 to 2.0.1, then to 2.0.2, then to 2.0.3, and finally 2.0.4. It would be way too much work to be able to go directly between arbitrary versions, because that would explode the script with all of the combinations; making all of the intermediate changes would suffice.

There are a few reasons why this isn't happening now. One is resource availability; it would be a lot of work, and it is more efficient to describe the changes required (which might be as simple as listing fixed bugs and new features in the form of a JIRA release notes page) than to spend engineering hours on a programmatic upgrade process, I'm sure most of you would prefer that we spend our time adding more features and fixing bugs. Another is the overall complexity of the task. It would be hard enough with a "boring" language like Java, but all of the configuration files and most or all of the application files in a Grails application are written in Groovy. It would be very difficult to edit a file that can contain arbitrarily complex logic in a safe way, and too easy to damage your application's code in cases where the code is valid but doesn't match the expectations of the upgrade script.

For a concrete example, consider a similarly complex but much smaller problem: changing the `install-plugin` script from adding entries in *application.properties* to programmatically adding a dependency in the `plugins` section of *BuildConfig.groovy*. Say we have this initial block:

```
plugins {
    runtime ":hibernate:$grailsVersion"
    runtime ':jquery:1.7.1'
    runtime ':resources:1.1.6'
    build ":tomcat:$grailsVersion"
}
```

and we want to install the `console` plugin. Running `install-plugin` will find the latest
version and add it to *application.properties*:

```
app.grails.version=2.1.1
app.name=my_cool_app
app.version=0.1
plugins.console=1.2
```

But that is problematic because we cannot choose the plugin scope, restrict its dependencies, or do any other configuration. So the `install-plugin` script could be made
intelligent enough to just add it to *BuildConfig.groovy*:

```
plugins {
    runtime ":hibernate:$grailsVersion"
    runtime ':jquery:1.7.1'
    runtime ':resources:1.1.6'
    build ":tomcat:$grailsVersion"
    runtime ":console:1.2"
}
```

That looks easy, but what if it were already installed? Or what if it were installed under
a different scope than "runtime"? Or what if it were included conditionally; for example:

```
plugins {
    runtime ":hibernate:$grailsVersion"
    runtime ':jquery:1.7.1'
    runtime ':resources:1.1.6'
    build ":tomcat:$grailsVersion"
    if (some logic here) {
        runtime ":console:1.2"
    }
}
```

And, what if it's there, but commented out?

```
plugins {
    runtime ":hibernate:$grailsVersion"
    runtime ':jquery:1.7.1'
    runtime ':resources:1.1.6'
    build ":tomcat:$grailsVersion"
    /*
    runtime ":console:1.2"
    */
}
```

The detection logic would likely see it in both of the previous two cases, and hopefully stop the process or start asking questions. But what if it were included using logic for the declaration itself:

```
plugins {
    ...
    String name = ...
    String version = ...
    runtime ":$name:$version"
}
```

This is easy compared to some of the changes that needed to be made when upgrading an entire application. In order to reduce or eliminate the risk of damaging your code during the upgrade, many changes will either have to be skipped or manual intervention will be required, and in both cases, that can only happen if the script detects that it can't do its work for some task. So other than a core set of changes, most real upgrade tasks will require manual work guided by (hopefully) helpful release notes and upgrade documentation.

A General Approach to Upgrading

For a small version delta, for example 2.1.0 to 2.1.2, it is often sufficient to just edit *application.properties* and change the version. The next time you run a script that triggers dependency resolution (most do, and `grails refresh-dependencies` is a good one to use) the Hibernate and Tomcat plugins will be upgraded for you—as long as you keep the default version set to the `grailsVersion` variable in *BuildConfig.groovy*—unless you have uninstalled one or both of them. Be sure to read the release notes for the intermediate versions to be aware of any changes you need to or might want to make. A larger delta requires a more formal process, however.

For bigger version differences, I favor an approach that uses a variant of a three-way diff. Say you're upgrading from version 1.2.3 to 2.1.1. It can be difficult to know what you changed or removed without searching through your source control commit history, so I create a new empty application using the old version of Grails (in this case, 1.2.3). The name doesn't matter, since you'll be deleting it. If you copied artifact templates into your application with the `install-templates` script, run it in the 1.2.3 application so you can discover the changes that you made in those. Using whatever approach you like, compare your application to the new one. There are good free and commercial diff tools, both command-line and GUI-based. Meld (*http://meld merge.org/*) is one that I like a lot, and it's cross-platform; and WinMerge (*http:// winmerge.org/*) is a popular Windows-only tool.

Next, I create a new empty application in the new version of Grails (in this case, 2.1.1). Name this the same as the application that you're upgrading, because it will replace your application. Once you determine what to keep and remove from the old application based on the directory diff, make those changes in the new application and replace your application with this one.

The diff that you run will show you files that you added, deleted, and modified (be sure to ignore generated files like classes, and version-control files such as the contents of the *.git* folder and *.svn* folders). Most or all of the files that you added can be copied into the new application, but some changes may be required. Files that were deleted will probably include the stock CSS, JavaScript, and images that are created by the `create-app` and `create-plugin` scripts, so you will likely want to delete the corresponding files in the new application. The files that were modified will require a bit more care though; you can't just make the same changes in all cases.

Because `install-plugin` is now deprecated and plugin dependencies should be added to *BuildConfig.groovy*, be sure to move any plugin entries from *application.properties* to *BuildConfig.groovy*. The "compile" scope is typically the one to use, but the plugin pages include the syntax to use for the latest version. For example, the entry for the `atomikos` plugin (*http://grails.org/plugin/atomikos/*) would be:

```
compile ":atomikos:1.0"
```

Doing this work will also give you a chance to update to the latest version. You can make this process a bit faster by using the `list-plugin-updates` script (*http://bit.ly/YL3qrZ*).

Upgrading Petclinic: A Case Study

A customer reported that he was using the Grails version of the Spring Petclinic application [one of the available sample applications (*https://github.com/grails-samples/petclinic*)], saying that he had run `grails upgrade` to update it to 2.1, but things weren't working. The latest version in the Git repository used Grails version 1.3.4.BUILD-SNAPSHOT, so it was a fairly big change. I updated the application to use Grails 2.1.1 (the most recent version of Grails at that time).

Step 1: Determine the changes in the application

The first step (after cloning the Git repo to get the current code) was to create a new empty application with the old version and compare it to the current code. I used Grails 1.3.4 for this, because it's close enough to the 1.3.4.BUILD-SNAPSHOT version that was used:

```
$ grails create-app empty134
```

Diffing the two applications showed that there were some changed files:

- *grails-app/conf/BootStrap.groovy*
  - — Sample data population logic
- *grails-app/conf/UrlMappings.groovy*
  - — The "/" mapping was changed from `view:"/index"` to `controller:'clinic'`
- *grails-app/i18n/messages.properties*
  - — Several application-specific messages were added
- *grails-app/views/layouts/main.gsp*
  - — UI updates
- *web-app/css/main.css*
  - — UI updates

and some added files:

- *grails-app/controllers*
  - — Three new controllers
- *grails-app/domain*
  - — Seven new domain classes
- *grails-app/views*
  - — Nine new GSPs and templates
- *test/unit*
  - — One new unit test
- *web-app/css/petclinic.css*
- *web-app/html/petclinic.html*
- *web-app/images*
  - — A few new images

and some deleted files:

- *petclinic.tmproj*
- *grails-app/views/index.gsp* and *web-app/index.gsp*
  - — Not needed with the `UrlMapping` change to use *ClinicController.index* as the root URL
- *web-app/images*
  - — A few images

In addition, there were some missing changes from previous upgrades that will be added as part of this upgrade, including:

- Some properties in *Config.groovy* (`grails.views.gsp.sitemesh.preprocess`, `grails.scaffolding.templates.domainSuffix`, `grails.spring.bean.packages`, etc.)
- Updates in *web-app/WEB-INF/tld/grails.tld*
- Updates in *web-app/WEB-INF/applicationContext.xml*
- Slightly old version of Prototype (which will be removed anyway)

Step 2: Make the first round of changes in a new application

Now we can create a new empty application using the version of Grails we're upgrading to:

```
$ grails create-app petclinic211
```

The name is based on the original, plus an indicator of the version used; it will be changed to the application name in a bit.

Now we can start making the corresponding changes in the new application. We start with deletions:

- *petclinic.tmproj*
  — Nothing to do because this is only created by the `integrate-with` script now
- *grails-app/views/index.gsp* and *web-app/index.gsp*
  — Only delete *grails-app/views/index.gsp* because there is no *web-app/index.gsp* in 2.1.1
- *web-app/images*
  — Delete the images that were previously deleted

Next we can work on the added files:

- *grails-app/controllers*
  — Okay to copy, but we will do some refactoring
- *grails-app/domain*
  — Okay to copy
- *grails-app/views*
  — Okay to copy, but we will do some refactoring

- *test/unit*

  — Okay to copy, but we will do some refactoring
- *web-app/css/petclinic.css*

  — Okay to copy, but there is a fix needed
- *web-app/html/petclinic.html*

  — Okay to copy, but there are updates needed
- *web-app/images*

  — Okay to copy

Next, we can look at the changed files:

- *grails-app/conf/BootStrap.groovy*

  — Okay to copy with some minor changes
- *grails-app/conf/UrlMappings.groovy*

  — Okay to copy
- *grails-app/i18n/messages.properties*

  — Cannot copy because that will revert new default messages; instead, edit the file and copy the added messages (`owners.not.found`, `owner.firstName.blank`, etc.) at the end
- *grails-app/views/layouts/main.gsp* and *web-app/css/main.css*

  — Cannot copy because that will revert several new changes; instead, manual edits are needed

Note that, because this is a demo application, *DataSource.groovy* just uses the in-memory (HSQLDB) database in all environments. Using this process, the default H2 databases will be used, but for most applications, some work configuring the database connection settings would be required.

Also, there are a few new files added for us; *grails-app/conf/ApplicationResources.groovy* (the config file for the "resources" plugin) and a few new message bundles in *grails-app/i18n*.

Step 3: Make the second round of changes

Some changed and added files cannot be copied unchanged, because some refactoring and updates are needed. For example, the controllers use the older style of defining actions with closures. This is still supported, but it's a good idea to change to methods; for example:

```
package org.grails.samples

class ClinicController {

    def index = {}

    def vets = {
        [vets: Vet.list() ]
    }
}
```

to:

```
package org.grails.samples

class ClinicController {

    def index() {}

    def vets() {
        [vets: Vet.list()]
    }
}
```

 Most of the time, changing closures to methods is the right thing to do, but there can be some unexpected behaviors. See Tomas Lin's blog post (*http://bit.ly/YL5PCV*) that discusses some pitfalls.

While we're looking at the controllers, there are some patterns to look for and update. One is that, because public methods are considered actions, any old public helper methods must be made private or protected. This makes sense anyway, because controller methods can only be called internally or within the class hierarchy. Also, specifying an unquoted action closure name as the argument to the redirect method was supported because it references a class property, but this fails in 2.0+ because methods cannot be referred to directly like fields can. So, if you do this, quote your action names. Finally, because command object properties are now not-null by default, to be consistent with domain class constraints, you may need to adjust the constraints in your command objects.

I opted to do some database persistence refactoring too. Controllers should be very dumb, capturing request query parameters and delegating to helpers (services, domain classes, etc.) to implement business logic. Then they should render the next view using what was returned from helper method calls (using a GSP, a JSON builder, or some other helper) or redirect to the next URL. Putting too much logic in controllers doesn't sufficiently separate concerns, makes the controllers overly hard to test, and can even result in unexpected behavior. For example, database updates, deletes, and creates in controllers are not run in a transaction, so if an exception occurs after some changes but before all have been done, you can end up with inconsistent database state.

So I created a new service, `org.grails.samples.PetclinicService`. I moved the logic for creating and updating a `Pet` and creating a `Visit` from `PetController`, and moved the logic for creating and updating an `Owner` from `OwnerController`. Rather than simply passing the `params` object to the service, which would somewhat couple the web and service tiers because now the service would need to know the "magic" map keys in the `params` map, I converted the `params` values to their expected types and passed them to the service methods, which can be called anywhere in the application, such as `Pet cre atePet(String name, Date birthDate, long petTypeId, long ownerId)`.

By adding a dependency injection for the service (`def petclinicService`), I can then convert this `Pet` creation logic in the add action from:

```
def pet = new Pet(params['pet'])
if(pet.save())
    redirect controller:'owner',action:'show', id:pet.owner.id
else
    render view:'add', model: [pet: pet, types: PetType.list() ]
```

to this:

```
def pet = petclinicService.createPet(params.pet?.name, params.pet?.birthDate,
    (params.pet?.type?.id ?: 0) as Long, (params.pet?.owner?.id ?: 0) as Long)
if (!pet.hasErrors()) {
    redirect controller: 'owner', action: 'show', id: pet.owner.id
    return
}

[pet: pet, types: PetType.list()]
```

For the new GSPs, they can for the most part be copied, but the `createLinkTo` tag calls must be changed to `resource` calls. Layout GSP changes are more involved, but for the most part, just involve copying changed sections into the new layouts. It's important in most cases to retain the new HTML5 tags to keep the benefits of the new UI changes. In this case, I changed the `title` tag text, removed the Grails logo image and "spinner" `div`, added a `link` tag for *petclinic.css*, and changed the "footer" `div` to include the Petclinic HTML.

`OwnerControllerTests` needed a lot of work. Previously, it extended `grails.test.Con trollerUnitTestCase`, but the preferred approach now is to use the new test mix-in annotations. I changed it to not have a base class (using JUnit 4 annotations instead) and added `@TestFor(OwnerController)` and `@Mock(Owner)` and the other changes related to these to take advantage of the new testing approach.

web-app/css/petclinic.css was okay except for one line:

```
li ul {
    list-style: square url(images/sub-bullet.gif);
}
```

The problem here is that there was no *sub-bullet.gif*, and I couldn't find it in the original Spring application either. It's not an important issue from a UI perspective, but it causes an error message in the console at runtime because the resources plugin renames files and changes URLs, so referenced files must exist to avoid this. So I hacked in a work-around to use an existing image:

```
li ul {
    list-style: disc url(../images/bullet-arrow.png);
}
```

I updated *web-app/html/petclinic.html* with various minor changes, updating some URLs and the descriptions of the technogies being used.

I changed domain class `save()` calls to `save(failOnError: true)` in *grails-app/conf/BootStrap.groovy*. I would almost never do this in application code that works with user input, because exceptions shouldn't be used for nonexceptional cases such as invalid user input. It's simple enough to check if the `save()` call failed by checking that the return value is null, or with the `hasErrors()` method. But in tests, *BootStrap.groovy*, and other places where you have hardcoded data that you expect to succeed, it makes sense to throw an exception and fail loudly.

Also there are a few new files added for us: *grails-app/conf/ApplicationResources.groovy* (the config file for the `resources` plugin) and a few new message bundles in *grails-app/i18n*. Similarly, some files are automatically updated, including *grails-app/views/error.gsp*, *web-app/js/application.js*, *web-app/WEB-INF/applicationContext.xml*, *web-app/WEB-INF/sitemesh.xml*, the TLD files *c.tld*, *fmt.tld*, and *grails.tld*, several *grails-app/i18n* message bundles, *grails-app/conf/BuildConfig.groovy*, and *grails-app/conf/Config.groovy*.

Note that, because this is a demo application, *DataSource.groovy* just uses the in-memory (HSQLDB) database in all environments. By using this process, the default H2 databases will be used, but for most applications, some work configuring the database connection settings would be required. `cache.provider_class='net.sf.ehcache.hibernate.EhCacheProvider'` becomes `cache.region.factory_class='net.sf.ehcache.hibernate.EhCacheRegionFactory'`, because the older value is deprecated in the more recent version of Hibernate that Grails now uses. *Config.groovy* and *BuildConfig.groovy* will usually require manual merging too, if you have made changes there.

application.properties now has setting `app.grails.version=2.1.1` and no plugins listed (they're all in *BuildConfig.groovy*). I also removed the `app.servlet.version` property because it is ignored (the setting from *BuildConfig.groovy* is used instead).

There were several new properties added in *Config.groovy* (some were pre-1.3.4 but hadn't been added):

- `grails.project.groupId = appName`
- `grails.resources.adhoc.patterns = ['/images/*', '/css/*', '/js/*', '/plugins/*']`
- `grails.views.gsp.sitemesh.preprocess = true`
- `grails.scaffolding.templates.domainSuffix = 'Instance'`
- `grails.json.legacy.builder = false`
- `grails.spring.bean.packages = []`
- `grails.web.disable.multipart=false`
- `grails.exceptionresolver.params.exclude = ['password']`
- `grails.hibernate.cache.queries = false`

Step 4: Finishing up

We can now delete the *empty134* application and make the *petclinic211* application the real *petclinic* application. If you're using Git, you can do this by renaming the old application directory (e.g., to *petclinic.old*) and changing the *petclinic211* directory name to *petclinic*. Then move the *.git* folder to the new application, and run all of the Git commands required to delete, add, and update the various files. The process for Subversion and other source control systems is more involved but similar.

Run the application's tests and run the app, testing various URLs and workflows. Hopefully, everything works as expected and you have successfully upgraded to Grails 2.1.

Running the upgrade script instead

Having upgraded the application this way, I was curious what the `upgrade` script would have done in this case. I made a copy of the preupgrade application and ran `grails upgrade --update-data-source` on it. Here's a summary of the changes that were made:

- `app.grails.version`, `plugins.hibernate`, and `plugins.tomcat` were updated to the latest version in *application.properties*
- TLD files *c.tld*, *fmt.tld*, and *grails.tld* were updated to the latest
- *applicationContext.xml* was updated to the latest to include the current parent application context beans
- *sitemesh.xml* was updated to the latest

- The CSS files *errors.css* and *mobile.css* were added
- Seven new images were added:
  — *apple-touch-icon.png*
  — *apple-touch-icon-retina.png*
  — *grails_logo.png*
  — *leftnav_btm.png*
  — *leftnav_midstretch.png*
  — *leftnav_top.png*
  — *springsource.png*

In addition, thanks to the `update-data-source` flag, *DataSource.groovy* was updated to use H2 instead of HSQLDB. The `driverClassName` property was updated, and the `url` property for the `development` and `test` environments were converted to H2 syntax. The `production` HSQLDB configuration wasn't changed, because it's unlikely that you would use HSQLDB in production; and, for applications that still use the default configuration, the production HSQLDB settings configure a file-based database instead of an in-memory one. Because this most likely contains data, you would need to manually migrate that to an H2 file-based database. If you still want to use HSQLDB you can, just add a dependency in *BuildConfig.groovy*.

Having done this, there are some steps that are required or a good idea:

- Convert the controllers to use methods instead of closures
- Refactor persistence from the controllers to a new service
- Update *BootStrap.groovy* `save()` calls
- Fix the production *DataSource.groovy* URL
- Update the GSPs and layout (*main.gsp*)
- Update *OwnerControllerTests.groovy*
- Update *petclinic.css*
- Update *web-app/html/petclinic.html*

There were many differences between the upgraded application (with the above fixes) and the end result of the previous exercise, though:

- *grails-app/conf/ApplicationResources.groovy* wasn't created, so we would need to do that manually
- The new default plugins `jquery`, `resources`, `database-migration`, and `cache` aren't installed

- *BuildConfig.groovy* hasn't been updated
- *Config.groovy* has several missing properties
- *DataSource.groovy* is missing the new `properties` section in the production environment block that configure pooling, and still has a `cache.provider_class` setting instead of `cache.region.factory_class`
- *grails-app/i18n/messages.properties* and other language bundles are missing several new messages and new language translations haven't been added
- *error.gsp* wasn't updated
- The Hibernate and Tomcat plugins are still in *application.properties* instead of *BuildConfig.groovy*
- The Prototype javascript files are still there but unused
- Several old images are still there but unused
- *web-app/js/application.js* still uses Prototype instead of jQuery syntax

On balance, it should be clear that although the `upgrade` script does some work for you, too much is not done, and an approach like the one I've described here makes a lot more sense.

A Short History of Grails

When upgrading a Grails application or plugin, it's important to know what changed between versions. The changes include breaking changes that can cause failures in your application if you don't adjust for them, changes that you don't need to adjust for at all such as performance increases, and new features and enhancements that you may wish to take advantage of. Release notes make for dry reading, so here is a summary of the highlights for the Grails releases since 1.2. Note that some of the minor releases (e.g., 1.3.x) aren't listed, because they were mostly bug-fix releases.

Grails 1.2

- Ivy (with a significant amount of Grails customization and fixes) is now used to manage JAR dependencies. This is configured in the `grails.project.dependency.resolution` block in *grails-app/conf/BuildConfig.groovy*.
- *BootStrap.groovy* now has environment support; instead of having to use if/else or switch blocks, you can use an `environments` block in the `init` closure just like in *Config.groovy* and *DataSource.groovy*.

- The Spring framework version has been updated to version 3, which adds support for many new features, including

  — Spring MVC controllers using the `@Controller` annotation

  — Spring beans defined in Java and Groovy using the `@Component`, using `@Auto wired` for dependency injection

  — Fine-grained transaction configuration in Grails services and other Spring beans with the `@Transactional` annotation

- You can now configure default mapping settings with the `grails.gorm.de fault.mapping Config.groovy` setting and default constraints with the `grails.gorm.default.constraints` setting.

- You can now define GORM named queries and conveniently reuse and compose them.

- For cases where a validation error should throw an exception, you can use the `failOnError` option in the `save()` method: `save(failOnError:true)`.

- GSPs are now precompiled when building a WAR file; this means that the permgen cost that is required when compiling is incurred during the build instead of on your server at application startup.

- You can define named URL mappings and refer to them in GSP tags.

- There is a new script to find available updates for your installed plugins, `list-plugin-updates`. It works well in general, but because of the way we release the Hibernate and Tomcat plugins for each Grails release, it can falsely report that there is an available update for those plugins.

Grails 1.2.2

You can configure JVM settings such as heap and permgen size and with the `GRAILS_OPTS` environment variable.

Grails 1.2.4

There's one small fix in 1.2.4 that addresses an issue that many users found frustrating. The artifact creation scripts assume that you will specify the logical name of the artifact, for example, `grails create-service user` to create a `UserService` class. But often users would run this as `grails create-service userservice` or `grails create-service UserService`, which would result in a `UserServiceService` class. This is easy to fix manually, but now the scripts detect this and adjust for it.

Grails 1.3

- You can now write tests with JUnit 4, using annotations instead of having to extend a base class.

- The `install-plugin` and `uninstall-plugin` scripts and specifying plugin dependencies in *application.properties* are still supported, but the preferred approach now is to declare the dependencies in *BuildConfig.groovy* in a similar way to how library dependencies are specified. This approach allows for a more fine-grained configuration; you can specify exlusions of transitive dependencies, specify plugin scope (build, runtime, compile, etc.).

- You can now publish plugins to and load from Maven repositories.

- Groovy 1.7 is now used, which adds support for many features including anonymous inner classes and nested classes, better support for annotations, and the "Power Assert" display from failed assertions.

- There are new GORM methods for dirty checking, including `isDirty()`, `isDirty(String propName)`, `getPersistentValue()`, `getDirtyPropertyNames()`, which can be used to know what has changed in a domain class instance since it was retrieved from the database.

- You can define derived properties in the `mapping` block in domain classes, for example, `finalPrice formula: 'PRICE * 1.155'`,.

- You can use the `load()` method instead of the `get()` method to create a proxy instead of retrieving the entire instance; this will load the data on-demand if you access any property other than the `id`, but if you only need the primary key, for example, to delete the instance, use it as a reference in another instance or use it in a query—it is more efficient than incurring an unnecessary extra database hit.

- Artifacts defined in plugins can conveniently be overridden in the containing application. Plugins are now compiled into a separate directory from application classes. The application's classes directory is listed before the plugins' in the `run-app` classpath, and application classes are copied to the WAR file's *WEB-INF/classes* directory after the plugins' so they can overwrite them. This also works for GSP views and templates.

- You can now chain named queries.

- The `dataSource` bean is now a `TransactionAwareDataSourceProxy`, and the "real" bean has the name `dataSourceUnproxied` for the rare cases where you need direct access. This means that, if you get a connection from the `DataSource`, if there is one in use in an active transaction or Hibernate session, you will get a reference to that one instead of a new connection. This is useful when you use `groovy.sql.Sql` for queries and updates and need to have access to changes made by GORM within the same transaction or session.

- You can specify your own Hibernate `NamingStrategy`. You can still configure table and column names in the domain class `mapping` blocks on a case-by-case basis, but if you have a consistent pattern, you can encapsulate that in one place with a custom strategy.

- You can set a default GSP template with the `grails.sitemesh.default.layout` setting in *Config.groovy* instead of adding `<meta name="layout" con tent="main" />` in every GSP.

- If you use the Grails documentation engine with **.gdoc* files (this is more common in plugins than applications), you can create a single PDF with the `pdf` flag; for example, `grails doc --pdf`. There is also an `init` flag that will create the directory structure and starter files for you: `grails doc --init`.

Grails 1.3.1

- You can partition filters into multiple classes and define the order that they run with the `dependsOn` setting; for example, `def dependsOn = [MyOtherFilters]`. The filters are still executed in the order specified in the class, but the `dependsOn` setting groups the filters.

- You can now nest named queries.

Grails 1.3.2

The 1.3.2 release contains a convenient feature to help recover from command-line typos. If you mistype a script name, all of the available scripts will be searched to find the five closest matches, and you will be provided a "did you mean" list to choose from; if you're reasonably close (e.g., `grails create-doman-class`), then the one you wanted will usually be the first choice.

Grails 1.3.4

- You can conveniently register event listeners for any various Hibernate events by defining a `hibernateEventListeners` bean in *resources.groovy*.

- You can enable GSP reloading when your application is deployed as a WAR file with the `grails.gsp.reload.enable` option in *Config.groovy*. This only makes sense if the WAR file is exploded. There is a small performance impact when using this because file modification times must be checked.

- The `GrailsApplication` instance is available in *resources.groovy* as the `applica tion` variable.

- The embedded Tomcat instance used by run-app can be configured with the grails.tomcat.jvmArgs setting in *BuildConfig.groovy*.

Grails 1.3.6

- You can create a beforeValidate event handler method in your domain classes.
- Groovy scripts can be run from the command line with the run-script command. These are different from Gant scripts, and can access application classes directly, use GORM, and access Spring beans.
- Exceptions that occur during controller requests are logged and include URI and request parameters to help diagnose the cause.

Grails 1.3.7

You can now disable request parameter logging when an exception occurs by adding grails.exceptionresolver.logRequestParameters=false in *Config.groovy*, and parameter name exclusions can be defined in the grails.exceptionresolver.params.exclude setting (e.g., grails.exceptionresolver.params.exclude = ['password']).

Grails 1.3.8

1.3.8 was a small release but includes two important changes:

- To protect against data binding security attacks, dependency injection in domain classes and command objects was moved from before data binding to after. So for example, when using the common idioms new Person(params), there is no risk that injected Spring beans can be modified by request parameters, because they won't be available yet. Further optimizations were made in the 2.0.2 release, including the new bindable constraint. See this blog post (*http://bit.ly/15g3hjk*) for a more complete discussion.
- Plugins are now published to a Maven-compatible Artifactory repository (*http://repo.grails.org/*), so the grailsCentral() repository will resolve to the old repository if you don't upgrade. The old repository is still online but only contains older plugin releases.

Grails 1.3.9

1.3.9 has one fix, related to the data binding fix in 1.3.8. The data binding order was further refined to do dependency injection before validation (but still after data binding), so injected beans will be available to custom validators.

Grails 2.0

Grails 2.0 was a significant release. Originally it was going to be called 1.4 and there was a 1.4-M1 release, but as development progressed, it was clear that, given the scope of the changes and new features, renaming it to 2.0 (and pushing some of the changes that had been planned for 2.0 to 3.0) was warranted.

- Many libraries were updated, the significant ones being Spring 3.1, Groovy 1.8, Hibernate 3.6, and Tomcat 7.0.

- Code reloading in the development environment is no longer limited to controllers, services, taglibs, and GSPs. Thanks to the reloading agent, all classes can be reloaded at runtime, even *src/groovy* and *src/java* classes. This is a significant productivity boost, because you can go a lot longer between server restarts while modifying code. One wrinkle is that because domain class changes may affect the database schema, the `SessionFactory` will be reloaded, and depending on your `dbCreate` setting, the database may be dropped and rebuilt.

- The Servlet 3.0 spec is now supported (although the default is still 2.5). I wrote a blog post (*http://burtbeckwith.com/blog/?p=1251*) demonstrating the new async features that are available in 2.0 if you enable Servlet 3.0 support, including the new `startAsync` method.

- You can now compile plugins and deploy them as JAR files instead of deploying as ZIP files, including source code. These are packaged with the `binary` flag, for example `grails package-plugin --binary`, or by adding `def packaging = 'binary'` in the plugin descriptor.

- The `datasources` plugin has been merged into Grails core to allow the use of multiple datasources in Grails domain classes. In addition, there is a new `atomikos` plugin that adds support for XA transactions and two-phase commit (2PC) to ensure that changes in multiple datasources (or even XA-aware technologies such as JMS) are committed together or rolled back together.

- The console experience has been significantly updated.

  — "Interactive" mode is started by just running `grails` instead of running the `interactive` script. And you can get a lot more done in interactive mode, because several memory issues have been fixed, and the new reloading approach means you need to restart the console less often.

  — In general, the output is far more condensed, because important output remains visible in the console, but less important output is displayed on a single line without scrolling. This results in dramatically less noisy output.

  — Colors are more effectively used in console output.

- You can autocomplete scripts using tab completion, and this tab completion also works for class names after the `create-*` commands.

- Command history is maintained within the console, and between runs. Use the up arrow to cycle through previous commands.

- You can use the `open` command in interactive mode to open files, with special handling of unit test output with the `test-report` name, and dependency report output with the `dep-report` name.

- You can run operating system commands and applications in the path by prefixing the command with a ! character.

• To help plugin authors know about plugin usage, there is now usage tracking of installed plugins. This is optional; you can easily opt out. But the data collected is trivial and helps to get a better sense of which plugins are popular.

• The CRUD pages that are generated by the `generate-views` and `generate-all` scripts were completely reworked with a new look and feel, and support for HTML5.

• jQuery is now the default Javascript library, replacing Prototype. The `jquery` plugin in installed by default, but can be uninstalled by removing it from *Build-Config.groovy*.

• The resources plugin (*http://grails.org/plugin/resources*) is installed by default and provides extensive resource (CSS, JavaScript, and image) management functionality. You can configure bundling, GZIP compression, versioning, and other performance-related settings with this plugin and its companion plugins such as `zipped-resources` and `cached-resources`.

• Unit testing support was completely reworked. Rather than relying on extending base classes (which requires a class hierarchy for each testing framework), you can now annotate test classes and enable AST transformation mix-ins, which add the methods and behavior that were previously made available with subclassing. This gives you the freedom to use JUnit 3, JUnit 4, or Spock tests. In addition, a new in-memory GORM implementation is available for testing domain classes, although integration tests should be preferred for persistence testing so your tests take advantage of a real database instead of a mock.

• GORM methods that were previously added to domain classes using runtime metaprogramming via the `MetaClass` (e.g., `save()`, `delete()`, `list()`, `count()`, etc.) are now added to the bytecode using compile-time metaprogramming with AST transformations. This exposes the methods to Java and other languages, making integration easier. Dynamic methods such as `findByFooAndBar` are still added to the metaclass, because they're only added the first time they are used.

• HSQLDB was replaced with H2 as the default database provider. H2 is more robust and is more similar to the databases that you're likely to use in production, which should result in fewer surprises and behavior differences when deploying to production.

- H2 includes a web-based database console that works with any database that you have a JDBC driver for. This is configured by default in development at the /dbcon sole URI but not in production, although it can be enabled or disabled per environment and the URI can also be configured.

- The new GORM methods findOrCreateWhere, findOrSaveWhere, findOrCreate ByXXX, and findOrSaveByXXX make it convenient to retrieve an instance if it exists, or create and optionally persist it if it doesn't, in a single method call.

- You can now conveniently send a permanent redirect (301 error code) in addition to sending a temporary redirect (302 error code) with the permanent attribute, such as redirect(controller: 'foo', action: 'bar', permanent: true).

- You can create links to Grails controllers and other resources in a service or other artifact that isn't in web scope like controllers and taglibs with the new grailsLink Generator Spring bean. Add a dependency injection (def grailsLinkGenerator). This is implemented by the org.codehaus.groovy.grails.web.mapping.Cachin gLinkGenerator class, which adds a caching layer to the default implementation.

- Spring bean scope defaults to "singleton," and typically, Spring MVC controllers are implemented as stateless singletons, but Grails controllers are "prototype" scope, so a new instance is created for each request. This is fairly inexpensive given how efficient modern garbage collection is at managing short-lived objects, but you can change the scope of your controllers to singleton either per-class with static scope='singleton' or for all classes with grails.controllers.defaultScope in *Config.groovy*. Make sure you have no per-request state before making this change (injected singleton beans are fine, because they are shared but not modified).

- Reverting changes made to MetaClasses in unit tests is now automatic, thanks to a registered instance of Groovy's MetaClassRegistryChangeEventListener. This causes an event to be fired when a MetaClass is changed, so Grails retains the original MetaClass and resets it after the test runs. This removes the need to manually manage this or use the registerMetaClass method in GrailsUnitTestCase.

- GORM dynamic finder methods and executeQuery can now specify a readOnly flag to make the returned results read-only. This is read-only in the Hibernate sense, in that they can be modified but there is no dirty checking for these instances, so changes won't be automatically flushed. You can explicitly save or delete read-only instances, though.

- Although they don't depend on Grails 2.0, the new db-reverse-engineer (*http:// grails.org/plugin/db-reverse-engineer*) and database-migration (*http://grails.org/ plugin/database-migration*) plugins were released at the same time as Grails 2.0. These can be used with Grails 1.3 or higher.

- By popular demand, the limitation to two expressions in dynamic finders (e.g., `findByFooAndBar`) was removed. This was an artificial limitation that was in place to keep method names from becoming very long, so you're now free to make method names as long as you like. You can only use all `Ands` or all `Ors`, however, because the lack of parenthesis or grouping indicators complicates resolution order.

- You can now use the Hibernate `DetachedCriteria` feature. This lets you decompose a criteria query and compose it as needed. This can be done explicitly by creating a new `DetachedCriteria` or indirectly with the new `where` queries that use `DetachedCriteria` under the hood but provide a more intuitive approach.

- Sending binary files to the response is much easier now with the `file` attribute for the `render` method. This can either be the path to a file in the filesystem, a `File` instance, an `InputStream`, or a `byte[]` array. If you specify the `fileName` attribute, it will be specified in the `Content-Disposition` response header and it will be used to determine the Mime type from the `grails.mime.types` map in *Config.groovy* unless you specify it explicitly with the `contentType` argument. So it is now as simple as `render(file: '/path/to/the/file.txt')` to render a text file or `render(file: person.badgePhoto, fileName: "${person.name}_badge.png", contentType: 'image/png')` to render an image stored in the database in the Person domain class.

- Command object properties now default to being not-null to be consistent with domain classes; add `nullable: true` in the `constraints` block to revert back to the old behavior.

- Controller actions can now be methods instead of closures, although closures are still supported. In addition, methods with arguments will have data binding conversions applied from the `params` object. This saves you the work of explicitly converting them or using command objects. You cannot have overloaded methods though, so if a parameter is optional, use a default value of null and it won't be bound if it is missing, such as `def someActionName(String param1, Integer param2 = null) { ... }`.

- Generated unit test methods now intentionally fail as a not-very-subtle reminder to write tests. The exception to this is the tests created for statically scaffolded controllers; the generation script creates a large amount of initial code for the tests covering all of the important controller actions, although there are some TODO instructions where you must finish the test, because it's not an entirely automatable process.

- The `production` section in *DataSource.groovy* now includes a default properties section with pooling properties configured to help you get started with the various advanced settings.

- For security reasons, GSPs cannot be directly accessed from a request; use a controller action or create a URL mapping instead.

- There is a new `refresh-dependencies` script (*http://grails.org/doc/latest/ref/ Command%20Line/refresh-dependencies.html*) that will install missing plugins, and optionally download source if the `include-source` flag is specified and `java doc` if the `include-javadoc` flag is specified, and can optionally generate an XML report.

- There is a new `groovyPageRenderer` Spring bean that can render a GSP as a string or to a Writer.

- The static holder classes (`ConfigurationHolder`, `ApplicationHolder`, `PluginMa nagerHolder`, `BuildSettingsHolder`, etc.) are now deprecated, and dependency injection should be used instead.

There were some breaking changes that you should be aware of:

- If your domain classes extend abstract base classes, move the base classes from *grails-app/domain* to *src/groovy* to use the same table structure.

- Criteria query joins are now INNER joins instead of LEFT joins.

- Because public controller methods are considered actions, helper methods that were unintentionally public should be changed to private. This is both as a best practice (the methods are only called internally) and also because of the overloading restriction that can cause startup errors.

- Because GORM methods are added to domain classes' bytecode, you cannot have a property called `count` because there now will be a static `getCount()` method.

- The `release-plugin` command has been removed. You must now use the `release` plugin and its `publish-plugin` script.

- When the resources plugin is installed, the `<g:resource>` tag will throw a `FileNot FoundException` if the referenced resource does not exist.

- The `redirect()` method no longer commits the response. This allows extra headers to be added after the call, but code that relies on `response.isCommitted()` may break and will need to change to use `request.isRedirected()` instead.

- The `redirect()` method uses the `grails.serverURL` setting in *Config.groovy* if it is set. Set it if you know the server URL at deployment time, but remove it to dynamically discover it from the current request.

- The loggers injected into artifacts (controllers, services, etc.) have changed from being added dynamically using runtime metaprogramming to being added with an AST at compile time, and this resulted in changes to some of the category name prefixes:

— `BootStrap.groovy` changed from `grails.app.bootstrap` to `grails.app.conf`

— Codecs (in `grails-app/utils`) changed from `grails.app.codec` to `grails.app.utils`

— Controllers changed from `grails.app.controller` to `grails.app.control lers`

— Services changed from `grails.app.service` to `grails.app.services`

— TagLibs changed from `grails.app.tagLib` to `grails.app.taglib`

— Loggers for domain classes and filters didn't change

- Use `request.withFormat()` instead of `withFormat()` to render different responses depending on the request content type.

- The resources plugin changes the behavior of some core tags including `<g:java script>`. Instead of directly rendering the tag output, it saves it and only renders the output with a `<r:layoutResources/>` tag.

- The resources plugin adds `/static` between the context and the URI, so any references to the old URL patterns will have to be updated.

- The dependency resolution logic has changed and plugin dependency repositories are not registered (although the dependencies are). The plugin portal pages will display the syntax needed to add the repository; for example, the `spring-security-kerberos` plugin page (*http://grails.org/plugin/spring-security-kerberos*) includes `mavenRepo "http://maven.springframework.org/milestone/"`, which must be added in the application's `repositories` block in *BuildConfig.groovy*.

- Domain class constraints declared for nonexistent properties now throw a `groovy.lang.MissingMethodException` at startup; this helps to detect typos.

- If you have defined a `beforeValidate()` callback method, it will typically be called two or more times during a request; be sure that the code can work correctly when called multiple times.

- You can still use the older unit test base class hierarchy (e.g., `GrailsUnitTest Case`, `ControllerUnitTestCase`, etc.), but you cannot use the new mix-in annotations (e.g., `@TestFor`) in test classes that extend these base classes.

- Output from Ant tasks using methods such as `ant.echo()` is now hidden by default; use `println`, or the event mechanism (e.g., `event('StatusUpdate', ['the mes sage'])` or `event('StatusError', ['the error message'])`), or if the plugin only supports 2.0+ applications, the new `GrailsConsole` methods (e.g., `grailsCon sole.addStatus('the message')`, `grailsConsole.updateStatus('the mes sage')`, and `grailsConsole.error('the error message')`).

Grails 2.0.2

- The data binding security fixes that were made in version 1.3.8 were also applied to version 2.0.2. See this blog post (*http://bit.ly/15g3hjk*) for a more complete discussion.

Grails 2.1.x

- Domain classes now have `first` and `last` methods.
- Groovy was upgraded to version 1.8.8.
- Spring Framework was upgraded to version 3.1.2.
- The default plugins in *BuildConfig.groovy* were updated; the `jquery` and `resour ces` plugin versions were updated and the `database-migration` and `cache` plugins were added.

Grails 2.2.x

- Groovy was upgraded to 2.0 (currently version 2.0.5), which adds the new `@Type Checked` and `@CompileStatic` annotations, as well as partial support for "invoke-dynamic" in JDK 7 and higher.
- *error.gsp* now only displays stack traces in development mode.
- The domain class `mappings` block now supports seting comments for database tables and columns, and default values for columns.

Notes on Upgrading

The best way to make upgrading easier is to stay aware of changes that are upcoming in future releases. Sign up for the Grails user mailing list (*http://grails.org/Mailing +Lists*) to see discussions about new features and fixes. You should also follow the *@grailsframework* Twitter account (*https://twitter.com/grailsframework*) since releases and other news items are announced there. Prerelease versions are made available before the final release (both beta releases and release candidates) and, if possible, upgrade your application early to help us find bugs and to discover changes you need to make in your application early.

Once the new version of Grails is released, read the release notes. A new page will be created for each release, and they are all collected at the Release Notes (*http://grails.org/ Release+Notes*) page. Click through to the JIRA issues and familiarize yourself with what changed. If something doesn't work or doesn't work as expected, search the mailing list archives (*http://grails.1312388.n4.nabble.com/Grails-user-f1312389.html*) and use your favorite search engine to do a search for previous discussions; it is unlikely that what you are seeing is specific to you unless you are a very early adopter.

We try to test library upgrades to the extent possible, but cannot test everything. So for example, when we upgrade Hibernate or some other library, if you use a feature that we haven't got a test for, a bug can sneak through. And, because Grails is a metaframework that wraps dozens of other frameworks, the combinations of interactions between libraries make detecting all of the impacts of library upgrades impractical. So you should also look at the release notes of the important libraries that you use to see if there might be impacts to your application. Groovy is another important library that Grails uses extensively, and changes in the Groovy language and libraries can affect how applications run. Be sure to stay aware of changes in Groovy.

There are also upgrade-specific pages in the online Grails documentation (*http://grails.org/doc/latest/*). For example, there is a section on upgrading (*http://bit.ly/YL6apg*) and, a page on new features and changes in Grails 2.0 (*http://bit.ly/ZsVcAl*) and Grails 2.1 (*http://bit.ly/15aUyhZ*), so you should expect a new section for each new major release.

Additionally, there is a page on the Grails How-Tos (*http://grails.github.com/grails-howtos/*) site with a lot of useful information about upgrading to Grails 2 (*http://bit.ly/ZwpuRR*).

More information is available in two blog posts that discuss users' experiences upgrading to 2.0; in particular, the breaking changes around unit testing are highlighted. See Rob Fletcher's post (*http://bit.ly/138KeD9*) and Ted Naleid's post (*http://bit.ly/YL6sfW*).

Index

We'd like to hear your suggestions for improving our indexes. Send email to index@oreilly.com.

GStrings, 19
GVM (Groovy enVironment Manager), 2, 38

H

hash functions, 248
hashCode method, 136
HDIV (HTTP Data Integrity Validator), 257
heredocs, 19
Heroku, 98, 277–284
    build packs, 284
    database applications, 278
    deployment philosophy, 277
    HTTP sessions, 283
    scaling, 282
Hibernate ORM library
    accessing session connection, 132
    caching, 137–143
    collections performance, 148
    creating an application in, 120–125
    custom configurations, 150
    customized data type storage, 129
    dialects, 117–119
    get(), load(), and read() methods, 156
    Hibernate Query Language (HQL), 143–147
    Hibernate sessions, 125
    Java type support, 128
    mapping domain classes in, 115
    mapping views, 153–156
    open session in view (OSIV) pattern, 126
    optimistic/pessimistic locking, 131
    optimizing performance in, 158
    overview of, 115
    proxies, 135
    schema-export, 132
    Session.createFilter(), 150
    SQL logging, 133
hibernate plugin, 44
Hibernate Query Language (HQL), 143–147
hibernate.cfg.xml, 120
HibernateUtil, 121
HTML emails, 172
HTTP Basic authentication, 259
HTTP filters, 290
HttpServletRequest metaclass, 55
HttpServletResponse metaclass, 55
HttpSession metaclass, 55
hyphenation syntax, 57

I

i18n message bundles, 104
i18n plugin, 53
IDE (integrated development environment)
    support, 41
imports, default, 17
in keyword, 17
in operator, 28
infrastructure as a service (IaaS), 263
injection attacks, 237
inline plugins, 220, 235
input validation, 256
insecure cryptographic storage, 248
insecure direct object references, 244, 257
installation
    Grails, 38
    Groovy, 2
integration tests, 221
IntelliJ IDEA, 42
interception logic, 51, 287, 294
interface coercion, 11
internationalization support, 53, 100
Inversion of Control (IOC), 87–89
invokedynamic, 33
InvokerHelper, 21

J

Java
    populating collections with Groovy, 4
    vs. Groovy, 1, 17–19
Java API for XML Web Services (JAX-WS), 177
Java Cryptography Extension (JCE), 249
Java Data Objects (JDO) support, 106, 128
Java DataBase Connectivity (JDBC), 106
Java Development Kit (JDK), 21
Java Enterprise Edition (JEE) technologies, 161
Java Management eXtension (JMX), 112, 190
Java Message Service (JMS), 112, 161–169
javac, 1
JavaMail API, 113
javap, 8
JAX-WS services, 177
JConsole, 191
JD-GUI, 8
JDBC database, 44
JdbcTemplate, 106
JFrog Artifactory server, 226
jms plugin, 166

jmx plugin, 113
jquery plugin, 44
JSON format, 48
JSP (JavaServer Pages) support, 52
JVM (Java Virtual Machine) classes, 21

L

layout conventions, 59
lazy-loaded collections, 127, 135, 159
life cycle callbacks, for plugins, 215
Liquibase database refactoring tool, 44
load() method, 157
lock contention, 131
lock method, 81
Log4j logging, 133, 174, 191
logging plugin, 53

M

mail, 113, 170
malicious text, 256, 258
malware, 252
many-to-many relationships, 79, 149
many-to-one relationships, 79, 127, 149
mapped collections, 79, 149
mapping closure, 13
MBeans, 191
MD5 hashing algorithm, 249
Meld diff tool, 235
messaging, 161–169
    Java Message Service (JMS), 161
    XA transaction support, 166
messaging service, 112
Meta Object Protocol (MOP), 1, 21
metaclass interceptors, 294
metamethods, 19
metaprogramming, 1, 21, 292
method call caching, 113
methodMissing, 25
methods
    adding, 22
    method reference, 29
    vs. closures, 32
mimeTypes plugin, 54
model-view-controller (MVC), 107
multiline strings, 19
multimethod dispatch, 19
multipart emails, 171
multivalued attributes, 18

MVC controllers, 108

N

NetBeans IDE, 42
non-primitive data types, 116
nonpersistent domain classes, 69
NoSQL support, 84, 273
null-safe dereference operator, 26
nullability, 116
nulls, conversion from blank strings, 77
nullSafeGet, 129
nullSafeSet, 129

O

object equality, 18
object references, evaluation of, 15
object-relational mapping (ORM) libraries, 115
onChange, 218
onConfigChange, 219
one-to-many collections, 127
onShutdown, 219
open classes, 21
open session in view (OSIV) pattern, 126
Open Web Application Security Project
    (OWASP)
    broken authentication/session management,
        243
    cross-site request forgery, 246
    cross-site scripting (XSS) attacks, 240
    failure to restrict URL access, 250
    injection attacks, 237
    insecure cryptographic storage, 248
    insecure direct object references, 244
    insufficient transport layer protection, 250
    security misconfiguration, 247
    unvalidated redirects/forwards, 252
operators
    operator overload, 29–31
    types of, 26–29
optimistic/pessimistic locking, 131
OSIV interceptors, 127
OWASP Enterprise Security API, 256

P

parentheses, 16
passwords
    authentication of, 153, 248, 249, 250

resources plugin, 45
resources.groovy, 198
REST (representational state transfer), 183–190
return keyword, 16
runtime metaprogramming, 22, 292

S

scaffolding plugin, 54
schema-export, 132
scope modifiers, 16
scope property, 55
script injection attacks, 240
Searchable, 273
security by obscurity, 259
security issues
    AntiSamy, 256
    best practices, 242, 249, 257
    HDIV (HTTP Data Integrity Validator), 257
    Open Web Application Security Project
        (OWASP), 237–252
    OWASP Enterprise Security API, 256
    security plugins, 252
security misconfiguration, 247
self-documentation, 32
semicolons, 16
sendMail method, 171
server-side validations, 257
service conventions, 61
services plugin, 54
Servlet 3.0, 259
servlet filters, 51
ServletContext metaclass, 55
servlets plugin, 55
session fixation, 244
session ID cookies, 250
session management, 243, 272, 283
Session.createFilter(), 150
sessions, 125, 132
setProperty, 24
setters, 5, 117
SHA-256/512 hashing algorithms, 249
Shiro plugin, 250, 252
shopping carts, 90
simple text emails, 171
simple web services, 177
singletons, 90
SOAP XML, 181
SOAP-based web services, 177–183
software as a Service (SaaS), 263

Sonatype Nexus server, 226
spaceship operator, 27
spread operator, 27
Spring AOP
    AspectJ-annotated aspects, 298
    compile-time weaving, 301
    configuration of, 296, 297
    enabling, 297
    overview of, 296
Spring Expression Language (SpEL), 88
Spring Framework
    AOP functionality, 296
    bean aliases, 99
    bean creation, 52
    bean declarations, 197
    bean definition, 2
    bean life cycles/interfaces, 96
    bean postprocessors, 97
    bean registration, 50, 61
    bean scopes, 90
    cache abstraction, 44, 113
    data binding/validation, 103
    database persistence, 104
    email implementation, 113
    Enterprise JavaBeans (EJBs), 112
    environment-specific Spring beans, 200
    integration with Grails, 48
    internationalization, 100
    Inversion of Control/Dependency Injection,
        87–89
    Java Management eXtension (JMX), 112
    Java Message Service (JMS), 112
    model-view-controller (MVC), 107
    overview of, 87
    remoting, 109
    resources, 101–103
    transactional services, 90–96, 296
    validation, 75
Spring MVC controllers, 108
Spring Security plugin, 250, 252
Spring Web model-view-controller (MVC), 107
SQL injection attacks, 237
SQL logging, 133
SSL authentication, 251
static resources, 45, 51
strings, 19
sub-select domain classes, 154
synchronous messaging, 112

About the Author

Burt Beckwith has been a software developer for 15 years (most of that as a JVM developer), and for the last five years, has been working with Grails and Groovy. He is a core developer on the Grails team at SpringSource, and has created over 50 Grails plugins. Burt is a frequent speaker at conferences and user groups where he shares his passion for Grails and other Groovy-based technologies, in particular those that are related to persistence, security, and performance. He blogs at *http://burtbeckwith.com/blog/*.

Colophon

The animal on the cover of *Programming Grails* is an Antarctic giant petrel (*Macronectes giganteus*), also known as a southern giant petrel. These large seabirds live in the southern hemisphere, nesting on subtropic islands around South America, Australia, and Africa, as well as the Antarctic continent. The name "petrel" is derived from Saint Peter, because this family of birds appear to run across water when they are taking off into the air.

This is the largest of the petrels, with an average wingspan of 73–81 inches. Males weigh around 11 pounds, and females range from 7–18 pounds. The majority of Antarctic giant petrels have a light head and neck, with mottled brown plumage on the rest of their body. On their upper beaks are "naricorns," tubular nostrils used to expel excess salt after drinking seawater (with the help of a gland that secretes concentrated saline).

Breeding season occurs in October and November, and the birds form loose colonies while they are nesting. Giant petrel nests are built on the ground, and are made of moss, grass, and stones. They only lay one egg at a time, which is incubated between 55–66 days.

Though the giant petrel catches squid and fish near the surface of the water and occasionally hunts other seabirds, it is largely a scavenger, eating whale, seal, and penguin carcasses that have washed ashore. This carrion diet is of note when considering one of their nicknames, "stinker": their defense mechanism is to regurgitate food and oil and spit it at whatever is threatening them. The northern and southern giant petrels are also the only petrels that are able to efficiently walk on land.

The cover image is from Wood's *Animate Creations*. The cover font is Adobe ITC Garamond. The text font is Adobe Minion Pro; the heading font is Adobe Myriad Condensed; and the code font is Dalton Maag's Ubuntu Mono.

Have it your way.

Get even more for your money.

Join the O'Reilly Community, and register the O'Reilly books you own. It's free, and you'll get:

- $4.99 ebook upgrade offer
- 40% upgrade offer on O'Reilly print books
- Membership discounts on books and events
- Free lifetime updates to ebooks and videos
- Multiple ebook formats, DRM FREE
- Participation in the O'Reilly community
- Newsletters
- Account management
- 100% Satisfaction Guarantee

Signing up is easy:

1. **Go to: oreilly.com/go/register**
2. **Create an O'Reilly login.**
3. **Provide your address.**
4. **Register your books.**

Note: English-language books only

To order books online:
oreilly.com/store

For questions about products or an order:
orders@oreilly.com

To sign up to get topic-specific email announcements and/or news about upcoming books, conferences, special offers, and new technologies:
elists@oreilly.com

For technical questions about book content:
booktech@oreilly.com

To submit new book proposals to our editors:
proposals@oreilly.com

O'Reilly books are available in multiple DRM-free ebook formats. For more information:
oreilly.com/ebooks

O'REILLY®

Spreading the knowledge of innovators   oreilly.com

CPSIA information can be obtained at www.ICGtesting.com
Printed in the USA
BVOW040509260413

319127BV00006B/6/P